THE DECORATIVE ARTS LIBRARY

FURNITURE

THE DECORATIVE ARTS LIBRARY

FURNITURE

EDITED BY LYDIA DARBYSHIRE

CHARTWELL
BOOKS, INC.

A QUINTET BOOK

Published by Chartwell Books
A Division of Book Sales, Inc.
114, Northfield Avenue
Edison, New Jersey 08837

ISBN 0-7858-0617-2

This book was designed and produced by
Quintet Publishing Limited
6 Blundell Street
London N7 9BH

Creative Director: Richard Dewing
Designer: Jill Coote
Project Editor: Clare Hubbard
Editor: Lydia Darbyshire

Typeset in Great Britain by
Central Southern Typesetters, Eastbourne
Manufactured in China by
Regent Publishing Services Ltd
Printed in Singapore by
Star Standard Industries (Pte) Ltd, Singapore

The material in this book previously appeared in:

A Guide to Art Deco Style, Arie van de Lemme;
Art Deco Source Book, Patricia Bayer; *The Arts and Crafts
Movement*, Steven Adams; *Encyclopedia of Arts and
Crafts*, Consultant, Wendy Kaplan; *Encyclopedia of
Chairs*, Simon Yates; *Encyclopedia of Sofas*,
Constance King; *Encyclopedia of Tables*, Simon Yates;
Illustrated History of Antiques, General Editor,
Huon Mallalieu; *Introduction to the Decorative Arts*,
Edited by Amanda O'Neill; *'20s & '30s Style*,
Michael Horsham.

The publisher would like to thank Michael Norman
Antiques Ltd., Brighton, England, for supplying items
of furniture featured on pages 2, 16–17,
24–5, 42–3, 80–1, 118–19, all photographed by
Jeremy Thomas.

CONTENTS

INTRODUCTION

ENGLISH STOOL OR TABLE

ENGLISH STOOL OR TABLE

▶ OAK

*c.*1580

The clover-leaf top of this piece is probably unique. It may be strong enough to be a stool, and the carved columnar legs are identical to joint stools of the Elizabethan period. However, the top is relatively thin, and therefore perhaps too weak to serve as a seat. Whether a chair or a table, it is a very rare, very pleasing relic.

With its stylistic variety and wide range of forms, furniture remains one of the most interesting and impressive categories of antiques. The first unified schemes of interior decoration began to appear during the Renaissance. By the 17th century such carefully contrived effects were quite usual among the *beau monde* in France, the Netherlands, and England, and those who wanted to be fashionable had pattern-books to guide them.

Books of engraved patterns and ornaments and of architectural styles had been available since the 16th century. The earliest furniture pattern-book was *Différents Pourtraicts de Menuiserie* (*c.*1588) by Hans Vredeman de Vries (1526–*c.*1604), and this was followed by another major work, *Oficina Arcularia* (1621) by Crispin de Passe the Younger (*c.*1593–*c.*1670). Early design books were mainly concerned with architecture or with architectural features. Increasingly, however, furniture was included.

Most engraved pattern-books were published in early centers of the printing industry –

Nuremberg, Augsburg, Amsterdam, and Utrecht, for example – but many of the late 17th- and 18th-century productions appeared in Paris. While early 17th-century architects and designers had looked to Italy for their models, and Italian craftsmen were enticed to countries all

FRENCH CONSOLE TABLE

▶ GILT WOOD

*c.*1740

This is a good example of a gilt wood and gesso console table in the Louis XV style. All curves and very asymmetrical, the table is pure rococo, with the elaborate decorations on the tapering inward legs and stretcher.

◀ TULIPWOOD AND ORMOLU
*c.*1900
The French passion for revivalist 18th-century furniture reached its peak *c.*1860, during the reign of Napoleon III. At first, good quality, authentic pieces were made, but later fidelity to the original patterns and spirit waned. This library table is in many ways similar to an English center table. It has a deep frieze, sits on a quadruped support, and is covered with rococo ormolu decoration.

over Europe to add Italian decorative refinements to the most luxurious schemes, by the late 17th century the French had secured the lead in both design and craftsmanship. French sophistication, embodied in the splendors of Versailles, became the goal of the fashion-conscious throughout Europe, and France remained the most potent influence on interior design throughout the 18th century.

Pattern-books were one way of disseminating fashion. The movement of craftsmen and designers around Europe was another. The Italian Domenico Cucci (*c.*1640–1705) and the Flemings Pierre Golle (1620–84) and Daniel Marot (1663–1752) were merely the most celebrated of many outstanding foreigners who were attracted to Paris in the 17th century. After the revocation of the Edict of Nantes in 1685, however, Huguenots were forced to flee to countries such as England, the Netherlands, and Germany, where Protestants were welcome. These craftsmen took both their skills and French styles with them.

Ambitious princes sent designers and craftsmen to Paris to assimilate the latest refinements so that they could introduce them in the purest possible form at home. French or French-trained architects and furniture designers found enthusiastic clients for their services in all parts of Europe. Examples include the attachment of

Marot to the court of the English king William III, of François Cuvilliès (1695–1768) to the courts of the electors of Bavaria, and of Nicolas Pineau (1684–1754) to the court of Peter the Great in Russia.

Those eager for the latest Parisian designs could receive them within just a few weeks, even if they lived as far afield as Poland or Sweden. The desire of the rich everywhere to adopt newly fashionable styles as soon as possible ensured the rapid spread of artistic movements such as the baroque, rococo, and neoclassical.

▼ MAHOGANY
*c.*1815
The bold carving and use of high quality mahogany are typical of the work of cabinet-maker Duncan Phyfe, whose ability to distill English and French neoclassical styles with equal confidence to an increasingly wealthy clientele in New York in the early 19th century ensured that his workshops prospered.

AMERICAN ARMCHAIR

► WALNUT
*c.*1760
This armchair, substantial without being heavy, was made in Philadelphia, and it is an example of some of the best craftsmanship to be seen before the War of Independence. The curvaceous design with its dramatic top rail is loosely based on chairs from the reign of William and Mary in England. The splat and cabriole legs are early Georgian, and the reeded lines carved on the edge of each rail are a unique adaptation of the Queen Anne style.

FRENCH COMMODE

▼ PAINTED AND SILVERED WOOD
1739
This marble-topped commode, from the hunting room at the Amalienburg, Palace of Nymphenburg, shows the palatial rococo at its most extreme. It was designed by François Cuvilliès.

These tended to have few national variations as long as they remained in the hands of those high on the social scale. As soon as they percolated down through society, they became first nationalized, then regionalized.

The downward filtering of styles may be seen most markedly in the way in which rococo was adopted around Europe. Developing in Paris during the early 18th century, it was soon taken up in an extravagant way at the courts of German princes such as Maximilian Emanuel of Bavaria and Augustus the Strong of Saxony. When it was adopted in England and the Netherlands, rather later, rococo became a style of the *nouveaux riches* rather than of aristocrats, and it emerged in a nationally identifiable form. It was not long before rococo elements – asymmetric C-scrolls and curlicues, cabriole and *bombé* shapes – filtered into the regional furniture forms of all the countries in Europe.

The adoption of the neoclassical style followed a similar pattern. The first manifestations were the most aggressively "new" and pure. Within 20 years or so the style had become watered down for the masses and modified according to national tastes and forms.

Two threads – status and comfort – weave their way through the history of furniture. Status could be embodied in the importance as well as the modishness of furniture – it was certainly often reflected in its cost. Comfort was also related to status. The most wealthy paid attention not just to changes in style but to developments in comfort and convenience. The increase in the number and function of small tables during the 18th century, for example, represented an aspect of this, but the evolution of upholstery was, perhaps, an even more important consideration.

UPHOLSTERY

The part played by the upholsterer in interior design is a somewhat neglected aspect of its history. Architects may have determined the shapes of rooms, the style of their decoration and sometimes even the furniture, but it was the upholsterer who had the last word in the finished effect. The 18th-century "upholder" was concerned not just with seat upholstery and bed hangings but also with wall and floor coverings, window blinds and curtains, and was usually responsible for the arrangement of furniture in a room.

Because textiles are so much more perishable than furniture, the emphasis that was placed on them in the 17th, 18th, and 19th centuries can easily be forgotten. Hangings for beds invariably cost much more than the bed frames themselves, and seat furniture was often made expressly to set off embroidery. The sums spent on curtains, hangings, and textile wall coverings in many instances far exceeded the amounts expended on woodwork. The very term furniture was, in the 18th century, used as much for hangings and coverings as for movables. This supremacy of the upholsterer over other furniture craftsmen was often enhanced by direct contact with the client rather than, as was often the case with the other members of the furnishing team, the client's agent. Indeed, the upholsterer's perceived superiority was often a cause of friction with architects, who felt their control over total schemes to be threatened.

The most powerful cabinet-makers were those, such as Thomas Chippendale (*d.*1779),

ENGLISH CHAIR

◄ EBONIZED WOOD
*c.*1890
This unusual Arts & Crafts chair is attributed to John Moyr Smith, but it shows similarities to the designs of the revolutionary architect and designer Edward Godwin. In spite of the turned stretchers and homely English look, there is an austerity about the piece that shows its oriental influence.

FRENCH CHAIRS

▼ GILTWOOD
*c.*1850
Their design has been attributed to Nicolas Heurtaut. The flat-back armchair was designed to stand against a wall.

FRENCH CHAIR

► *c.*1920
Robert Mallet-Stevens
(1886–1945) was a French
architect and designer,
and most of his chairs
were made to fit his
interior schemes. They
were of primarily tubular
construction, placing
great emphasis on
simplicity and plain
design.

BRITISH CHAIR

► 1903
Black chair by Charles
Rennie Mackintosh.
Mackintosh was reluctant
to incorporate natural
wood grain into his
design.

William Vile (*d.*1767), John Cobb (*d.*1778) and
Samuel Norman, whose businesses embraced
both cabinet-making and upholstery. Chippendale, for example, supplied his important clients
not only with furniture but also with wallpapers
and borders, curtains and blinds, bedding, carpets, and other items of household equipment.

Curtains, cushions, and wall hangings were
in widespread use among the status- and
comfort-conscious nobility of Europe during
the Middle Ages, but upholstered chairs, with
stuffing and fabric fixed to their frames, did not
come into use until the 16th century, and they
were not adopted widely until the 17th century.
The typical farthingale (joined and upholstered
chair) of this period had a stuffed back as well as
seat, with covers of leather, patterned turkeywork, or embroidery, and with added embellishments in the form of fringes or brass-headed nails.

In its early stages the technique of upholstery
was still relatively primitive, with luxurious
effects achieved through the use of rich and
colorful fabrics rather than through any particular artistry in applying them. From the late 17th
century, however, the upholsterer in France
emerged as a craftsman, establishing standards
of excellence that were maintained through the
next two centuries in Europe and America with
surprisingly little change.

Forms of seating more luxurious than the farthingale chair were soon designed – tall-backed wing chairs, some with adjustments for reclining; sofas with down-filled cushions and arms padded with horsehair; and chairs with upholstered seats and full-length backs. Even cane-seated chairs of the early 18th century were generally made more comfortable with mattress-like tufted squabs tied on with tapes. From the mid-18th century tufting was used to secure the square-edged, even shape of English upholstered chair seats. At this time French chairs differed in having domed stuffed seats, and it was not until the 1780s, when the neo-classical period was well advanced, that the French generally adopted squarer forms of stuffing to harmonize them with linear neo-classical style.

For trimming the edges of upholstered chairs fringes, gave way to braids, often home-made. But the most usual form of chair edging during the second half of the 18th century was decorative brass nailing. Loosely fitting cotton covers were placed over upholstery to protect precious materials from sunlight and dust when a room was not in formal use for a grand occasion, and such attention to conservation has ensured the survival of a number of important suites of upholstered furniture.

During the 19th century upholstery grew more luxuriously thick, and tufting on chairs and sofas was increasingly replaced by buttons, which secured the horsehair padding inside more firmly. Upholstery reached its deep-buttoned peak of comfort, if not of elegance, during the 1840s, by which time coiled springing had also come into widespread use. The French *crapaud* (toad chair) and the English Chesterfield sofa epitomize the overstuffed technique of upholstering, in which no vestige of the seat frame is left visible.

By this period the 18th-century upholsterer had turned into the interior decorator, who was now in charge not only of the supply and co-ordination of furnishings and decorations but also of the planning and design of schemes. In England, Morris & Co. was an important

example, and the earlier firm of Crace was also influential. The work of Crace at Chatsworth, Longleat, and several Astor residences in the late 19th century showed a thoroughgoing approach to historical revivalism, including extensive research, providing designs for ornament, furniture, and upholstery as well as having them made. This approach also relied on collecting and restoring antique furnishings where appropriate. In this last function such firms heralded the practice of early 20th-century decorating companies, such as Lenygon & Morant, which were also antique dealers. Purposeful collecting of antique furniture in the 19th century, greatly stimulated by antiquarianism, rather than its mere accumulation by families, meant that interior decoration henceforth was concerned as much with antique furnishings as with new ones.

◄ OAK
*c.*1935
Gigone is the French word for a mother of many children. This nest of tables, designed by Michel Frank and Adolphe Chanaux, was originally created in oak and covered in vellum and straw marquetry.

ENGLISH TABLE

▼ HYEDUA
*c.*1979
This table, which was made by English cabinet-maker and designer Jeremy Broun (b.1945), is made from hyedua, an oriental hardwood. It exploits the markings of traditional manufacture, as seen by the joints at the points where the top meets the legs, and is innovative in its center joint in the table top. It is based on traditional craft design. Tables based on the principle of three have been made since the 16th century, but the triangular component has more usually been the tripod base rather than the top.

THE BEGINNINGS: ANCIENT TIMES

▼ *c.*3000 BC
This is a reconstruction
of one of the earliest free-
standing chairs. The
original was excavated
from the tomb of the
Egyptian pharaoh in
1922. Beneath the
embossed metal and
enamel, it has a simple
wooden frame, basically
identical to those found
in most western homes
today. There are many
fine examples of ancient
Egyptian chairs and
stools in the Cairo
Museum.

Before 1500 few Europeans had even seen a
chair, let alone sat on one. Chairs had existed, however, and one of the earliest recorded
pieces of surviving furniture is a folding chair of
ash with a seat of otter skin, which was found in
Muldbjerg, Denmark, and is believed to date
from before 1000 BC. This piece is particularly
unusual not just because of its early date but also
because climate has destroyed almost all wooden

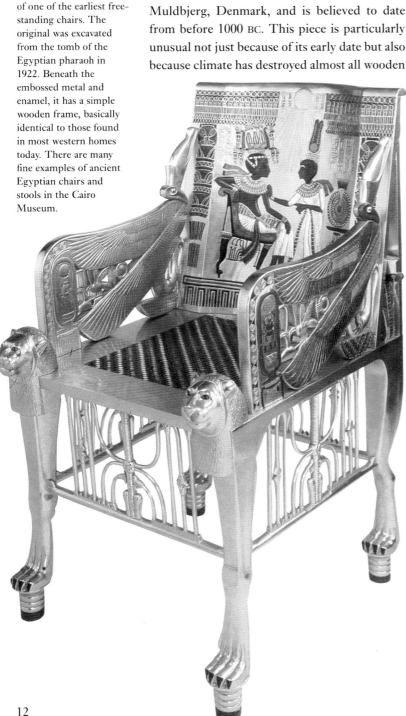

seat furniture made before 1500. Consequently,
tracing the development of furniture has largely
to be done through surviving paintings and
other art works.

Artifacts from ancient Egyptian, Roman, and
Greek civilizations provide clear evidence of
contemporary furniture. Both chairs and
couches were standard practical equipment for
royal Egyptians, and pharaohs were buried with
examples for use in the afterlife. Ordinary
people would have owned only the simplest
items, such as wooden coffers and stools. Most
of these early couches seem to have been low
and sloping down to the foot, but those used by
Tutankhamen were very high, perhaps as an
indication of his rank. Both cushions and linen
covers appear to have been used, although the
double benches that seated a man and his wife in
tomb reliefs were left plain. The Egyptians used
veneers, marquetry, and inlay.

Greek and Roman drawings on vases and
wall paintings show that chairs, couches, and
small tables were in common use then, too, although virtually none has survived.

Little is known of European furniture
between AD 500 and 1000. In Europe the use of
formal seating was generally restricted to kings
and bishops. Church influence on the development of the chair is clear, and what was possibly
St. Augustine's chair from the 6th century can
still be seen in Canterbury Cathedral, England.
Illuminated medieval manuscripts show
Romanesque monks using chairs in the 12th
century, but they rarely used tables. King Richard
II (reigned 1377–99) is depicted on his, and
Leonardo da Vinci (1452–1519) painted Jesus'
disciples on stools. By 1550 boisterous peasants
using stools in the fields appear in the works of
Bruegel, and just before 1600 Caravaggio places
St. Matthew in an identifiably X-framed chair.

The likelihood is that most of the pieces used
in this early period were of rough construction,
with thickly sawn planks and four legs. Tables
were not used for storage as they are now, and
they were, therefore, less necessary than other
pieces of furniture, such as chests, coffers or
even built-in cupboards.

THE MIDDLE AGES

After the fall of the Roman Empire in the 5th century AD many of the skills and materials used in the furniture of the ancient world disappeared. Between the 11th century and 15th century, however, furniture steadily regained its importance. Most of our evidence for this period comes from paintings, sculptures, and illuminated manuscripts, but a few pieces have survived, although they are often damaged or much changed from their original appearance because of repairs and, especially, the loss of the bright colors with which much early furniture was decorated.

During this period, homes – even the great households – were scantily furnished, and what furniture there was was simply and sturdily made. Furniture was limited to meeting the basic needs of eating, sleeping, and sitting, and storage. In addition, although to a limited extent, it was made to meet the needs of those who could read and write. It also served the less direct purpose of indicating rank in society or status within a household. Oak was the most commonly used wood for furniture. There were abundant supplies of walnut, cypress, and fruit-woods of various kinds in Spain and Italy, and conifers were plentiful in the Alpine regions.

Carved decoration was based on architectural motifs, first the Romanesque, with its classically inspired round-headed arches, then, in the 14th and 15th centuries, the gothic, with its pointed arches, buttresses, crockets, and tracery.

SEAT FURNITURE

Chairs were often reserved for the lord of the manor and favored guests. Later, chairs for nobles had a canopy to show the status of the occupier, and this was reinforced by being placed on a dais to give extra height. Chairs and stools constructed with X-frames have a long pedigree, and the style was used throughout Europe in the Middle Ages, although there were distinctive regional variations. In Italy, for example, the style was known as the Savonarola chair. The earliest X-framed stools were of a folding type, with brightly painted leather slung between the side rails to form a seat. The addition of a back support formed a fixed chair, and the use of padding, cushions and a footstool afforded greater comfort.

A few throne-like chairs – such as the 14th-century coronation chair in Westminster Abbey, London – were also made. They were often constructed on a box-like principle, with upward projections forming the back and sides, and were generally decorated with architectural motifs such as pinnacles and crockets. A third type was the barrel chair; the most primitive examples were made from part of a barrel, with a few boards added to form a seat.

Stools were probably the only form of seating in humble houses. They were made from a circular or triangular slab of wood with three or four turned or square legs driven into the seat and secured by pegs. The back legs were elongated upwards and provided with a curving back rail to form a chair. As an alternative to solid seats, rushes were sometimes woven around the seat rails. Rather more sophisticated slab-ended stools with rectangular seats were made, their solid supports sometimes decorated with gothic ogee arches cut into the bottom. In some examples the seat had a circle with a cross-bar cut into it for easy carrying.

ANCIENT ROMAN WALL PAINTING

◀ *c.*50 BC
In the fresco, known as *Noblewoman Playing a Cithera*, a woman sits on a small sofa, similar in size to the love seats of the 18th century. The seat is supported on turned legs, strengthened with a brace, and its slatted back is curved for greater comfort. This piece reveals the complexity of form that was possible at the time.

▶ ITALIAN

*c.*1480

This painting entitled *The Birth of the Virgin* shows a very sparsely furnished room as was common in the 15th century. St Anne sits up in a bed which has simple chests placed in pairs around it, all set on a low dais. The chests were useful for storage and doubled as seats or tables. The bed itself is of box form, with panels of equal height forming head and foot-boards, which are decorated with ball finials.

Benches were either slab-ended, like stools, or were solid and chest-like with a lid, a form that later became known as settles. These had hinged lids and were cushioned.

TABLES

Dining tables were used, but they were often nothing more than trestles, with long, narrow, softwood boards resting on easily movable square-cut or V- or A-shaped supports.

CHESTS AND CUPBOARDS

By far the most numerous pieces of early furniture were chests of varying sizes, and because of the strength of their construction, early examples are not uncommon. Chests were used not only for storage and for securing valuables, but also as seats, tables, and even beds. The earliest were made from hollowed-out tree trunks (giving an alternative name), with iron bands added for strength. By the 13th century, construction methods had become a little more refined, and chests were made from planks, split or sawn lengthwise down a log and joined together in box form by nails or oak pins. They were made secure not only by ironwork (by this time decoratively scrolled) but also by locks. In the second half of the 15th century, framed con-

struction became more usual, and lighter panels sit in the grooves of a mortise-and-tenon frame.

All houses in the Middle Ages were cold and damp, whatever the rank of the occupant, and furniture had to be raised above floor level to prevent rotting. From the 12th century on, therefore, chests often had stiles (uprights) projecting downward to act as legs. Decoration was often done by chip carving, a simple technique using a gouge and chisel to chip out Romanesque arcades in relief across the front panel.

In the gothic period, carving, like architecture, became more elaborate, and the front surfaces of chests were carved with pointed arches and tracery. Some examples even had small "buttresses" that were fixed to the stiles with wooden pins. In the prosperous Low Countries, where there was a thriving wool and cloth trade and merchants' houses were well furnished, carving was especially fine. Many 15th-century English inventories refer to "Flaunders chests," which were often carved with a linenfold motif. The so-called "tilting" chests produced in France and England in the 14th and early 15th centuries are carved in relief with figures of armor-clad knights jousting. In Italy simple chests were used not only for storage but as a step up to the bed or as a seat or table.

Early cupboards were simply shelves attached to the wall. By the 15th century small chests with doors and long legs were being made, as were livery (food) cupboards, with doors pierced for ventilation, often in gothic patterns. To keep out vermin, small hanging livery cupboards were also made. Some larger dressers for storing linen appeared in the 15th century, and a few survive in churches.

BEDS

Few beds survive from the Middle Ages, largely because they depended on perishable textiles for their grand appearance. It is clear from pictorial sources that beds played an important part in expressing status, and rich hangings – furs, silks, and tapestries – are listed in inventories. At this time the state bed emerges as the most costly and extravagant piece of furniture in a great household, but it was often intended less for sleep than for show.

In northern Europe beds were often raised from damp floors. During the Romanesque period low railings were added, joining the four short bedposts, and with a lower section in the center of one side to permit the occupant to get in. Burgundian carvings in the 12th-century cathedral at Autun clearly show a simple wooden bed frame, with a hide lashed to a frame with leather thongs – a style known in ancient Egypt.

By the 13th century, sleepers in northern Europe were looking for greater comfort. Beds were made with warm hangings, which could be detached and packed in chests when a great household traveled. Such beds were of two types. The sparver, or tent bed, had a conical, textile-covered softwood bowl that was suspended from the ceiling above a couch bed and to it were attached rich hangings that were pulled around the bed in tent-like fashion. The other type of bed had hangings suspended from a rectangular canopy, on which they ran on iron rails to be drawn into pear-shaped bundles during the day. Manuscripts and paintings from the 15th century onward indicate that feather beds and pillows were increasingly used.

FRENCH TAPESTRY

◀ *c.*1500
The Lady and the Unicorn shows a circular pavilion, similar in form to the canopies of state and those of sparver beds, where the dome and hangings would have been suspended from the ceiling, with the hangings drawn around a couch bed.

THE 15th & 16th CENTURIES

Unified schemes of interior decoration, revealing harmony between architecture, ornamental features, furniture, and upholstery, began to appear during the Renaissance. One of the main ways by which styles were disseminated throughout Europe was by means of pattern-books. Furniture was transformed into more heavily worked, highly decorated pieces.

Florence, Milan, Rome, and Venice became important centers of cabinet-making, and the idea of furnishing and decorating the home as a place of comfort and beauty was for the first time given serious consideration. The Low Countries and Germany influenced ornamentation, and extravagantly decorated designs appeared on furniture. The Moorish style prevalent in Spain and Portugal also exerted an influence.

In England and elsewhere, craftsmen were making fine tables and chests, especially using only local woods, and developing along traditional lines their national style: English chests, inlaid with scenes worked in several woods; huge, sturdy refectory tables, smaller chests for churches and large houses; bedsteads, which reveal the transition from useful Tudor to ornate Jacobean styles.

England

During the 16th century England's geographical isolation from the rest of Europe was reinforced by the cultural isolation following Henry VIII's break with Rome. One result of this was that Italian artists who had helped to embellish palaces left the country. Only a few of the luxurious pieces that furnished these buildings survive – the bright colors of Henry VIII's writing box in the Victoria & Albert Museum, London, serve as a reminder that much 16th-century furniture was painted. Oak was the most commonly used wood, but imported walnut was used for the grandest pieces, especially beds.

Portraits of Tudor monarchs show the continuing use of the X-framed chair and canopy. In most ordinary households chairs were few in number, benches and stools being the most usual type of seating. In the 1520s the decoration of heavy box-chairs, constructed like chests and often with hinged seats, combined gothic linenfold carving on the panels of the base with Renaissance Grotesque motifs or romayne work on the stiles or rails of the paneled back. The French-inspired *caqueteuse* (gossip-chair), which evolved in the 1530s, had a seat that was narrower at the back than the front, a tall back and, instead of the side panels of the box-chair, splayed arms. Later in the century, the back-stool appeared; this had an upholstered square seat and rectangular back, and straight-cut or turned legs joined by stretchers.

The use of sturdy, fixed bedposts and wooden headboard and tester (canopy) made the 16th-century bed more ponderous than its

ENGLISH JOINT STOOL

▶ OAK

*c.*1580

This beautifully decorated stool, constructed with sturdy mortise-and-tenon joints, is not only early but also extremely rare. The arcaded rails are characteristic of the Elizabethan era. The fluted legs are unusual in the way that the beaded ring forms the capital.

ENGLISH DINING TABLE

▶ OAK

*c.*1620

This is a typical example of a joined table, with a fixed top, six legs, and stretchers between the feet. It has a little turning on the legs, some carving on the frieze where the rails meet the legs, and mortice-and-tenon pegged joints throughout.

predecessors. In the latter part of the century the posts were often carved with a bulbous ornamentation known as cup and cover.

Standing tables of joined construction with a strong underframe were used for dining, although trestle tables were still used in most households. In the 1580s table supports were carved with cup and cover decoration. Draw tables, with extendible leaves supported on slides, became popular from the 1540s, and small tables were in use by the end of the century on which to play cards and board games for example. The use of inlays spread during the Elizabethan period, especially with the arrival of immigrant German craftsmen in London in the 1580s.

France

As in the rest of Europe, little furniture of note was produced in France before *c.*1400. The few chairs, stools and tables that did exist were plain and gothic in style, made of thick planks and

joined with pegs. This changed when the Renaissance spread from Italy to France at the end of the 15th century. As a result, French artists and craftsmen rediscovered classical antiquity adopting two features in particular – the Grotesque style of ornament and the use of architectural forms, notably columns, cornices, and pediments.

French Renaissance style can be divided into two main periods. The first was roughly during the reign of François I (1515–47), when carving in the Grotesque style of ornamentation was used on almost every available surface and architectural forms were subordinate to decoration. The showpiece of the new style was the palace at Fontainebleau outside Paris. This was the center for the school of Fontainebleau, greatly influenced by the Italian Francesco Primaticcio (1504–70), and was responsible for introducing Italian designs in furniture production. These included carved motifs and table friezes, which were decorated with designs such as slender nymphs, chubby angels with garlands of flowers, satyr masks, strapwork, and scrolls.

▲ WALNUT
mid-16th century
The carving and
architectural decoration
on this provincial table
are equally important.

Similarly, chairs at first had a wide, tall back and were supported by side pieces. In later chairs, which are often known as *caqueteuses* (gossip-chairs), the back became narrower, the arms were widely-splayed, and the side pieces were replaced by slender columns.

Beds, especially the headboards, were often extravagantly carved.

The most important regional style in French Renaissance furniture is that of the Ile de France. It was characterized by refined architectural proportions. Also significant were the styles of Burgundy, which was marked by massive shapes and bold carving, and of the south, in which multicolored painting and marquetry predominated.

The second period began with the reign of Henri II (1547–59), by which time the applied arts in France were in turmoil, and it lasted until the French Wars of Religion (1562–98). In addition to the highly decorated pieces to be seen at Fontainebleau, another style, emphasizing graceful proportion and geometric, restrained design, emerged in reaction to Renaissance excess.

Oak, which had been the principal material used during the gothic period, was replaced by the darker, oilier walnut, which was not only easier to carve but also produced a high sheen when polished. Carving was supplemented by other decorative techniques, such as inlays of wood, precious stones, ivory, and other materials. Metal mounts – i.e., hinges, handles, locks, and corner pieces – were generally eschewed as being too obtrusive.

The principal showpiece of the period was the buffet or sideboard. Typically this had two compartments, one above the other and each with two doors, but there were other forms. The door panels were carved and framed with architectural features.

Tables, supported during the first period by elaborately carved end pieces, became more elegant by mid-century and stood on legs in the form of slender, turned columns on plain bases.

▶ WALNUT
late 16th century
The sparse and elegant
architectural forms of
this gossip-chair,
including the *trompe l'oeil*
arcade carved on the
back, are characteristic of
this period, when chairs
were not upholstered but
would have had
removable cushions.

Italy

Although Italy was renowned for the splendor of its decorative arts during the Renaissance, furniture remained sparse, even in the grandest palaces.

The production of fine chests flourished, however, and their makers were considered superior in rank to the makers of more rudimentary pieces. Certain areas of Italy excelled in the production of marriage chests (or *cassone*) as objects of great status, and specialist workshops flourished, one of the best known being that of Apollonio di Giovanni in Florence. The chests were painted with the arms of the two families and with scenes of courtly love. The front panels were painted in tempera (a mixture of pigment and egg yolk), and they showed romantic scenes, such as the meeting of Solomon and Sheba, often set within architectural vistas that reflected the Renaissance interest in perspective.

In the 16th century the gilded and painted *cassone* were superseded by a richly carved type, the front panel of which was often decorated with high-relief scenes of battles or triumphs – in time such carving became Mannerist, with contorted poses and elongated figures. Some chests were also decorated with gilded gesso (plaster base) designs in relief, usually with Grotesque motifs.

The ancient Roman technique of *pietra dura* (hard-stone inlay) was revived in the 16th century, the most celebrated workshop being the Opificio della Pietra Dura, which was founded in Florence in 1588. The craft involved cutting hard stones – lapis lazuli, porphyry, and agate, for example – and laying them out in interlocking, mosaic-like patterns. They were used on table tops, which at the time had supports in the form of lions, griffins, sphinxes, or human figures. *Scagliola* – imitation marble made by mixing powdered selenite with size – was also developed at this time. Skillful craftsmen were able to imitate costly *pietra dura* work in this cheap material, and the technique spread throughout Europe in the 17th century.

Simple chests were not only used for storage but were placed in pairs around a bed dais, as a step up to the bed and as a seat and a table.

The *cassapanca* (settle) derived from the *cassone* by raising its back and sides to form supports for the back and arms, evolving in much the same way as settles in northern Europe had done. However, the sarcophagus form of the *cassapanca* gave it a distinctly "antique" appearance.

A characteristically Italian chair began to appear in the early 17th century. This rested on cartouche-shaped supports at front and back, and the backrest was also shaped like a cartouche, although examples with shell backs are also known. This style was taken up by the English, who mistakenly called it *sgabello*.

The walls of grand rooms in Italian palaces were often decorated with panels painted to imitate costly tapestries, and similar painted decoration was used on *desci da parto* (trays commemorating births). Another important form of decoration that evolved in Italy at this time and that was used on cupboard as well as chest panels was intarsia (inlay), in which a design was gouged out of a carcass wood (often walnut) and then filled in with different color

ITALIAN *CASSONE*

◀ INTARSIA WALNUT AND OTHER WOODS
*c.*1500
The two coats of arms suggest that this was a marriage chest. The geometric inlay is similar in design to that of the *certosina* work of Lombardy and the Veneto, although it is executed entirely in different colored woods and does not have the mother-of-pearl or silver popular in those areas.

▶ *SCAGLIOLA* WITH EBONIZED AND PARTLY GILT MOLDINGS

mid-17th century

In the 16th century the grand-dukes of Tuscany revived the Roman art of making *scagliola*, a composition material of ground marble, gypsum, plaster of Paris, and glue. This was applied like paint, allowed to dry, then polished. It was so like marble and *pietra dura* that it was known as counterfeit marble. The architectural treatment of this cabinet, with the pediment over the central cupboard and ripple moldings, is similar to contemporary work from other areas, but the *scagliola* decoration of birds and flowers and the geometric pattern on the sides have their origins in the distinctively Italian craft of *pietra dura*.

woods, such as fruitwoods, yew, and olive. The designs were often pictorial and frequently demonstrate skill in depicting perspective.

The warmer climate meant that hangings were less necessary, and privacy was assured by curtaining off part of the room. Most beds were of a box type, with end panels heightened to form head and foot boards. As in other Italian furniture, the panels were often decoratively treated, either painted or inlaid.

Spain and Portugal

 During the 16th century the arts flourished throughout the Iberian peninsula. The vocabulary of the decorative arts was enriched by the *mudéjar* (Moorish) style, which in furniture took the form of geometric inlay, often using as a ground wood the walnut that grew throughout Spain. The influence of Moorish decoration can be seen both in the Italian *certosina* work, which was popular in Venice, where mother-of-pearl inlays enlivened surfaces, and in the geometric moldings of late 16th- and early 17th-century Dutch furniture. In Spain *mudéjar* decoration co-existed with Renaissance ornament and other types of Islamic decoration.

Territorial acquisitions in the New World brought great wealth to Spain and Portugal, and the grandest furniture was inlaid with silver. Exotic woods – including ebony and mahogany – were also used. The 16th-century chair, known in England as a back stool, may have originated in Spain, where it is called the *sillón de fraileros* (monk's chair). Early Spanish types were strongly constructed, with square-cut legs and sturdy stretchers. Covers were of velvet, damask or the tooled and painted leather associated particularly with the city of Cordoba. Later, this style of chair took on the French-inspired characteristics of elaborate and decorative spiral-turned uprights and stretchers, but the distinctive use of leather continued.

The rise of the cabinet as a display piece was as marked in Spain as elsewhere in Europe. The *vargueño* (a 19th-century term) was a cabinet with a drop-front resting on slides drawn out from the decorative stand, often of arcaded form. Exteriors were often relatively plain, but interiors were sometimes ornamented with Moorish motifs, silverwork-style reliefs, or inlay.

Germany and Austria

 In the 15th century the predominantly Catholic cities of Augsburg and Nuremberg in the south of Germany, already known as centers of artistic excellence, became famous for woodcuts and engraved designs. The Augsburg-trained Peter Flötner (c.1490–1546), who worked in Nuremberg from c.1522, had visited Italy, and some of his designs relate closely to the decorative painting of Raphael at the Villa Madama in Rome in their use of Grotesque motifs, acanthus scrolls, and putti. His furniture designs also incorporate architectural forms.

Craftsmen and designers from Augsburg were noted for the exuberance and vitality of their work, as may be seen in the inlay work based on the designs of Lorenz Stöer (fl.1550–1621), who added a Mannerist twist to Renaissance interest in ancient architecture and perspective by producing designs of ruined buildings in deliberately distorted perspective. These often included borders of strapwork, a form of decoration developed by Italian stuccoists at the palace of Fontainebleau in France and taken up by designers across northern Europe. The skills of the inlay worker and carver combined to produce extravagantly decorated cabinets, using not only woods of various colors but also amber and precious metals. These cabinets were at first placed on tables, later on stands. The *Kunstkammer*, a cabinet for displaying precious objects, replaced the *Wunderkammer*, in which merely bizarre objects were placed.

In the mainly Protestant north, cabinet-makers retained their strong gothic tradition of vigorous wood carving, but this was often combined with the use of Renaissance architectural motifs.

The Low Countries

The Low Countries (Belgium and the Netherlands) passed from Burgundian to Habsburg rule in 1493. The largely Protestant Northern Provinces broke away in 1579 leaving the Catholic south under Spanish rule. In the Low Countries Grotesque ornamentation, originating in Renaissance discoveries of Roman decoration in a supposed grotto, assumed an increasingly exaggerated character in the hands of Antwerp designers. One of these, the prolific Hans Vredeman de Vries (1526–c.1604), produced designs of fantastic architectural vistas, cartouches of strapwork and variations on the classical orders. He influenced English craftsmen and was the author of the earliest furniture pattern-book, *Différents Pourtraicts de Menuiserie*, which was published at Wolfenbüttel c.1588.

▼ PAINTED AND PARTLY GILT
16th century
This cabinet has a chest base with a pair of drawers over a pair of cupboards, rather than having the more commonly seen trestle base. Behind the fall-front there are 12 small drawers grouped around a cupboard with three more drawers inside. The writing surface is supported on shell-fronted lopers, which are pulled out when the front is opened. The piece is elaborately painted in the *mudéjar* (Moorish) style.

THE
17th
CENTURY

This was a century of change. The refinement that had begun in England and France in the mid–16th century continued. By 1700 there were gilt chairs in France, marquetry in Flanders, sculptural carving in Italy, regular trade between Europe and the Far East, and constant contact between Europe and the Americas. Perhaps the most significant change, however, was that furniture was no longer simply a symbol of power and status — it had become the property of the populace.

ENGLAND

The Stuart kings James I (reigned 1603–25) and Charles I (reigned 1625–49) introduced continental standards of luxury to England. Huge sums were spent on royal palaces, and agents abroad sent back paintings and sculpture and lured foreign artists to work in England. All this was swept away in the Civil War of 1642–9, when country houses were ransacked by troops, families fled into exile and, after the execution of Charles I in 1649, his goods were systematically sold off.

It is difficult to imagine the palaces and grand houses as they existed before 1640, because almost all the exquisite pieces made for the king and court have disappeared. The great hall of a house retained its role of an entrance from Tudor times, but it was no longer used as a dining room. It was traditionally furnished with a long, heavy oak table and benches. Leading off the hall was the parlor, furnished more comfortably with tables, one or two chairs, stools, and perhaps a chest or cupboard. The main or "state" rooms were usually on the first floor. Chief among them was the great chamber, which served as both dining and reception room and which had the finest furniture – a draw-table, armchairs, stools, and cupboards displaying silver dishes and flagons.

The bed, together with its hangings, was by far the most expensive item in the house. Otherwise bedroom furniture was similar to that in other rooms. The long gallery was sparsely furnished, with chairs and stools against the walls, a few small tables and chests, perhaps a cabinet, and paintings. The most private room was the closet, which might contain a day-bed, a small writing table, and a cabinet for papers or precious objects.

Very few types of furniture were used: tables, chairs, and stools, chests, coffers and cupboards, and beds. Most of these had barely changed from those in use in the late 16th century, and they were made from the same woods – oak and occasionally walnut – and using the same construction techniques.

In 1660 the monarchy was restored with Charles II (reigned 1660–85), and palaces and great houses were rebuilt and refurnished. This activity was combined with the massive rebuilding of ordinary houses after the Great Fire of London (1666), which provided a large market for good furniture in fashionable styles. New items of furniture were largely based on Dutch models. Later, in the reigns of James II (1685–8) and William and Mary (1689–1702), French style came to dominate, and many skilled Huguenots, French Protestants fleeing from persecution at home after the revocation of the

ENGLISH GATE-LEG TABLE

▶ OAK

*c.*1670

Although it was made during the reign of Charles II (1660–85), this table shows Puritan influences in its plain lines and lack of decoration. The shapes are geometric – the top is round and the stretchers are rectangular – and even the turned legs are simple. The only decorative elements are minimal – the aprons hanging from the frieze. The table has two single gate-legs, one on each side, and a drawer in the frieze. The advantage of the two flaps is that the table folds away to quite a small size. Tables such as this were made for a variety of purposes, from card playing to dining, and in a variety of sizes. The fashion for formal gate-leg tables died away in the early 18th century, but was revived after *c.*1770, and they continued to be produced to about the mid-19th century, especially for country and common use.

Edict of Nantes in 1685, brought their cabinet-making and metal-working crafts to London, raising the level of craftsmanship to continental standards.

During this period a great house had an imposing staircase, leading from the entrance hall up to a saloon (the old great chamber), on each side of which were apartments, sets of rooms consisting of an anteroom, bed-chamber, and closet, some with a withdrawing room and presence chamber for royal use. For these splendid rooms the finest furniture was made, including tables, looking-glasses, and *torchères* (candlestands) set against the piers (spaces between tall windows), lavishly upholstered beds and chairs, exquisite cabinets and writing desks. Furniture became increasingly specialized, with chests of drawers, bookcases, and other pieces made for specific purposes. Walnut replaced oak as the standard material, and other woods – laburnum, kingwood, ebony – were used for exotic effects. Oriental lacquer and its European imitations were fashionable, and their dark tones contrasted with carved and gilded wood. Textiles became less important.

New fashions in tables in the 17th century included the draw-table, whose two ends could be drawn out, which gradually replaced the long, heavy oak table. Most draw-tables were of oak, but some were of walnut. The legs were bulbous, perhaps shaped as Ionic capitals, a decoration sometimes continued on the frieze. Gate-leg tables, which had been introduced in the 16th century, were popular throughout the 17th century. The tops of these tables folded and could be opened out and supported on the gate-leg. By the 1660s walnut gate-leg tables, with spiral turned legs began to replace draw-tables for dining.

Small movable tables, made of oak or pine and covered with leather or textiles, were also used. These sometimes were of much finer quality and made of carved and silvered wood, occasionally overlaid with embossed metal. Marble-topped tables on stone baluster stems or strong wooden frames were made in the early 17th century, some by the sculptor Nicholas

Stone (1587–1647). Charles I owned several similar tables (the makers are not known), some of black marble, some of white, some inlaid. Later in the century marble-topped tables became rarer but were sometimes used for dining rooms.

After 1660 the most striking new furniture arrangement was the side table with a looking-glass over it, placed against a pier and often flanked by a pair of matching candlestands. Pier tables were rectangular and small. In the 1660s a walnut veneer was used, sometimes inset with panels of oyster veneer or parquetry – both veneers with geometric patterns – and the legs were spiral and connected by flat stretchers. By the 1670s panels of floral marquetry were used to decorate the tops of tables, and sometimes the friezes, which occasionally had shallow drawers. The legs formed S-scrolls and had serpentine stretchers. Other tables were made of ebony, sometimes with plaques of embossed silver, and a few were of imported lacquer or japanned. In the 1690s French fashion dictated a straight tapering leg with a gadrooned capital and scrolled stretchers, which rose in the center to an urn shape. By the end of the century these tables were of carved and gilded wood, and their tops bore elaborate carved or punched designs.

ENGLISH TABLE

⬛ OYSTER VENEER
*c.*1670
The unusual decoration of small circles of veneer (from which the term "oyster" derives) is produced by cutting the branches of a tree across the grain. Like tree trunks, branches show annual growth rings, and an economical way of making the most of a special tree was to slice the branches and enclose the rings in a frame of lighter wood. This technique is generally found on English furniture, with woods as varied as laburnum, lignum vitae (*Guaiacum* genus), olive wood, and various fruitwoods. The shape of this table is standard for the period, with barley-twist legs, inward-curving, cross-framed stretchers, and bun feet.

MARQUETRY

Marquetry, a decorative technique, became popular in England toward the end of the 17th century when it was practiced as part of the new craft of cabinet-making. It entails gluing a thin veneer of different colored woods or other materials to the carcass of a piece of furniture. The most popular type of marquetry was the floral panel, depicting a vase or spray of flowers. At first made of contrasting light and dark woods, floral panels later became brilliantly colored by the incorporation of bone or ivory stained green for leaves and red for exotic birds. This emphasis on decoration influenced the design of furniture because large, flat areas were needed for the increasingly elaborate marquetry panels. Occasionally, especially in Dutch pieces, marquetry covered the entire surface, but typically it was contained within oval panels, with the spandrels (the spaces between the panel and the corners of the surface) decorated with a simpler design.

Seaweed marquetry, which was popular in the 1690s, consisted of small-scale, stylized arabesque designs, usually of yellow sycamore contrasted with a darker walnut background. A difficult and expensive technique, it was used mainly on fine pieces of furniture such as small writing tables and small longcase clocks.

ENGLISH WRITING CABINET

▶ WALNUT WITH FLORAL MARQUETRY
*c.*1690

The base of this William and Mary piece is made of two short and two long drawers beneath a fall-front writing compartment containing drawers and pigeonholes arranged around a central cupboard. There is a further concealed drawer with a cushion-shaped marquetry front in the frieze just below the overhanging cornice. Fall-front desks of this kind are often called escritoires, but their original owners may have called them scrutoires. They were fashionable in the late 17th century but seem to have been generally superseded by the bureau-bookcase in England in the following century. Luxuriant floral marquetry of this kind is typical of the period, and it was inspired by the veneering skills of immigrant craftsmen from the Netherlands and France.

In the 17th century, armchairs were symbols of status – the great chair and footstool were reserved for the head of the household with perhaps one other for his wife or an important guest. By *c.*1610 an upholstered chair would have replaced the wooden one in aristocratic households, and this was usually *en suite* with a footstool, armless chairs, and stools. The most common of the upholstered chairs were farthingale chairs, which had a padded back and seat, with a gap between that enabled women wearing hooped whale-bone petticoats (farthingales) to sit comfortably. The covering was of turkeywork (knotted pile fabric), cloth or leather. Carved wooden chairs with two solid supports in place of legs, usually made of walnut, often partially gilded, and known as *sgabello* chairs, were made in England in the 1630s and imported.

Caning for chair backs and seats was introduced from the Netherlands in the 1660s. At first the caning was of a wide mesh. The front stretcher, the supports flanking the cane panel of the back and cresting rail were all carved, and cushions covered the cane seat. By the 1670s the

mesh became finer and the back higher, reaching extreme heights by the end of the century. Straight stretchers and cresting rails were replaced by pierced and arched forms.

Armchairs were solidly upholstered and lost their farthingale gap. The most comfortable form were wing chairs. Most late 17th-century chairs were of walnut, but some were beech, painted black or "ebonized" to resemble expensive imported wood.

Day-beds, dating mainly from the second half of the century, had cane seats and single cane ends, carved cresting rails and eight legs each, the legs united by stretchers. Later examples have padded seats and ends; couches have two ends and backs. By the 1690s they were comfortably padded and had high, shaped backs.

Chests, made by joiners and usually made of oak, were the traditional storage for all kinds of objects. Some, used as strong boxes, were entirely cased in iron and had massive locks, while others were bound with iron. Most were paneled, and some had carved decoration. The style of chests was less affected by changing fashions than that of other items of furniture, and in the following century provincial chests still resembled those made a hundred years before. The coffer was a type of chest with a domed lid,

ENGLISH ARMCHAIR

◄ WALNUT WITH CANE BACK AND SEAT
*c.*1670
The wide mesh of the cane seat would have been covered by a cushion. The spiral turned supports of the legs and back later gave way to scroll legs and carved decoration. The cresting, back panel frame, and front stretcher of this transitional chair are treated as decorative areas.

ENGLISH DAY-BED

▼ GILT WOOD
*c.*1695
This day-bed was made for Thomas Osborne, 1st Duke of Leeds, for his manor at Kiveton Park, Yorkshire. The French taste is evident in the elaborate fringing and braiding, and the back is crested by an escutcheon bearing the duke's cipher and coronet. It was an interest in comfort that fostered the construction of day-beds such as this, and this is an especially fine example.

made of wood encased in leather or fabric. Large coffers were used as traveling trunks. Their leather covers were held in place by brass studs, which were arranged in decorative patterns, and their corners were strengthened with metal mounts. Small coffers, covered in velvet or embroidered silk, sat on dressing-tables and were used as jewel boxes.

By the early 17th century, cupboards, which were open-fronted, had three shelves with decorated friezes and stood on carved supports. One type with an enclosed upper section is known as a court cupboard. Cupboards were used in halls or great chambers to display silver.

The press, which was practical rather than decorative, was an oak cupboard enclosed by doors, with shelves and pegs for clothes.

Bookcases hardly existed in the early 17th century – a set of hanging shelves or a chest were considered sufficient. As book buying increased, however, so did the need for efficient and accessible storage. In 1666 Samuel Pepys recorded in his *Diary* that he had ordered bookcases from a joiner, and they survive, as do similar examples. They have a bold cornice, blazed doors, and adjustable shelves.

There were few innovations in British furniture in the 17th century, but the period did see the development of a compact, practical new piece – the chest of drawers. Early examples were massive and heavy, usually of oak, occasionally with an inlay of bone or mother-of-pearl. Some had double doors, which opened to reveal the drawers inside; others had one very deep drawer, which could be at the top or bottom. Drawer fronts had Flemish-inspired decoration, either with faceted panels or with geometric moldings and applied baluster decoration, in which sections of turned wood were split vertically and glued to the surface. Handles were simply small wooden knobs.

From the 1660s the design of chests of drawers was refined. Walnut was used instead of oak, brass drop handles were added and, by the end of the century, when the chest of drawers became known as the commode, panels of floral or seaweed marquetry were applied to the sides and front, making it an expensive, decorative, and useful piece. Some examples were built on stands and, with their spiral, turned legs and curved stretchers, resembled cabinets.

The cabinet on stand was the most fashionable new piece of furniture to appear in the 17th century. In the 16th century, a cabinet was a small portable box with either two doors or a fall-front, which was placed on a table in the closet or study and used to store jewels, miniatures or papers. The cabinet on stand, which was used to furnish bedrooms, great chambers, and long galleries, was much more substantial and highly decorative.

ENGLISH BOOKCASE

▼ OAK
*c.*1670
Glazed doors protect the books, while finely carved moldings separate the lower and upper stages and form a deep cornice. This design continued to be made into the 18th century.

In the 1620s and 1630s most cabinets were imported from Europe. Paris makers specialized in ebony veneers, as did those in Augsburg, where the veneer was enriched with silver mounts (handles, corner pieces, and so on). Other fine cabinets came from Italy, and the diarist John Evelyn (1620–1706) possessed a particularly fine one made in Florence. It is in-laid with panels of *pietra dura* and decorated with gilt bronze mounts. The cabinet is unusual in having outer doors enclosing the smaller drawers, which had become standard by mid-century. In the later years of the 17th century a cornice formed another, handle-less drawer.

Because of the expensive hangings, the most valuable item in a 17th-century house was the bed. Grand beds had a tester (wooden canopy supported on posts) and curtains, and some had

VENEERING AND LACQUER

After the Restoration production of cabinets increased. They were usually made with a matching stand, which had six legs and stretchers. The design of the leg developed from spiral-turned to scrolled to tapered. Some cabinets were of walnut, either oyster-veneered or with inset panels of floral marquetry; others were of exotic woods or of other native woods which, cut in transverse sections, produced a strongly contrasting pattern of light and dark.

The fashion for lacquer – a hardy, glossy finish, often black with gold decoration – originated with cabinets and screens imported from China and Japan. By the 1670s this fashion had become a craze and supply could not match demand, so a substitute process, japanning, was introduced. Lacquer and japanned cabinets were usually set on richly carved and gilded stands, and sometimes had matching cresting rails above the cabinet.

ENGLISH CABINET ON STAND

◄ LABURNUM WOOD WITH SILVER MOUNTS
*c.*1670
The strong markings of the oyster-veneered laburnum make a dramatic pattern. Only the spiral-turned legs are plain. The silver mounts are particularly fine.

carved headboards and two bedposts left visible at the foot. Such beds were superseded by the more fashionable French bed, which had no visible woodwork, but after 1660 beds became increasingly elaborate and costly. The neat exterior of the French bed acquired a richly decorated, deeply fringed valance around the tester. One of the finest surviving examples, probably made by the joiner Thomas Robins (or Roberts), is a state bed made for James II, now at Knole, Kent. It was made *en suite* with a pair of armchairs and six stools, all covered in Genoese cut velvet. Both the bed and seats have gilt wood legs carved with putti and the royal coat of arms.

By the 1690s beds, like chair backs, had become impressively high – the Melville Bed (now in the Victoria & Albert Museum, London) is, at 15 feet and with its elaborate draperies, a remarkable example of this style.

FRANCE

EARLY 17TH CENTURY

In the reigns of Henri IV (1589–1610) and Louis XIII (1610–43) Spanish, Dutch and German styles, techniques and materials joined those from Italy in influencing French art, particularly that of the court. So well were these influences assimilated in furniture that it is often difficult to determine the country of origin of pieces from this period. At the same time, the Renaissance style continued to be used, although in modified form: the architectural structures and elaborate ornament of the previous century gave way to moldings, geometric carving, and lathe-turned legs, pedestals and so on.

The principal piece of furniture was the box-like cabinet, with two doors that opened to reveal drawers, that was made of ebony and

ENGLISH CHEST OF DRAWERS

▶ OAK INLAID WITH HOLLY AND BOG OAK
*c.*1660
The drawer fronts are inlaid with contrasting colored woods in simple foliage designs, and the side panels have applied baluster decoration of a style used in the early 17th century on beds and tables.

stood on table-height, turned legs. The favorite material for decorating cabinets was ebony, an expensive wood of which craftsmen made lavish and clever use. Thick sheets of ebony veneer were decorated with low-relief carving, then applied to the cheap wood carcass of the piece. The interior was sometimes crafted in ebony to resemble architectural façades with turned columns, pediments, and doorways. It might incorporate tortoiseshell and silver ornaments or classical perspective decoration executed in wood and ivory marquetry.

Large cupboards and buffets also featured at this time. Many were of the same basic construction as during the Renaissance, but they tended to be decorated with heavy moldings framing panels of geometric carving or, in the case of buffets, with veneer.

Chairs, tables, and much of the decoration of cabinets and cupboards were made of fruitwood or walnut. The construction of some pieces included spiral twists and other complicated lathe turning, which was by this time in widespread use. Chairs became more comfortable, with both seats and backs covered with brightly colored embroidered velvet, patterned to match the decoration of the rest of the room.

The engravings of Abraham Bosse, which provide the most vivid views of interiors of this time, reveal the extent to which textiles were used to cover furniture. Tables were draped with cloth, chair legs were covered in the same upholstery fabric as the back and seat, and beds were so heavily draped that no wood was visible. The increased convenience and comfort of the furniture depicted by Bosse is reflected in the large number of small tables that survive. These have oblong or octagonal tops and turned legs.

LOUIS XIV

The reign of Louis XIV (1643–1715) is famed for the splendor of the king's courts at Versailles and Paris. After *c.*1660 the dominant cultural figure was the interior designer Charles Lebrun (1619–90), who was the first director of the Gobelins tapestry workshop. The workshop, later known as the Manufacture Royale des Meubles de la Couronne, contained a cabinet-

FRENCH ARMCHAIR

◀ GILT WOOD
mid-17th century
Leaf scroll carving, "hairy" paw feet, and "mutton bone" legs and stretchers are typical of the period, as is the cut velvet upholstery.

FRENCH CABINET ON STAND

▼ EBONY
early 17th century
The carving and moldings enhance the shape of this cabinet and stand. French cabinet-makers were strongly influenced by Italian inlaid work, and the technique of veneering allowed them to cover carcasses of wood with sheets of ebony that were sufficiently thick to permit low-relief carving.

making department run by the Italian Domenico Cucci (*c.*1640–1705). This specialized in the production of elaborate cabinets decorated with panels of *pietra dura* and mounted with ormolu.

The Dutch cabinet-maker Pierre Golle (1620–84) worked in Paris from the 1640s. He belonged to a different tradition – his pieces are a development of the great ebony cabinets of earlier in the century. Golle created court furniture of simple, usually traditional shapes, such as cabinets on stands, tables, and kneehole desks, using colorful marquetry of woods, ivory, shells, and metals.

As in the first half of the century, sets of seat furniture, *ameublements*, together with matching bed and wall hangings are found in profusion, but cabinet-work is rare. Large chairs and arm-chairs were carved with scrolls and gilded, and then covered with velvet or silk embroidered with gold and silver thread. The gilt wood side table made its first appearance at this time. Such tables often have straight, tapering legs, a scroll-shaped stretcher and a frieze carved with strap-work and other stylized motifs. They were known as *pieds de table* (table supports), because the costly marble top was considered to be more important than the comparatively inexpensive support.

FRENCH CABINET

▶ EBONY, GILT BRONZE, TORTOISESHELL, MOTHER-OF-PEARL, IVORY, AND LACQUER

*c.*1650

Flemish influence is apparent in this piece, which is attributed to Pierre Golle, the Dutch cabinet-maker who worked in Paris from the 1640s.

Cabinets, cupboards, and desks of the second half of the century are notable for their opulence and size. The Gobelins workshop produced cabinets in ebony inlaid with Florentine *pietra dura* panels. Gilt bronze was used to frame the panels and also for figural mounts, which supply architectural shape. Cabinets were also made with wood marquetry, with a central door, drawers at the side and often gilt wood figural supports. Matching sets, sometimes known as triads, consisting of a table, two candlestands, and a mirror frame, in wood marquetry or lacquer, were extremely popular.

The use of metal and tortoiseshell marquetry, generally known as boulle, was named after its prime exponent, André-Charles Boulle. The decoration had become popular by the 1680s and was used on various types of furniture, particularly on *armoires* (large cupboards) and *bureaux à caissons* (kneehole desks), which were later known as *bureaux Mazarin*. The *bureau Mazarin* is the most often seen piece of Louis XIV furniture. It usually has eight legs, either square and tapering or scroll-shaped, each set of four being joined by an X-shaped stretcher. There are three or four drawers at each side and

▲ GILT WOOD AND RED MARBLE
*c.*1715
Inspired by a design of Nicolas Pineau (1684–1754), the light-hearted motifs – the dolphins, masks of bearded men, and hoof feet – are typical of the lightening of style at the beginning of the 18th century.

one long, shallow drawer above the kneehole. A variation, which is known as the *bureau brisé* (folding desk), has a top that folds back in the center to reveal further small drawers inside and a writing surface.

Towards the end of Louis XIV's reign Boulle began to experiment with new furniture shapes, and two designs in particular were to prove especially popular in the next century – the *bureau plat* (writing table) and the commode (chest of drawers). The *bureau plat* is large, stands on four legs, and has three drawers in the frieze or

🝆 BOULLE MARQUETRY 🝆

*B*oulle marquetry is a brass veneer set in tortoiseshell. It was invented by Pierre Golle (fl.1644–84), but it was named after its most noted practitioner, André-Charles Boulle (1642–1732). Boulle originally trained as a cabinet-maker, architect, engraver, and bronze worker, and he published a series of engravings that helped to promote his work throughout Europe. He never signed his pieces, and although they often sold for vast sums, he was often in debt, largely because he indulged his passion for collecting works of art, especially Renaissance paintings.

The veneer was produced by tightly fastening together a sheet of brass and one of tortoiseshell, placing on top a sheet of paper marked with a pattern, then cutting with a fretsaw around the pattern and through the sheets of material below. The cut-out pieces of brass then fitted perfectly into the spaces left in the tortoiseshell. Much of Boulle's furniture was made in pairs, the piece with brass-in-tortoiseshell marquetry being known as première partie, *and the other piece, veneered with the "negative" of the cut-out tortoiseshell-in-brass being known as* contre partie. *Sometimes a mixture of both types was used in the same piece.*

The marquetry pattern was usually one of scrolled foliage within geometric borders or of fanciful scenes inspired by the work of the designer and decorator Jean Bérain (1640–1711). Brass patterns were usually engraved with, for example, tendrils or shading to produce a three-dimensional effect, and the tortoiseshell was often colored, usually red or blue, by placing painted paper beneath it on the carcass of the furniture.

FRENCH TABLE

▶ BOULLE
*c.*1695
This table top is in *contre partie* – that is, the background is of metal with a tortoiseshell underlay. Boulle work remained popular from the end of the 17th century, peaking in the 18th century, and enjoying a revival in the 19th century. One of its disadvantages is that it is easily damaged. Because different metals expand at different rates, the work can lift from the surface on which it is laid, and it is very difficult to replace. The wrinkle across the central oval of this table top has been caused in this way, but this is, nevertheless, a fine example of 17th-century work, showing a wealth of decoration. The central armorial, mythological figures, strapwork, floral and scroll inlay, together with the engraving, enhance the colorful effect.

the front, usually genuine at one side and dummies at the other. Much more than the chest of drawers to which we are accustomed today, the finely ornamented commode was the focal point of a room, often being placed at the center of the longest wall. Both these pieces were originally decorated with boulle marquetry, but by the time of Louis XIV's death in 1715 this had been replaced by simpler geometric wood veneers.

ITALY

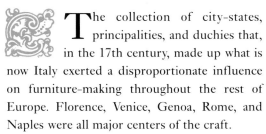The collection of city-states, principalities, and duchies that, in the 17th century, made up what is now Italy exerted a disproportionate influence on furniture-making throughout the rest of Europe. Florence, Venice, Genoa, Rome, and Naples were all major centers of the craft.

Many of the furniture forms developed during the Renaissance persisted into the 17th century, but the embellishments became increasingly elaborate, in keeping with the baroque style that was flourishing in other arts in Italy at the time. Chests, chairs, and table supports were massively carved with such motifs as caryatid figures, putti and gods, eagles and dolphins, fruit and plants in sumptuous garlands, supported by spiral scrolls and shells. Beds were magnificently gilded and hung with silk or velvet. Table tops were made of exotically colored marble.

The leading practitioners of these sculptural effects were Andrea Brustolon (1662–1732) in Venice, Domenico Parodi (1668–1740) in Genoa and Antonio Corradini (1668–1752), who took the full-blown sensuality of the Venetian baroque into the 1730s. Their furniture represented the peak of the grand effect for which many aristocrats strove. The wealthy citizens of Rome, Genoa, Florence, and Turin made sure that their state rooms reflected their worldly success – galleries with painted ceilings had antique statues ranged along the walls, interspersed with carved and gilded console tables, throne-like chairs, and fantastically decorated cabinets.

◄ 17th century
This armchair, which was made in Venice, is in the manner of the sculptor Andrea Brustolon (1662–1732), whose heavily carved furniture with figure supports established a showy tradition for Venetian *palazzo* furniture. Pieces known to have been designed by Brustolon include frames, tables, and vases, and religious items such as crucifixes, tabernacles, and a baldachin.

Such cabinets were designed not only to house the collections of curiosities owned by all rich connoisseurs of the time but also to display the craftsmanship of their makers, and they were adorned with gilded bronze sculptures of the drawers and borders, carvings in boxwood or lignum vitae or tortoiseshell panels. Most, especially those made in the Opificio della Pietra Dura in Florence, were inset with naturalistic birds and flowers in *pietra dura*. These cabinets were commissioned not only by wealthy Italian patrons but royal aristocratic families throughout Europe. Unmounted panels of *pietra dura* or *scagliola*, which could be used for cabinets or table tops, were bought by rich travelers on the Grand Tour.

By the end of the 17th century the leading stylist of hard-stone furniture was Giovanni Battista Foggini (1652–1725), a sculptor who set off flat hard-stone panels with elaborate gilt bronze mounts. Equally exuberant were the three-dimensional swags of fruit and leaves with which he provided a colorful and light-hearted foil for ponderously baroque ebony furniture.

In contrast to the show rooms of Italian *palazzi*, the living rooms were, like those of middle-class houses, much more sparsely and simply furnished with solid, sturdy pieces, mainly of walnut. Nevertheless, few could resist decoration of some sort, and inlays of ivory, pewter and mother-of-pearl were favored for some of the more important pieces made in the areas around Venice and Lomardy. Like much Italian furniture, they are rather crudely constructed compared with similar pieces from northern Europe, but the decoration has a pleasing vivacity.

Venice was famous throughout Europe for the production of mirror glass, and until France and England developed their own industries in the late 17th and early 18th centuries, the city effectively enjoyed a monopoly. The manufacture of elaborately carved and gilded frames to complement the looking-glasses was an important industry in both Venice and Florence, and Venetian mirrors were regarded as essential features in all well-appointed Italian rooms.

SPAIN AND PORTUGAL

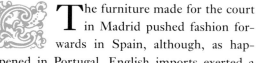

The furniture made for the court in Madrid pushed fashion forwards in Spain, although, as happened in Portugal, English imports exerted a strong influence.

In Spain the dominant inspirations were from France and Italy, both dynastically linked to the Spanish kings, but the country's Moorish past and the associated decorative forms lived on in provincial and country furniture. The rococo fashion for console and side tables, heavily carved and gilded and complemented by ornate mirrors, was appropriate for the lofty Spanish rooms and led to the establishment of a mirror factory.

The *vargueño* (cabinet) continued to be popular as a luxury object but was replaced as a show piece in the mid-17th century by the *papeleira*, a type of cabinet lacking the characteristic Spanish fall-front and closer in style to Dutch and French pieces. Spanish cabinets on stands at this time are remarkable for their rich veneers, usually of ebony and tortoiseshell but sometimes of carved ivory.

GERMANY AND AUSTRIA

Strong regional differences are discernible in the furniture made throughout central and eastern Europe. Like Italy, Germany was a collection of more or less independent states rather than a unified nation. Italian influence was strong in the predominantly Catholic south, while Dutch influence was felt in the Protestant north. The patronage of princely bishops and other ecclesiastics was often as lavish as that of secular princes, especially in western Germany. In the north much furniture was produced to reflect the wealth of rich merchants from flourishing city states like Danzig, Hamburg, and Lübeck.

Nuremberg and Augsburg continued their tradition of fine furniture craftsmanship, producing cabinets decorated with ivory, ebony, tortoiseshell, metals and semi-precious stones. They were works of art in their own right and were exported to rich connoisseurs all over Europe. Toward the end of the 17th century these two towns also became known for the publication of ornamental engravings of interiors and of books of designs for furniture and interior decoration. In the early 18th century the influence of French courtly fashions was to be seen in the engraved and embossed silver furniture produced in Augsburg for export to the more flamboyant courts of Germany. Little survives.

BAROQUE

Munich was also a major center of furniture craftsmanship, particularly in the Italian-inspired baroque style of the later 17th century. Tables with inlaid marble tops and robustly carved figure supports were among the most lavish pieces and were produced there under the influence of architects and artists from Turin.

Toward the end of the century, the inspiration of Paris and particularly of the cabinet-maker Boulle, is apparent in much of the furniture produced in southern Germany. A leading exponent in boulle marquetry was H.D. Sommer (*fl*.1666–84) of Kunzelsau in Swabia, whose preferred materials included ebony, brass, tortoiseshell, pewter, and ivory. The Augsburg partnership of Esser and Wolfhauer combined boulle marquetry with marble mosaic.

The magnificence of the baroque style found a ready acceptance all over Germany, and persisted well into the 18th century. It was embodied most often in the *Schrank* (large cupboard), which graced the hall or landing of every wealthy burgher's house. Heavy cornices, architectural pilasters, and paneling were usually embellished with carving. This was often

in the fleshy auricular style – *Knorpelwerk* – for which designs were published by the Frankfurt cabinet-maker Friedrich Unteutsch *c*.1645.

Small cupboards included the *Geschirr-schrank* (china cupboard) and the *Stollenschrank* (cabinet-on-stand). The *Tabernakel* was a cupboard enclosing drawers, which by the 18th century became part of a multi-purpose piece consisting of the *Tabernakel* above and a slope-fronted desk with a three-drawer chest beneath.

The auricular style found its way on to chairs in the 17th century. The plank-seated, splayed-legged variety, progressed to upholstered chairs that later had very tall carved backs.

DUTCH CABINET-ON-STAND

◄ WALNUT AND ROSEWOOD
late 17th century
This piece is lavishly decorated with floral marquetry enclosed within oyster veneer borders.

THE LOW COUNTRIES

 The Dutch were supreme masters in the absorption of styles. Influences came from many quarters – France, Germany, the East (where the Dutch enjoyed great trading success), and Moorish southern Europe (resulting from a long period of Austro-Spanish domination of the Netherlands) – and were discernible in the arabesque patterns and geometric motifs in Dutch furniture. Britain was particularly important, and the exchange of influences was strengthened when the Dutch William of Orange and the English Mary became joint monarchs of England in 1688.

Cabinet-making was as prized in the Netherlands and Belgium as elsewhere in Europe, and in the early 17th century both Antwerp and Amsterdam emerged as major centers of the craft. There was an increasing use of exotic woods, especially ebony, which was mainly used as a veneer or decorative molding, especially on mirror and picture frames. Tortoiseshell, colored on the back, was also used as a veneer. Inside, cabinets often had painted panels and stacks of small drawers.

In the early 17th century X-framed and rectangular chairs were made more comfortable by fixed padding and upholstery. Chairs were covered with velvet or with tooled and gilt leather fixed with large, decorative, brass-headed nails. The traditional carved lion finial continued to be used on chair backs, and stretchers were used in double rows to give strength while legs were turned to resemble balusters.

AMERICA

American furniture design is marked by its independence. Of course, European styles, particularly ones from Britain, did have some influence on American designers, but they were outweighed by original ideas, brought about as much by new circumstances and materials as by native inventiveness.

For the first British settlers of the New World the needs of providing shelter and food for their communities left little time for advanced craftsmanship in furniture-making. Simplicity and sturdiness were the keywords, and most of the few chairs, benches and stools that survive from about 1650 to the 1670s are very basic. Among the few early pieces that did extend the skill of the artisan were the oak or ash wainscot chair (so called because of the high-paneled back, which could be plain or carved) and more ornamented Carver and Brewster chairs, which were named in honor of the first governor and premier elder of the Plymouth Colony and whose backs and arms were ranged with spindles (see next chapter).

The almost medieval character of these chairs was exceeded by that of the trestle tables, some of which were more than 8 feet long. These large pieces had removable tops, secured

INDO-DUTCH ARMCHAIR

▶ HARDWOOD
17th century
This chair is an intriguing variant on the style of James II of England, but it was made in the Dutch East Indies (now Indonesia). The fundamentals are the same, with the barley-twist columns and stretcher, the foliated ends on the arms and the caned seats, which derived, in any case, from the East. The difference is seen in the carving. In a European chair of this period the panels, in particular the crested top rail, back splat and pierced stretcher, would have been of Renaissance cherubs, with urns sprouting flowers. Indonesian craftsmen carved dragons, lions, and elephants among lotus flowers and trailing tropical plants.

with pegs and either a third trestle or removable vertical supports. Few of these anachronistic tables survive, because they were soon supplanted by the refectory-style table with immovable top and supported on four turned legs, connected by stretchers. Such full-sized pieces were echoed on a smaller scale in the common tap-room or tavern table, made in oak, maple, pine, cherry, butternut, and other fruitwoods. This was also popular for domestic use, when it often incorporated a decorated frame or skirt.

In the late 17th century an even smaller piece appeared, the ancestor of many an occasional table to follow. This was the "stand" – a plain rectangular or round top, set on four vertical or splayed legs – which was used for both hearth- and bedside. The gate-leg table – a table with framed legs that swing in to let down a drop leaf – was popular and gave rise to a uniquely American version, the butterfly table, so called from its butterfly-wing-like drop leaf supports. Both types of table are first found in maple, wal-nut or oak. Leg and stretcher turning became more elaborate towards the end of the century. The best examples have numerous legs, ingeni-ously arranged to aid both storage and use.

In the days of early settlement the educated few wrote either at the single large table in the house or on a writing box that was also used to store writing materials. By 1675, the writing stand or desk-on-a-frame had been introduced. Although this continued to be made into the next century, it was supplanted in popularity by the fall-front desk. During the William and Mary period, which in America lasted from 1695 to 1720, desks of this type were made of a mixture of woods – for example, a top of straight-grain maple, sides of curly (feather-grain) maple, a front of knot-patterned maple, feet and string borders of walnut, pigeonholes and small drawers of cherry, and pine linings for the main drawers. In grander furniture marquetry made the most of the varying hues of the local woods.

In the initial settlements the "best" bed took pride of place, first in the parlor but later in the main upstairs room. Made of oak, maple or pine, it had hangings in crewel (a fine worsted

AMERICAN HADLEY CHEST

◄ WOOD
*c.*1680–1710
This Hadley-type chest has the typical three panels across the low-relief carved front, short legs, and two drawers. Hadley chests, named after the town in Massachusetts, were often painted black, red, brown or, as here, green. Their production was especially associated with John Allis and his son Ichabod, Samuel Belding, and John Hawkes.

yarn) or, in poor families, homespun fabric. The late 17th century saw an innovation in the day-bed. Early examples were in the English Carolean style (1625–49) – that is, caning was used on the adjustable back and seat, and eight turned legs were connected by ornate crested rails and ended in small ball feet. This style, however, soon gave way to simple turned stretchers in place of rails, while the number of legs was reduced to six and given Spanish (knuckle-like) feet.

Among the most numerous surviving items of furnishing of the early colonial past are blanket chests (storage chests) of oak and/or pine, which also served as seating. Usually 25 to 30 inches high and 4 or 5 feet long, they fre-quently had bracket feet and flat lids, and the fronts were often divided into sunken panels and stylized floral carvings. There were four main types of chest. The Hartford or "sun-flower" chest, attributed to Nicholas Disbrowe (1612–83), had a central panel, carved with a sunflower and usually flanked by two tulip and leaf scrolled panels, and two paneled drawers with applied spindles, bosses, and turned knobs. Existing examples date from *c.*1660–80.

Contemporary with the Hartford chest was the Ipswich (Connecticut) chest, which is also sometimes called a Dennis-style chest after its originator. The stiles (vertical members be-tween sunken panels) of these chests and rails carried ornate guilloches (interlacing bands) and leaf designs.

THE
18th
CENTURY

W**hile the 17th century had been marked by its variety of furniture forms, especially tables, the 18th century is noted for its craftsmanship, and new craftsmen and designers in America emerged as a force to be reckoned with.**

BRITAIN

The trends that had appeared in the late 17th century – the emergence of an Anglo-Dutch style, the importance of cabinet-making skills and the predominating use of walnut – continued into the reigns of Queen Anne (1702–14) and George I (1714–27). One of the hallmarks of the period was a lack of pretension, and this trait continued to be evident throughout the century. There was, however, no shortage of color. Seat furniture was lavishly covered with needlework, damasks, silks, and velvets, and windows and beds were hung with luxurious curtains. Japanning continued to be in favor in the early part of the 18th century, especially when applied to small items such as dressing mirrors, corner cupboards, and ladies' cabinets, but it continued to be used on major display pieces such as cabinets on stands.

Different crafts developed to make the new styles. Joiners, who had made most early 17th-century furniture, began to be rivaled by carvers and gilders and, most importantly, by cabinet-makers, who used marquetry. These craftsmen, working in London, made the finest furniture, but many pieces continued to be made using traditional methods and materials and ignoring new fashions. Simple oak chairs, stools, chests, and tables were made well into the 18th century. The details of a chair back or the panels of a chest might differ from 17th-century examples, but the basic type altered little. Regional variations continued too, and a chair or chest from Wales or the northwest of England would have decorative motifs peculiar to that area. Although often attractive and always useful, these pieces were not stylistically important – it was the furniture made for royal palaces and great houses that set new trends.

One of the most important pieces to evolve in the early 18th century, by way of the chest on a stand and the chest-on-chest (tallboy), was the large bureau cabinet. Some examples of this were double-domed, while others had a straight cornice. The disposition of storage space also varied – a kneehole arrangement of drawers with a central recessed cupboard was one change from the more customary form of three or four drawers below the fall-front bureau section. Above this there was sometimes a pair of mirror doors concealing shelves or small compartments and sometimes plain veneered or japanned doors. Such pieces were designed to grace the *salons* of gracious houses, and they were given the most lavish treatment, including veneers of strongly figured (grained) or burr (knotted) woods, such as mulberry, walnut, elm, or laburnum, together with japanning in brilliant red or lustrous black, with gold Chinese-style ornamentation (chinoiserie) in relief.

Bun feet (slightly flattened ball feet) were usual for cabinets and chests in the early 18th century, but they gradually gave way to bracket feet (shaped like a right-angled bracket), and

ENGLISH ESCRITOIRE

▼ WALNUT
early 18th century
Like much furniture of this period, this escritoire relies on the well-figured (grained) veneers and cross-bandings for its decoration.

this style persisted into the 19th century. The chest-on-chest also continued to be made for storage purposes, evolving in the mid-century into the gentleman's wardrobe – that is, an arrangement of drawers below with shelves within a cupboard above.

What has come to be known as Queen Anne style is most closely associated with the evolution of the cabriole (double curved) leg. The H-shaped stretchers of the earliest cabriole-legged chairs were soon abandoned, and both tables and chairs stood on gently serpentine legs terminating in pad feet. More robust curves developed later, and knees or bulges at the tops of legs were often decorated with carved shell medallions. By George I's reign, feet were usually of the lion's paw or ball-and-claw variety. The backs of Queen Anne and early Georgian chairs were also serpentine in outline, with vase-shaped splats of well-figured walnut or with carved shells at the top; they were occasionally partly gilt. Upholstered seats added color, while japanned chairs, which were more or less the same overall shape, more often had caned seats and backs.

Still more comfortable and colorful were the sets of chairs made for the houses of gentlemen. Side chairs had shaped seats and rounded backs, upholstered in brightly colored needlework,

sometimes with arms of sinuous walnut. Matching upholstered settees were also made, but most luxurious of all were the all-over upholstered and cushioned wing chairs.

An innovation of the Queen Anne and early Georgian periods was a proliferation of small, well-made pieces, such as tables for taking tea or displaying china or needlework. Dressing-tables, small chests of drawers – known as bachelor's chests – small kneehole desks, and small cupboards and cabinets for displaying china were also popular.

In any house, grand or humble, the bed was the most costly item. Few "ordinary" beds of the early 18th century have survived. The frameworks, concealed by the much more valuable hangings, were made of soft wood or beech, easy prey for woodworm and rot. More state beds have survived from the first half of the 18th century, and these show the influence of the Huguenot decorator and furniture designer Daniel Marot (1663–1752). Most have a tester (canopy) supported by four posts, which were concealed by the rich hangings, but others had only a half-tester, projecting from the head of the bed and supported from the ceiling.

Gerrit Jensen (*fl.*1680–1715) is regarded as
the first English cabinet-maker to achieve fame.
Established before 1688, he is known to have
made a table, stands, and looking-glass for
Charles II. These have not survived, but
examples of the marquetry he made for William
and Mary (reigned 1689–1702) and Queen Anne
(reigned 1702–14) are still in the royal collections. His intricately crafted metal marquetry
was influenced by that of the French cabinet-
maker André-Charles Boulle, but it is relatively
muted in its opulence, the silver and brass inlays
being interspersed with dark and light woods
and tortoiseshell. In his later furniture,
including some pieces for Queen Anne, Jensen
abandoned the use of metal inlays in favor of
japanning and complex seaweed marquetry.

The partnership of John Gumley (*fl.*1691–
1727) and James Moore (*c.*1670–1726) supplied
grand looking-glasses and lavishly gilded table
stands to noble households. Gumley's looking-
glass shop in the Strand, London, became a
fashionable meeting place, where people could
buy tables, cabinets, desks and bookcases.
Moore specialized in furniture on which low-
relief patterns of strapwork or leaves were built
up in gesso before being gilded. Moore's son
James (*c.*1690–1734) became cabinet- and chair
maker to Frederick, Prince of Wales, and is
known to have worked with the architect
William Kent (1685–1748). Kent was one of the
first designers to consider furnishings as a part
of the total scheme. His furniture is ponderously architectural, with a baroque and gilded
grandeur that made it suitable only for palatial
interiors, but his influence on subsequent designers and on the emergence of the neoclassical
style in England was considerable.

Fashionable, as distinct from regional, furniture can rarely be attributed with any certainty
to individual makers – it was neither obligatory
nor customary for English makers to stamp
their work – and most cabinet-makers who produced fine pieces for gentlemen's houses remain
anonymous. Of the few who did use trade labels
or who stamped their names, Hugh Granger,
Samuel Bennett and Coxed & Woster are associated with fine case furniture, mostly veneered in
walnut or burr woods, produced between about
1700 and 1730. Giles Grendey or Grendy
(1693–1780), who had a large workshop in
London, used both walnut and mahogany.

PALLADIAN TO ROCOCO

The Palladian movement of the 1720s and 1730s, which reflected a revival of classic Roman styles, coincided with a gradual transition from walnut to mahogany. The luster and strength of mahogany made it the ideal material to be used for chairs, which were ornamented with crisply carved motifs, and for the architecturally conceived furniture of William Kent and his contemporaries, among whom the royal cabinet-maker Benjamin Goodison (c.1700–67) was the most important.

Even as the sober discipline of classical form was being promoted by the supporters of Palladian principles, the French rococo was gaining ground in England, a move encouraged by both the influx of immigrant craftsmen and the increasing availability of pattern-books depicting the work of leading French designers. Engravers such as the French immigrant Hubert Gravelot (1699–1773) were widely influential. The new ideas took root in cabinet-making, and furniture began to show the restless, asymmetrical twists and curves of the rococo. Carved and gilded woodwork was adorned with waterfalls dripping on to rocky piles amid fronds of palm or acanthus. Birds of paradise were shown hovering above flowery garlands, while putti and Chinamen peered through gilded vistas of shells and foliage.

Among the most influential of the many English rococo design books of this period were those of Thomas Johnson (1714–c.1788) and Matthias Lock (fl.1740–65), both of whom were teachers and master-carvers as well as designers of great vivacity. Johnson's pattern-book, published in 1758, was dedicated to Lord Blakeney, the president of the Anti-Gallican Association, which had been founded in 1745 to oppose French influence on English furniture. In the preface, Johnson attacked "French paper machée." By the 1750s the rococo had embraced gothic as well as Chinese fantasies, and these were added to the design styles purveyed by the pattern-books published in the 1750s and 1760s, the most important of which was *The Gentleman and Cabinet-Maker's Director* (1754, 1755 and 1759–62) by Thomas Chippendale (1718–79), the greatest of Britain's cabinet-makers and furniture designers.

◀ c.1750
This design, which is in the style of Thomas Chippendale, is a classic of its kind. Little more than two chairs joined together, it is notable for its elegance rather than its comfort. The "chairs" are typical Chippendale, with elaborate, interlace ribbon backs, leafy back rails, and all on gothic, triple-column front legs. Much of the woodwork is ornamental rather than structural – for example, the small corner struts between the legs and front rails are stylish but offer little support.

▶ MAHOGANY
early 18th century
The large C-scroll, which
forms the back and ends
just above the seat, is
carved all over the rocaille
and acanthus. The splat
is similarly decorated in
low relief around the
central interlacing
strapwork. The arms are
carved both outwards and
then in and also upwards
and then down. The
front legs are cabriole
with a cabochon on each
knee, terminating in hairy
hooves.

▼ MAHOGANY
c.1756
These fine mid-18th-
century chairs are by
John Gordon, and they
are in the style known as
Gainsborough armchairs,
a type of chair supplied
to a number of great
houses at this period.
Although they are of the
same proportions as
armchairs today, these
have an unusual design.

THOMAS CHIPPENDALE

Chippendale devoted his life to producing beautiful and robust furniture, and his *Director* revolutionized furniture-making in Britain. It was the first design book to cover all kinds of furniture, and its success in distilling the current styles of decoration into a form that was both workable for the cabinet-maker and acceptable to his clients led to the adoption of the name "Chippendale" as a generic label for mid-18th-century furniture. Practically all the furniture covered in the *Director* alludes to the rococo – even the sober designs for library bookcases in the Palladian idiom have rococo flourishes as well as gothic tracery or Chinese fretwork in the glazing bars.

From the 1720s chair backs became less elongated as the influence of Marot declined, and by the 1750s they were a squat, rectangular shape, slightly flaring at the top. The top rail, which often terminated in projecting "ears," and the pierced back splat were carved into sinuous organic forms, acanthus foliage, ribbons, shells, gothic arches, or geometric Chinese patterns. All these were echoed in the carving on the knees and front cabriole legs. Scrolled feet were now more fashionable than ball-and-claw or pad feet. Some chairs of this period have straight front legs, decorated with fluting or carved borders, and reinforcing stretchers. Seats were generally upholstered, but narrow-backed "hall" chairs usually had wooden seats.

Chairs with upholstered backs and seats were known as French chairs, whether they were of the round-contoured, cabriole-legged variety, with frames carved and gilded in the French rococo manner, or of the minimally ornamented, squarish-backed type that are now often called Gainsborough chairs.

In the Queen Anne and early Georgian periods claw (round tripod) tables were made in various styles, while tables with folding tops often had decoratively quartered veneers. Tables – breakfast, shaving, tea, gaming, sewing, writing, china, and "claw" – were made in a profusion of designs, as were beds. China cabinets, stands, mirrors, screens, and much else were produced for the growing numbers of the wealthy middle-classes.

It was a golden age of cabinet-making. Hundreds of craftsmen were kept busy all over the country, but it was to London that talented craftsmen wanting to better themselves were drawn. Among the most successful were John Channon (1711–c.1783), whose specialty – large-scale carcass pieces with ingenious hidden gadgetry and richly chiseled gilt mounts – reflected a continental influence; William Vile (c.1700–67) and John Cobb (c.1715–78), William Hallett (c.1707–81), Samuel Norman (fl.1746–67), James Whittle (fl.1731–59), William Ince (d.1804) and John Mayhew (fl.1758–1804), and

William Linnell (*c.*1703–63) and his son John (1729–96), all of whom supplied furniture of the finest quality in the latest styles.

Fashions changed quickly in 18th-century England. The rococo flowered late and briefly. No sooner had the smartest houses been fitted out with "French" chairs, lacquered or marquetry *bombé* commodes, and fantastically carved and gilded mirrors, than the new classicism was being urged.

NEOCLASSICISM

Classical ideals were already well rooted in England, most recently through the Palladian movement, whose archaeologically based designs remained fundamental to much furniture of the 1750s, however much decked out in rococo ornament they might be. Archaeological discoveries at Herculaneum and Pompeii during the mid-18th century coincided with a decline in interest in rococo ornament and generated a new fascination with classical antiquity. Engravings, such as Giambattista Piranesi's

evocative visions of Roman ruins, and illustrated books on archaeology fueled the enthusiasm, and a whole range of new motifs, many of them derived from Roman wall paintings, entered the repertoire of architects and furniture-makers. For the remainder of the 18th century and for the first decade of the 19th century there was a striving toward greater archaeological accuracy in classical interpretation.

ENGLISH ARMCHAIR

▶ MAHOGANY
*c.*1785
This unusually elaborate armchair has an intriguing combination of motifs. The pierced back is carved with a most unusual splat of a central urn above an anthemion with interlaced ribbons. The front legs are distinctly Adam, and the arms have a strong but elegant scroll in the French manner, clearly showing the fashionable influences of the time.

Among the first exponents of the neoclassical style was the architect James "Athenian" Stuart (1713–88), who had spent more than a decade immersed in the ruins of Rome and Athens and who published the important guide *Antiquities of Athens* (1762). Stuart designed furniture for Kedleston Hall, Derbyshire, and Spencer House, London. He used carved griffins, fluting *paterae*, anthemion forms, and other motifs, soon to be adopted by others. Sir William Chambers (1723–96), another traveler who had produced *Designs of Chinese Buildings, Furniture, Dresses, Machines and Utensils* (1757), also contributed to English neoclassical development.

No designer, however, was more important than Robert Adam (1728–92). Like Stuart and Chambers, Adam had acquired his knowledge of classical design during the years he spent in Italy, and his subsequent employment by many

ENGLISH CHAIR

▶ YEW WITH ELM SEAT
*c.*1850
This good, if slightly late, example of the Windsor chair, perhaps represents the final stage in the development of the style. Like most of the early models, the back is of yew and the seat of elm. The yoke, which forms the top of the back and the central splat, is fairly standard. By this time, the Windsor chair had been adapted to include the Victorian habit of turning. Not only are the turned legs robust, but the central hoops, which form the arms, are also on turned spindles.

❀ REGIONAL FURNITURE ❀

*D*uring the early 18th century, there came into widespread use a type of chair known as the Windsor chair. Characterized by a solid wooden seat, simple turned legs, and a stick back – this

robust form of seating gave rise to a host of regional variants. These Windsor, or stick-back, chairs were only part of a rich rural tradition of chair-making that included the spindle- and ladder-back chairs of the Midlands and northern England and the button-back chairs of East Anglia. The styles of these chairs were governed more by geography than by period fashions.

Because new styles eventually percolate downwards through the social strata, regional or traditional chairs often display the characteristic decorative features of "town" furniture, such as padded feet, cabriole legs, and vase-shaped splats. Some East Anglian chairs can be associated with Sheraton designs. Even so, most regional chairs were built for durability rather than elegance, and their legs are usually reinforced by stretchers.

Other rural pieces, particularly tables and chests, of solid oak, elm, or fruitwoods, continued to be made in earlier styles throughout the 18th century of the richest and most powerful property owners in Britain gave him immense prestige and wide influence. In his all-embracing approach to building schemes, in partnership with his brothers John (1721–92) and James (1732–94), he took responsibility for all aspects of interior decoration – the painting of walls and ceilings, stucco work, furniture, carpets, curtains, and lighting – and by doing so gave patronage to some of the best craftsmen of the time. Among the cabinet-makers who collaborated with him were John Linnell, Thomas Chippendale, Ince & Mayhew, Vile & Cobb, and Samuel Norman.

The light elegance of the Adam style was well suited to the domestic interior and enhanced the skills of the furniture craftsman, giving unprecedented scope for marquetry decoration. The asymmetrical flourishes of rococo plasterwork were translated on furniture into well-regulated borders of anthemion or *paterae*, scrolled acanthus, looped garlands, and graceful arabesques. Painting and gilding were also widely used, and decorative ceramic plaques as well as finely chiseled gilt bronze mounts were applied to surfaces veneered in finely figured mahogany or satinwood.

The style was distilled most successfully in *The Cabinet-Maker and Upholsterer's Guide* (1788), the posthumously published design book by George Hepplewhite (d.1786), which took the Adam style not only to the furthest corners of Britain but to many parts of North America and Europe. Hepplewhite's express aim "to unite elegance and utility" was fulfilled in nearly 300 patterns, 40 of which were for chairs, most with decorated shield or square backs and upholstered seats. Hepplewhite drew attention to the Adam-inspired fashion for "finishing them with painted or japanned work" and "assorting the prevailing color to the furniture and light of the room."

Hepplewhite's essentially conservative approach is seen in his retention of the cabriole leg in some instances. Serpentine-fronted chests and side tables appeared alongside those of half-round neoclassical shape. Chairs, small tables,

and parlor pieces such as tea caddies and trays were given most decorative attention. Utilitarian furniture – wardrobes, library bookcases, chests and drawers, and pot cupboards – is classically simple. Although large tables were beginning to appear as permanent fixtures in dining rooms, they did not yet feature in design books. They signaled a more formal approach to dining habits, replacing the movable, multi-purpose tables of smaller but often adjustable sizes that had been used for the past century.

Hepplewhite's *Guide* and others of the period, such as the anonymous *Cabinet-Maker's London Book of Prices* (1788), reflect the elegant, well-made furniture that was being produced in huge quantities by firms such as Gillow (established *c.*1730) and George Seddon (1753–1868). Gillow's archives provide a detailed source of knowledge about furniture-making practices in the late 18th and most of the 19th century. The firm's habit of stamping its furniture has enabled many items to be identified.

George Seddon (*c.*1727–1801) was already regarded as "one of the most eminent cabinet-makers in London" in 1768, and his firm was the largest in London. Its name is associated with a wide range of well-made furniture and particularly with fine cabinets and tables in satinwood and mahogany. Some of these had

▼ MAHOGANY
*c.*1785
This Pembroke table in the Hepplewhite style, has three unusual features – the dappled grain of the mahogany veneer, the geometric loops of the drawer handles, which have chamfered corners where the washers meet the wood, and the contrast of flat, two-dimensional figuring and crisp carving, seen on the legs. The table has striking folding leaves with instepped quadrant corners.

FRENCH *TORCHÈRES*

▼ GILT WOOD
*c.*1725

Torchères such as these
were used to augment the
main lighting of a room
whose chief source of
light would have been a
chandelier or sconces.
This substantial pair
is cream painted,
heightened with gilt, and
features sculptural
carving. They are
probably made of a
softwood such as beech,
and they are in Régence
style, which was popular
in both France and
England in the early 18th
century. The blackamoor
guéridon is a 19th-century
copy of a late 17th- or
early 18th-century Italian
or French figure. An
original would have held
a candlestand rather than
a basket of fruit.

patent mechanical fittings of the type much in
vogue in the late 18th and early 19th centuries,
a time known in English furniture as the
Sheraton period, after the designer Thomas
Sheraton (1751–1806).

Relatively little is known of Sheraton's working life. Unlike Chippendale and Hepplewhite,
he probably never had a workshop of his own,
although he must have been trained as a cabinet-
maker. His trade card read: "T. Sheraton/
Teaches Perspective, Architecture and Ornaments, makes Designs for Cabinet-makers and
sells all kinds of Drawing Books etc." His first
pattern-book, *The Cabinet-Maker and Upholsterer's Drawing Book* (1791–4) echoes the
distinctly francophile neoclassicism of the
architect Henry Holland (1745–1806). The
Drawing Book was seen as a digest of the most
refined neoclassical taste and, like Hepplewhite's *Guide*, influenced furniture all over
Europe, as well as in America and Britain.

FRANCE

RÉGENCE AND LOUIS XV

❧ Furniture of the Régence and Louis XV (1715–74) rejected the weighty and grandiose, becoming more graceful and with exuberant but simplified rococo curves. This tendency appeared in
the last years of Louis XIV's reign, and was
reinforced during the first eight years of Louis
XV's reign, a period known as the Régence.
Plain wood veneer replaced boulle marquetry
and gilt bronze ornamentation was simplified.

Curvilinear motifs, such as water, plants,
dragons, and shells, proliferated in carved wood,
marquetry, and gilt bronze, and the structure of
pieces became all but invisible. On a Louis XV
chair, for example, legs, arms, seat, and back
contribute to a single, flowing curve, inter-
rupted by an occasional carving of, say, a leaf or
rococo scroll. Seat furniture and architectural
furniture (that is, furniture that forms part of
the wall decoration), such as console tables
(tables with no back legs attached to a wall by
brackets), and mirrors, were made of beech or
walnut, invisibly joined or pegged and gilded or
painted to harmonize with the rest of the room.
The carcasses of case furniture were often made
cheaply from pine, but sometimes oak, and were
veneered with exotic woods in geometric patterns known as parquetry because of the re-
semblance to parquet floors.

By the 1740s, flower marquetry had become
popular. One technique consisted of tinting the
inlays with dyes or in hot sand; another, producing finer results, used inlays cut across the grain
of a wood whose grain itself formed the desired
pattern. Veneering was sometimes carried out
with lacquer, Japanese or Chinese, or a French
imitation known as *vernis Martin*. Case furniture also incorporated gilt bronze mounts as
ornaments on projecting corners and on feet, as
handles and as frames for marquetry panels.

Many new types and shapes of furniture
appeared during Louis XV's reign. The most
often seen style of chair, the *fauteuil* (armchair),
had a scrolled, heart-shaped seat and back, and

curved legs and armrests. If the back was flat, it was a *fauteuil à la reine*; if it was curved, it was a *fauteuil en cabriolet*. The *bergère* (easy chair) was large and comfortable and had upholstery under as well as on top of the armrests. It is interesting to note the variation in the style of arms found on *bergères*. They are sometimes the same height as the back, forming a kind of tub, or they can be much smaller, resembling more closely the kind of easy chair we would find today.

Console tables stood on exaggeratedly curved legs, which would be decorated with, say, foliage on the legs themselves and a basket of flowers or a rococo scroll on the stretchers.

The commode was the principal piece of case furniture of the period. It had a curved front,

❁ MENUISIERS AND ÉBÉNISTES ❁

*U*ntil 1789, all furniture-makers in France belonged to the guild of woodworkers. Furniture-makers consisted of two distinct categories: the menuisier, who made chairs, tables, and other plain items, and the ébéniste, who made cabinets and other case furniture, which was usually veneered. The word ébéniste derives from the early use of ebony as a veneer. Each was a specialized activity, and a craftsman would work in one area or the other.
Strict legislation governed furniture-making. A maître (master craftsman) had

to serve a long apprenticeship, produce a chef d'oeuvre (masterpiece), and pay a considerable sum before he could practice under his own name. He had to mark each piece with his name – a procedure that has simplified establishing the provenance of French furniture – and officers of the guild held periodic quality checks, stamping approved pieces with the guild mark JME (Juré des Menuisiers-ébénistes). The practice of stamping furniture as a guarantee of quality was enforced by an edict of 1751.

FRENCH CONSOLE TABLE

▲ OAK
*c.*1720
The bare wood table, which is one of a pair, has been carved with a courtly mask decoration, an ornate frieze and heavy, square-section stretchers. It may originally have been gilt but have been stripped in the 19th century. It is unlikely that the marble top seen here is the original; it would be more likely to have been of finely patterned marble.

FRENCH *CANAPÉ*

◀ *c.*1775
The frame of the *canapé* is carved with leaf tips and continuous laurel banding, and the seat rail is sculpted with leaf tips and berried laurel. It stands on circular, tapering, stop-fluted legs, which are headed by *paterae* and gadrooned capitals. They end in *toupie* (top feet). The suite is stamped *G. Jacob*, the mark of Georges Jacob (1739–1814), an innovative maker of carved seat furniture.

▶ WALNUT
*c.*1715
This *fauteuil*, which is one of a pair, has many of the characteristics of 17th-century continental furniture – for example, the curving, X-framed stretchers, the cabriole legs, the hoofed feet, and the gently curving arms. The open arms and contrasting curves give the chair a light, airy feel, an effect that is heightened by the decoration. The scallops on the arms are echoed by the scallops and trellis work on the seat rails. There is also an extra finesse in the scrolled feet, which rest on their own feet below.

▼ KINGWOOD AND GILT BRONZE
*c.*1735
This commode is a fine example of the bold gilt bronze mounts favored by its maker, Charles Cressent (1685–1768), who was France's most talented cabinet-maker of the Régence period.

sides and legs, and either two or three rows of drawers. The *bureau plat* competed with various new types of desk, such as the *secrétaire à abattant* (fall-front writing desk), which had two doors and a writing surface flap that pulled down to reveal small drawers inside.

Small *tables à écrire* (writing tables), with one drawer at the side and sometimes a slide under the top, are found in a variety of shapes and sizes, including the *bonheur du jour* (small writing table with a recessed superstructure) and the *bureau à cylindre* (cylinder-top desk) reveals a writing surface when the quarter-cylindrical cover is slid back. *Tables à transformations*, a specialty of German cabinet-makers, contained locking devices, drawers, flaps, and recesses, which could have many uses, including writing, holding secret papers or needlework or, when some drawers converted into kneelers, praying.

Toward the end of Louis XV's reign, rococo style gradually gave way to neoclassical ornamentation, a style known as Transitional. It was characterized by the use of classical architectural forms and motifs, such as straight lines, symmetry, pilaster, fluting, rosettes, lion masks, and leaf or bead moldings. At first furniture was curvilinear in the rococo style, but it acquired neoclassical ornamentation. Then the shapes began to incorporate neoclassical elements – commodes became rectilinear, for example,

while the heart-shaped backs of seat furniture were often supported on straight legs. The neoclassical shapes came to be increasingly decorated in the same style. The body of the commode, for example, was adorned with formal flower marquetry and a severe scroll frieze. Gilt bronze corner mounts were sometimes modeled on the triglyph, and mounts on the apron were modeled on a smoking cassolette (incense vessel).

By about 1770 neoclassicism had almost completely superseded the rococo. Classical forms and motifs were, however, not applied to interior decoration with great seriousness. They were used in fanciful way that produced an elegant style that was well suited to the light architectural interiors of the day.

LOUIS XVI

In the reign of Louis XVI (1774–93) furniture was mainly adapted from earlier pieces and few new types were introduced. Seat furniture lost all traces of the rococo, as legs were turned, tapered and fluted, the joint between the legs and the rails was made in the form of a cube with a rosette, and the square backs and seat

◀ KINGWOOD INLAY
*c.*1745
The name *table à ouvrage* (work table) often refers to needlework tables such as this one. The top is covered with leather, as are the drawers, and the table is decorated with elaborate rococo inlay designs of organic motifs in kingwood. This would have been considered the height of rococo taste – restrained but lively.

examples are half-moon shape or have a break-front façade, in which the central part of the façade is shaped as a projecting panel. The *bureau plat*, *bonheur du jour*, *table à écrire*, and *secrétaire* were all made with square shapes and straight, tapering, turned or square legs. They usually had a Grecian frieze in the upper part and gilt bronze molding framing the main panel. Among the few new pieces to emerge at this time was the *console d'ébénisterie*, which was supported on column legs.

Pictorial marquetry continued to be used on case furniture, and popular motifs were ruins in landscapes, exotic objects, such as Chinese tableware, and complex geometric patterns. Gradually, however, plain veneer, especially in mahogany, began to supplant marquetry. Well-figured woods, outlined with finely chiseled gilt bronze, were used, as was oriental lacquer. Panels of *pietra dura* or boulle marquetry, often scavenged from pieces of Louis XIV furniture, were fixed to commodes and cabinets and given surrounds of ebony veneer. Plaques of Sèvres porcelain were also applied to case furniture.

frames were molded and decorated with classical freizes, such as ribbon twists. Beds and console tables had slender fluted column uprights and architectural friezes.

Case furniture also acquired an angular look. Commodes were often square, although some

◀ GILT WOOD
*c.*1780
Both chairs bear the maker's stamp of Jean-Baptiste Sené, one of the greatest French neoclassical chair makers. The spirally fluted legs, the shield-shaped backs, and the delicate carving are all characteristic of his work.

DIRECTOIRE AND EMPIRE

The years following the French Revolution of 1789 were turbulent. The political upheavals were mirrored by artistic ones. The dissolution of the guilds had a dramatic effect on furniture-making, opening up the trade to anyone who wanted to practice it. In addition, the difficult economic conditions of the times imposed austerity on a hitherto luxurious craft. Elaborate veneered and gilt bronze-mounted pieces were no longer commercially possible, and as a result simpler, painted furniture was made.

The style of design prevalent from *c.*1793 to 1804 is known as Directoire, after the Directorate. Its principal characteristic was the use of arabesque and Etruscan forms and motifs, such

❋ MARCHANDS-MERCIERS ❋

In the 18th century, a group of dealers known as marchands-merciers *emerged. Their function was to supply furniture and decorative objects to a rich clientele, and through their position they exerted considerable influence not only on the making of furniture but also on its design. Lazare-Duvaux, one of the best known* merciers *of Louis XV's reign, had a considerable hand in the design of the pieces he provided for the king's mistress Mme de Pompadour and others.* Marchands-merciers *eventually came to control the*

work of all the specialists involved in the manufacture of pieces of furniture. Dominque Daguerre, the greatest mercier *of the late 18th century, commissioned drawings, ordered porcelain plaques of specific shape and decoration from the Sèvres factory, bought lacquer cabinets that were then dismantled for their panels, and arranged for gilt bronze mounts to be made by leading metal workers. This left only the making of the carcass and the final assembly to the* ébéniste, *who was thereby reduced from designer to executor.*

FRENCH SECRÉTAIRE À ABATTANT

▶ JAPANESE LACQUER AND GILT BRONZE

*c.*1780

This fall-front writing desk bears the stamp of Martin Carlin (d.1785), who became a *maître ébéniste* in 1766. Little is known about him, but he is believed to have worked almost exclusively for the *marchands-merciers*. The desk originally belonged to Mlle Laguerre, a well-known Parisian opera singer and courtesan. She died in 1782, when she was just 28 years old, *épuisée par des excès du tout genre* (worn out by every kind of excess).

as fanciful animals, sea lions, eagles, serpents, lozenges, and palmettes. Commodes were plain, often with paw feet. For the first time dining tables, of mahogany, were made to be seen and not hidden under a cloth. Seat furniture, usually painted in light colors, is perhaps the most original and graceful feature of the period. Legs were often shaped like sabers or cornucopias or were turned and tapering (but not usually fluted). Backs were usually openwork, with the top rail curling over like a scroll.

The personal influence on the arts of the Emperor Napoleon Bonaparte was considerable. He encouraged the development of a monumental style, based on massive, solid shapes and bold decoration. An enormous quantity of furniture was made for the imperial palaces, and much surviving Empire furniture closely resembles known imperial commissions. The main source of inspiration for the Empire style was the heavy, carved marble outdoor furniture of the Graeco-Roman world. Another major influence was Egypt. Included in Napoleon's expedition to that country in 1799 had been artists who recorded what they saw, and this began a craze in France for anything Egyptian. Decorative motifs on furniture began to include winged scarabs, mummies, sphinxes, and hieroglyphs.

Seat furniture was made either of mahogany or gilt wood. With their square backs and boldly carved front legs rising to form the supports of the armrests, such seats appear to have been designed more to fit in an imposing interior than with the comfort of the sitter in mind.

Large stools also survive, often with an X-frame structure in the form of crossed sabers. Sets of commodes and *secrétaires* were often made with matching beds, dressing-tables and looking-glasses. The fine mahogany veneers set off elaborate gilt bronze mounts, pierced plaques or panels with military motifs. Large writing tables stood on carved end supports. Adding to the generally somber effect created by these heavy pieces were large, architecturally shaped bookcases.

FRENCH *GUÉRIDON*

◀ MAHOGANY
*c.*1805
The decoration and style of this example is purely neoclassical although the form is essentially the same as in the reign of Louis XVI. Mahogany was a favorite wood of the Empire period, but, because of the English blockade of French ports, it was scarce and expensive, leading to an increased used of indigenous woods. The table top is plain grained granite surrounded by a gilt bronze rim, which had, by this time, taken the place of a gallery. The saber-shaped supports end in Greek key pattern and sit on a concave tripod base. The tripod frieze itself has typical classical architectural panels.

FRENCH *CHAISE LONGUE*

◀ MAHOGANY
*c.*1800
This *chaise longue* is a superb example of the classically styled furniture design that emerged after the Revolution. Attributed to Jacob Frères, it has shaped, rectangular, out-curved open sides with turned and tapered lotus-carved crest rails. The molded splat is carved with the lozenge enclosing a central mask of Mercury and four *paterae*, each carved with a perched griffin and berried anthemion, one of the most popular early 19th-century motifs. It has a loose rectangular cushion above a conforming seat rail. It is fitted with a paneled *demi-lune* apron carved with a mask of Apollo. It stands on tensed animal legs with paw feet.

❈ PROVINCIAL FURNITURE ❈

*F*rench provincial furniture can be attributed stylistically to particular regions, but most pieces are anonymous because the Paris guild system did not extend to the provinces, and few country craftsmen stamped their names on their work. Distinctive styles are restricted to the period 1650–1850, although precise dating is difficult because popular forms continued to be made for long periods. Regional furniture was rarely veneered. It was made by the menuisier, who worked in solid, native woods.

The armoire (cupboard or wardrobe) was usually made to match the boiserie (paneling and other woodwork) of the room. Constructed in sections and assembled with pegs driven into holes, it could be easily dismantled. A style reminiscent of a Louis XIII or Louis XIV type, with geometric moldings, remained popular in central France until it was replaced c.1750 by the Louis XV type with asymmetric rococo panels. A small version of the armoire was known as the bonnetière or, in Normandy, the coëffière. It usually had only one door, enclosing an interior fitted with shelves to hold the wide-brimmed hats worn by the local women.

The buffet-bas was a waist-high cupboard, used as a sideboard. The doors, decorated with rococo panels, hung on pin hinges, and above were two or three doors. The buffet-vaisselier or dressoir was a buffet with a rack of shelves above. Examples from the Auvergne have restrained decoration, while those from Brittany have turned spindles forming plate-guards on shelves, and those from Normandy are rich in well-carved detail. Many of the buffets-bas from Alsace are decorated with painted flowers.

The buffet-à-deux-corps was a buffet with a cupboard above. The doors of the upper section could be glazed or paneled. Some later examples include a weight-driven clock.

The coffre (lidded chest or coffer) was usually made of oak, and in some areas 16th- and 17th-century designs continued to be made well into the 18th century. The style favored in Lorraine has a paneled front carved with floral motifs.

Provincial examples of the commode (chest of drawers) are only rarely found with the full bombé shape of the sophisticated Louis XV pieces, but many are shaped from side to side in serpentine or arc-en-arbalète (cross-bow) form. Some are richly carved, but many, especially those in Louis XVI style, are relatively plain. The top is usually wood, not marble.

The lit clos ("cupboard bed") continued to be made in the 17th-century style in rural areas, especially Brittany, until the late 19th century. The paneled doors are pierced for ventilation, and the vents are made into decorative features with turned spindles. Other examples resemble Louis XV armoires.

Small food cupboards, known as panetières, were often made to be fixed to the wall. They were often composed mainly of turned members to permit maximum ventilation, while affording some protection to the food from domestic animals. The turnings are generally socketed into horizontal rails that, in good Provençal examples, are fancifully shaped and carved.

FRENCH COMMODE

▼ CHERRYWOOD
*c.*1740
This provincial chest of drawers has a carved frieze and *arc-en-arbalète* (cross bow) front.

ITALY

In the 18th century the furnishing of smaller rooms in both palaces and houses became more important, and a variety of furniture types was introduced from north of the Alps. Long sofas, upholstered or caned, and chairs were imported from France, while bureau bookcases were imported from England and the Netherlands, and chests of drawers became more widely used. However, while the emphasis in northern Europe tended to be on solid quality and good craftsmanship, many Italian pieces from this period are colorfully embellished but shoddily constructed.

The enthusiasm for oriental lacquer, imported to Europe through the East India companies, was shared by the Italians, but the difficulty and expense involved in acquiring the genuine article inspired Italian furniture-makers not only to adopt japanning as an alternative but also to develop their own method of imitating its effect. The technique known as *lacca povera* (or *lacca contrafatta*) involved pasting cut-out and painted pictures – chinoiserie or rustic scenes were most often used – on the painted surfaces of pieces of furniture and then lavishly coating the whole with varnish. (This process was revived as découpage in the 19th century.) The

resulting decoration resembles the texture and sometimes also the color of japanning, although it rarely deceives. Painting – landscapes, flowers and figures – was another favorite form of decoration for chests, tables, and cupboards.

ROCOCO

In the 1730s the Sicilian architect Filippo Juvarra (1676-1736) gathered together a group of outstanding craftsmen to work on the Palazzo Reale in Turin. They included the sculptor Francesco Ladatte (1706–87) and the cabinet-maker Pietro Piffetti (*c.*1700–77). Together they produced some of the most unrestrained ornamentation on furniture ever seen, even in Italy, but at least it was well made.

Piffetti's confections of inlaid ivory, mother-of-pearl, and some exotic woods, with their finely chiseled bronze mounts, were among the earliest manifestations in Italy of the lightening of the baroque style into the rococo, which was much favored for the still showy but less grandiose furnishings of living rooms. It led eventually to the enthusiastic adoption of *bombé* fronts and serpentine shapes. These taxed the abilities of many Italian craftsmen, but they camouflaged defects in workmanship with gay painting or *lacca* and lavish gilding.

ITALIAN COMMODE

△ WALNUT
mid-18th century
The exuberant inlays and decorations of ivory, mother-of-pearl, and gilt metal on this north Italian *bombé* commode belong to a style already popular in the late 17th century. Together with the elaborate handles and escutcheons, the inlaid flowers and other motifs illustrate the enthusiasm for decorative effects.

ITALIAN SIDE-TABLE

◁ *LACCA POVERA*
*c.*1760
Like much 18th-century Italian furniture, this table is in the French style – Louis XV, in this instance. The decoration is, however, uniquely Italian. Also typically Italian is the table's sculptural quality – the cabriole legs start with an angelic head and end in leafy hooves. It has two tiers and is a variant on the *chiffonière*, a table form that had space for books or a drawer for needlework.

▶ CARVED WOOD AND GILT
1775
This fire screen was made for the Palazzo Reale, Turin, by Giuseppe Bonzanigo, a wood sculptor whose furniture contains elements of rococo and neoclassical styles. The painted decoration was by Michele Rapous.

The *bombé* front took different forms, ranging from a full curve high in the carcass of Venetian chests to the almost restrained undulation low in the sides, typically seen in work from Lombardy. The cabriole legs of chairs, tables, and commodes were more exaggeratedly curved in Italy than elsewhere in Europe. Other rococo touches, such as cartouches, leafy flourishes, and shell forms, were widely used.

NEOCLASSICISM

In the mid-18th century, Italy – specifically Rome – attracted archaeologists, artists, and designers from all over Europe in search of the "antique" and became the chief source of neoclassical ideas and models. Despite this, Italy lagged behind France and Italy in the development of neoclassical style. Straight lines and disciplined ornament were alien to Italian exuberance, and it was not until the end of the century that neoclassicism was widely adopted. Even then, less grand furniture often retained rococo elements in carved, marquetry or *scagliola* decoration.

▶ 1741
This wooden desk, which is inlaid with ivory and precious woods, was made by Pietro Piffetti, a cabinet-maker whose pieces had highly decorated surfaces. He often used exotic woods, ivory and mother-of-pearl, and his lighter style, seen in the furniture he designed for the Palazzo Reale in Turin, took the Italian rococo to its most fantastic extremes.

◀ *SCAGLIOLA*
1756
This beautiful table top is one of a signed pair and is, therefore, extremely rare. It is inscribed *D P Belloni A Florentia F 1756* ("Don Pietro Belloni made this at Florence in 1756"). The table shows rococo at its best. It uses light colors, and the border features flowers, scallop shells, small animals, and human figures.

❧ REGIONAL FURNITURE ❧

Everyday furniture was produced by household carpenters in various regional styles, and it was often extremely robust. The furniture of northern Italy was greatly influenced by the styles popular in southern France, and walnut was the most often used wood in both regions. The area was traditionally famous for intarsia work.

In Alpine regions painted furniture was popular, and japanning and lacca povera was practiced throughout Italy.

As one of the chief ports of the Mediterranean, Genoa was open to Spanish influence, and imported woods such as palisander were used alongside walnut. The same influence can also be seen in Sicilian ivory-inlaid ebony cabinets, which were modeled on the Spanish vargueño. The furniture of Tuscany tends to have a solidity of form and decoration that contrasts strongly with the exuberant shapeliness and shallow decoration of Venetian pieces.

The furniture of Emilia Romagna (the region south of Venice) was also of a solid character, for which oak was used in addition to walnut, but its most conspicuous feature was the geometric ornamentation of metal studs and roundels that was applied to the fronts of chests and cupboards together with interestingly turned wooden knobs. Like most furniture built for comfort and convenience rather than for fashion, Italian regional furniture is almost impossible to date.

▽ WALNUT
early 18th century
This piece from Ferrara features three drawers and a serpentine front. Its features are typical of furniture from this part of Italy.

The work done by Giuseppe Maria Bonzanigo (1745–1820) in palaces around Turin in the late 18th century shows elements of both neoclassical and rococo styles. Although he used rectilinear shapes and classical motifs, his own special skill was as a wood sculptor, and this is seen in the elaborately carved and gilded pieces he made. Painted decoration, usually of rococo-style flowers, was also a hallmark of his work, and his furniture for the Sardinian royal family is unmistakably Italian in its florid delicacy.

When the French-inspired version of neo-classical style was eventually adopted in the state rooms of the most fashionable *palazzi*, it was dominated by just a few great exponents, among whom the greatest was Giuseppe Maggiolini (1738–1814), who worked in Milan. No curving or carving are to be seen on his severely rectilinear commodes and cupboards. He relied instead on an array of differing woods – in one piece as many as 86 – to create pictorial marquetry panels of astonishing virtuosity, many of them designed by painters.

Close to Maggiolini in the production of good quality furniture were Ignazio Revelli (*b.*1756) and his son Luigi (*b.*1776), who worked in Turin. Noted for their half-round commodes, they also specialized in marquetry decoration.

PORTUGUESE COMMODE

▼ MARQUETRY
late 18th century
This piece, known as a Donna Maria commode, is typified by its linear design, finely crafted marquetry, deep apron, and marble top.

SPAIN AND PORTUGAL

❀ The furniture of 18th-century Spain and Portugal was rich in references to colonial expansion and cultural cross-currents. In Spain the influence of France and Italy continued to dominate, but Moorish traditions lived on in provincial and country furniture.

The palace of Philip V (reigned 1700–46) at La Granja, Segovia, was the most sophisticated manifestation of the French-inspired rococo in Spain. The fashion for console and side tables, carved and gilded and complemented by ornate mirrors, was particularly appropriate for lofty Spanish rooms, and it led to the establishment of a mirror factory at San Ildefonso in 1736.

The *vargueño* was gradually superseded as a show-piece by the commode. Although the commode had originated in France, its shape and decoration in Spain were Italianate, especially after the Neapolitan decorator Matias Gasparini became director of the royal workshops in Madrid in 1768. Later in the 18th century, however, Spanish neoclassical furniture acquired an extravagant severity all its own. Marquetry was generally detailed and delicate, and although painting and gilding were used, metal mounts were seldom seen.

In the first half of the 18th century, furniture imported from England influenced Spanish design, particularly that of chairs. Japanned pieces were popular imports, and the English cabinet-maker Giles Grendey sent a consignment of japanned furniture to the Duke of Infantado in the 1730s. Early Georgian and Thomas Chippendale designs were translated by the Spanish into walnut or poplar, or given carved and gilded rococo ornamentation and H-form stretchers. Later, Hepplewhite and Sheraton designs were echoed but less obviously.

In Portugal, where the riches of the South American colonies were more obviously enjoyed – at least, at court – English influence was most powerful. When the widowed consort of Charles II, Catherine of Braganza, returned to her native Portugal in 1693, she took English furniture

PORTUGUESE CHAIR
◀ WALNUT
*c.*1730
This chair, one of a set of five, has an interlacing strapwork splat, carved legs with ball-and-claw feet and a drop-in seat. English influence is evident, but the stretchers and low-slung effect of the exaggerated cabriole front legs are distinctly Portuguese.

After the disastrous Lisbon earthquake of 1755 and the subsequent restructuring of the Portuguese economy by the Marquess of Pombal, much fine furniture was produced to complement the neoclassical architecture. Cylinder-topped commodes and bureaus with well-crafted marquetry and parquetry decoration, as well as a profusion of occasional and games tables, with matching mirrors and console tables, also reflected the comfort and prosperity of late 18th-century Portugal. Chairs and settees made in a sturdy version of the Hepplewhite and Sheraton styles, many of them beautifully painted, suggest a familiarity with English pattern-books of the period.

GERMANY AND AUSTRIA

Germany's long tradition of wood carving continued in much of the furniture produced during the 18th and 19th centuries, but from the early 18th century veneers of walnut, ebony, and other woods were increasingly used. By this time the seeds of the rococo were being sown by certain princes in Germany, even through the baroque showed little sign of fading from favor for the majority. Contributing to this late continuance of the baroque in Germany were the widely influential designs of Johann Jacob Schübler (d.1741), published in Nuremberg and Augsburg in the 1720s and 1730s. In this furniture, ingenious gadgetry was disguised by baroque ornament that would not have been out of place 50 years before.

By the early 18th century, chairs produced in northern Germany showed evidence of both Dutch and English influence, with cabriole legs, shaped backs and caned seats and back panels.

During the first two decades of the 18th century palaces continued to be built in the baroque style, culminating in the Schloss Pommersfelden, built for Lothar Franz von Schönborn, prince bishop of Bamberg.

with her. The fashion she introduced was reinforced by mercantile treaties between the two countries that resulted in large consignments of English furniture finding their way into Portuguese homes.

Japanned pieces were popular, as in Spain, and the Portuguese also carried out their own imitations of oriental lacquer. English styles were reflected most often in Portuguese chairs, but these were generally more exuberantly carved than the originals and usually had H-shaped stretchers, which were discarded in England in the early 18th century. In many examples, English taste merges with French rococo influence, but the interpretations are distinctively Portuguese and often carried out in non-European woods such as the hard, dark jacaranda that was imported from Brazil.

In commodes and beds the Portuguese gave a distinctive and original interpretation to the rococo, with an emphasis on embellishment in carved wood rather than applied metalwork. Portuguese commodes were taller than those of other European countries, nearly always with a depth of four drawers.

▶ LACQUERED
early 18th century
This cabinet is in the
style of Gerard Dagly,
and it may have been
made in Berlin.

ROCOCO

The magnificent Palace of Würzburg, the Residenz of the electors of Mainz, was begun in 1720 in the baroque style, but the furnishings and decoration embodied the finest manifestations of the early rococo in Germany. Among the craftsmen who contributed were Franz Anton Schlott of Bamberg, the four Guthmann brothers of Munich, Johann Wolfgang van der Auvera, Carl Maximilian Mattern (*fl.*1733–70), Johann Georg Nestfell and Johann Kohler. Their elaborate confections of virtuoso marquetry, with lavish use of carving and gilding, look clumsy when compared with later rococo pieces, but they are of consummate craftsmanship and certainly meet their purpose of princely ostentation.

The Residenz at Ansbach was another influential gathering place for purveyors of early rococo, as was the Residenz of Bamberg. One of the chief Ansbach cabinet-makers was Martin Schumacher (1695–1781), whose restrained, linear furniture, which was sometimes veneered in mahogany, has a peculiarly English feel.

The rococo flourished at Bayreuth, home of the margrave Friedrich and his wife Wilhelmine (the sister of Frederick the Great), who were both enthusiastic builders of palaces. The most important cabinet-makers they patronized were the Spindler brothers, who later worked for Frederick the Great.

Augustus the Strong, elector of Saxony (1694–1733) and king of Poland (1697–1733), favored English-inspired designs, especially early on, but the influence of the French rococo supervened before long, and from the 1720s onwards much of the furniture for his court at Dresden was strongly French in flavor. Among the more distinctively Saxon pieces were writing cabinets with mirrors on the upper doors. Martin Schnell (*fl.*1703–40), lacquermaker to the royal court, produced japanned work of great richness, decorated with relief figures of lacquered and gilded copper.

The most extreme francophile manifestations of the rococo in Germany were without doubt those undertaken for the electors of

❧ JAPANNING ❧

*T*he late 17th- and early 18th-century enthusiasm for japanning was as strong in Germany as it was in the rest of Europe. One of the most skilled exponents was Gerard Dagly (fl.1687–1714), who was employed in Berlin, first by the elector Frederick William of Brandenburg and later by Frederick I of Prussia (reigned 1701–13). Dagly was a native of Spa (now in Belgium) where japanning flourished for most of the 17th and 18th centuries. His output of finely decorated cabinets, clocks, keyboard-instrument cases and stands, which were produced while he served as Directeur des Ornements to the royal court, surpassed almost all other European japanning in its quality. He created fine work in black and gold, but his most characteristic pieces, japanned in bright greens, reds, and other colors on a creamy white ground, are more reminiscent of porcelain than furniture decoration.

Bavaria in Munich. The elector Maximilian Emmanuel (1662–1726), formerly exiled at the court of Louis XIV, introduced the most advanced French taste into his surroundings at Munich. His chief architects and designers, first Joseph Effner (1687–1745) and later François Cuvilliès the Elder (1695–1768), both Paris trained, decorated the Munich Residenz and the Palace of Nymphenburg in an airy, dazzling rococo style. Cuvilliès published his designs for ornament, paneling, and furniture, which became known all over Europe, and he dominated rococo design in Germany until his death.

An altogether more robust rococo than that of Cuvilliès was that produced for Frederick the Great (reigned 1740–86) at Potsdam and Berlin.

GERMAN BUREAU-CABINET

◀ WALNUT

*c.*1740

Probably made in Würzburg or Mainz, this piece of furniture is of the type known as a *Tabernakel-Schreib-kommode*. The marquetry inlays and cross-bandings are of walnut, pear, and ebony. The piece includes rococo elements – the *bombé* shape of the *Tabernakel* section and the rocaille scrolls and carved cresting – but its mood is still ponderously baroque.

▲ CARVED AND GILT
1739
This table, in the full-blown rococo style, was made by François Cuvilliès for the Amalienburg hunting lodge at the Palace of Nymphenburg, Munich.

GERMAN *SECRÉTAIRE À ABATTANT*

▶ SYCAMORE
*c.*1780
The crisply chiseled gilt bronze mounts are an elegant foil for the timber of this piece. The sycamore veneer is decorated with marquetry flowers and ribbons. The piece was made by David Roentgen, and, as in much of his work, sophisticated mechanisms for opening drawers and secret compartments are concealed in the decoration.

At first under the direction of Frederick's superintendent of palaces, George Wenzeslaus von Knobelsdorff (1699–1753), and later under their own impetus, a gathering of consummate craftsmen, led by Johann Michael Hoppen-haupt (1709–*c.*1755) and his brother John Christian (1710–86), Johann August Nahl (1710–73), Johann Melchior Kambli (1718–73) and Johann Friedrich Spindler (1726–*c.*1799) and his brother Heinrich Wilhelm (1738–*c.*1799), filled the palaces of Charlottenburg, Potsdam, and Sans-Souci with boldly cur-vaceous furniture of unparalleled magnificence. Commodes, veneered with tortoiseshell or exotic timbers or decorated with marquetry of wood, mother-of-pearl, ivory, and even silver, were profusely ornamented with gilt bronze mounts made in Kambli's workshops, and chairs of painted or gilded softwood were carved with often Italianate confidence.

All this courtly extravagance had a varying effect on the styles of furniture further down the social scale. Regional characteristics were preserved, especially in the design of the *Schrank*, which remained an important symbol of a household's affluence. On the whole, the Hanseatic towns and free cities of the north showed the greatest conservatism. Even by the mid-18th century the *Schrank* as interpreted in Brunswick, for example, was still an essentially baroque piece, with an architectural cornice, classical pilasters, and symmetrical door panels of intarsia. The cupboards of Frankfurt and

Hamburg also kept their solidly baroque char-acter until the mid-18th century. On the other hand, the solid oak cupboards of Aachen, like those of Liège, were carved with *boiseries* (leafy carving) of surprising lightness.

In Mainz the rococo was embodied in a par-ticularly elaborate, three-stage *Schreibkommode* (form of writing bureau), a specialty of the cabinet-maker Peter Schuss. The serpentine-fronted commode section in the base was sur-mounted by a concave-shaped, sloping-topped bureau, and above this was a two-door cup-board, all decorated with marquetry. The canted corners, the cornice above and the apron below were all carved into volutes and twists, with asymmetrical cartouches and moldings wher-ever the opportunity offered. In the most extravagant examples, some of these carved appendages were gilded. The fine craftsman-

GERMAN *TABLE À ÉCRIRE*

◀ KINGWOOD, YEW, AND
AMARANTH
*c.*1750
This little writing table is
given its French name
because of its obvious
debt to French design.
The piece is discreetly
rococo, with gently
curved legs and apron
and up-turned feet. The
German influences can
be seen in the inlay and
marquetry, especially the
unusual choice of
materials.

was still popular in central and eastern Europe in mid-century. Alongside this, cabriole-legged chairs of both English and French derivation were usual.

At a higher level, the two most influential cabinet-makers of the second half of the 18th century were Abraham Roentgen (1711–93) and his son David (1743–1807), whose workshops in Neuwied-am-Rhein produced furniture of exquisite virtuosity and complexity. Through Abraham's experience in the Netherlands and England and, later, David's travels throughout Europe, the Roentgens cultivated an international, largely royal, clientele, and they bridged the rococo and the neoclassical styles. Their marquetry was unsurpassed, and complex internal mechanisms – locks, secret drawers, clocks, and so forth – were included on many of their pieces.

ship lavished on these pieces cannot, however, disguise their basically ungainly shape.

Other southern German bureau-cabinets were less elaborate in their carved detail, but they were still impressive. Walnut with marquetry of other woods, often in geometric patterns, was usual, and canted corners and concave fronts for the drawers in the base and a *Tabernakel* section on top gave a solidity to many such pieces. In these areas of Germany and Austria the influence was predictably Italian, and many pieces of carcass furniture made in the mid-18th century borrowed Italian features, such as exaggeratedly stumpy cabriole legs and plump *bombé* shapes. However, most pieces made for the middle-class market were relatively restrained and solid.

In the areas to the south and east of the region, traditional painted furniture continued to be produced. Relatively simple forms and construction were enhanced by an uninhibited use of color and pattern.

English and Dutch influences were apparent in the north, particularly on chairs. The tall, straight-backed form with H-shaped stretchers and, often, with caned seat and back, which was associated with 18th-century English designs,

THE NETHERLANDS

ANGLO-DUTCH FURNITURE

In the late 17th and early 18th centuries, when Dutch influence on English furniture was particularly strong, the Dutch in turn absorbed what they liked about English styles and types. The result was what has come to be known as Anglo-Dutch style. Caning for chairs was a Dutch introduction that became equally popular in England, and the vogue for oriental lacquer and the development of japanning in imitation of it was also popular in both countries.

Dutch cabinet-makers became leaders in the new craft of veneering, and by the end of the 17th century they had developed a specialized form of this – floral marquetry – using imported and native woods of many different and subtle shades. One of the first and greatest exponents of the art was Jan van Mekeren (*fl.c.*1690–*c.*1735) of Amsterdam, much of whose work was exported.

The Dutch passion for porcelain led to the invention of the glass-fronted display cabinet. Corner cupboards, some with lacquered panels in the doors, were also used for displaying china.

▶ WALNUT
mid-18th century
This piece features
carved cresting in the
rococo style and
decoratively scrolled
glazing bars. The Dutch
invented the glass-
fronted cabinet to meet a
national passion for
displaying collections of
ceramics.

▶ WALNUT
18th century
This side chair in the
Anglo–Dutch style has a
vase-shaped splat, carved
shell motifs on the top
rail and knees on the
front legs and ball-and-
claw feet. The floral
marquetry is typically
Dutch.

Both types were adopted in England. Another
characteristic piece of Anglo–Dutch furniture
was the bureau-bookcase with a sloping fall-
front at the top of the bureau and, above, a
bookcase with two doors and a double-arched
pediment. The piece was often japanned.

Dutch and English chairs also ran a parallel
course. Typical of the last quarter of 17th century were carved frames in oak or walnut with
caned seats and backs. By the early 18th century
Dutch chairs had taken on the flowing lines of
English examples, with cabriole legs, ball-and-
claw feet, and shaped backs with decorated
splats, some of which had panels of floral marquetry. The burgomaster or roundabout chair
was imported from the East Indies into the
Netherlands during the late 17th and early 18th
century. It had a round caned seat, a low back
with a carved splat and turned supports; the
carved cabriole legs were united by turned

stretchers. Dutch examples, usually of walnut or oak, and Indian versions were exported during the 18th century and copied, usually in a lighter form, by English chair-makers.

BAROQUE AND ROCOCO

In the 17th and 18th centuries many craftsmen left the Netherlands to seek their fortunes in France and England. At the same time, just as many artisans from abroad came to the Netherlands, often as a result of religious persecution in Catholic countries. One such was Daniel Marot (1663–1752), who spent his formative years studying the baroque style of the French court in Paris, then successfully transposed it to the Netherlands. His furniture, which ranged from costly state beds festooned with luxurious materials to elaborately carved chairs with elongated backs set in rows around rooms, was sculptural in inspiration. Marot's attachment to the court of William of Orange, both in the Netherlands and, later, in England, made him an important contributor to the Anglo-Dutch style, and his engraved designs for all kinds of furnishings were influential on both sides of the English Channel.

By the 1720s, Marot's heavy baroque style was already being supplanted in the Netherlands by the lighter exuberance of the rococo, and the influence of France was beginning to overtake that of England. By the 1740s, bureau-cabinets were characteristically *bombé* in the lower stage, with curvaceous cornices and scrolled moldings on door panels. Walnut, with its elaborate and irregular figuring, was the preferred timber for veneered pieces, with mahogany, oak, elm, and fruitwoods being used for solid pieces and carcasses. The southern Netherlands were more influenced by France than the north, as can be seen in a specialty of the Liège region – paneled oak cupboards decorated with lively carving of rococo scrolls, cartouches, and asymmetrical tendrils.

Flowers, whether in the garden, in paintings, on china and textiles or on furniture, have always been a great love of the Dutch, and floral marquetry was one of the Netherlands' most

striking bequests in furniture ornamentation. Bureaus, chests of drawers, cabinets, chairs, and clock cases were all decorated with fabulous veneers of naturalistic flowers in vases, baskets, swags, or bouquets. Such pieces show a distinctively Dutch combination of craftsmanship with serviceability, of solidity of form with exuberance of decoration.

NEOCLASSICISM

With the onset of neoclassicism, the extravagantly veneered decoration that had been such a feature of Dutch furniture became more restrained. Flowers now appeared only in small

DUTCH SOFA

▲ MAHOGANY
*c.*1790–1800
This marquetry-decorated mahogany sofa stands on semicircular molded bracket feet.

DUTCH COMMODE

▼ WOOD, MARBLE, AND GILT BRONZE
18th century
This French-style *bombé* commode features kingwood and tulipwood veneers on the sides and across the two-drawer front.

bouquets or sprays on inset lacquer panels. The fashion in the Netherlands for both French and English furniture continued in the second half of the 18th century, to the extent that Dutch cabinet-makers felt that their livelihoods were being threatened by imports, particularly from France. In 1771 the protests of the Amsterdam Guild resulted in a ban on all foreign imports of furniture. The high standards of Dutch cabinet-making were maintained by the Amsterdam Joseph's Guild, which required that all furniture made there be branded.

During the last decades of the 18th century, when Dutch cabinet-makers were especially prosperous, a French-inspired version of neo-classicism prevailed. Rococo curves gave way to rectangular shapes and straight, tapered legs for chests, tables, and chairs. Mahogany had by this time supplanted walnut for most furniture, but satinwood was much used, too. The Dutch continued to make a specialty of marquetry in other exotic woods, often including *trompe l'oeil* architectural details such as fluting. Gilt bronze mounts were used sparingly, but lacquer panels were sometimes incorporated into marquetry.

A typically Dutch item of this period was the *Opfluptafel*, a type of buffet-commode with a two-door cupboard below, a lift-up top revealing shelves in the lid and, sometimes, a basin set into the center of the carcass. Side flaps provided additional serving space.

RUSSIA AND EASTERN EUROPE

In Russia the most fashionable European furniture styles were enthusiastically adopted for palaces and country houses. What kind of furnishings were used in ordinary homes is not well documented, but they probably contrasted more starkly with those of the aristocracy than in other contemporary European countries. Russian cabinet-makers themselves were usually bound to particular houses as serfs, and they were not free to seek their fortunes elsewhere.

In the late 17th century, Russia began importing fine-quality pieces and having them copied by local craftsmen in native woods. The ambitions of Peter the Great (reigned 1682–1725) to establish a great cultural and economic center at St Petersburg, which was founded in 1703, prompted him to send cabinet-makers to England and the Netherlands to study the styles and techniques of the best craftsmen there. A blend of mid-European styles and peculiarly Russian characteristics developed during the 18th century and lasted into the 19th century.

DUTCH BUREAU-CABINET

▼ WALNUT
mid-18th century
This piece exhibits the combination of strong proportions and the exuberant marquetry of naturalistic flowers that has come to be associated with Dutch cabinet-making.

It was the French rococo that had the greatest direct impact on the furnishing of Russian palaces. Between 1716 and 1726 the French sculptor and woodcarver Nicolas Pineau (1684–1754), one of the leading exponents of rococo design, worked in Russia, introducing carved

RUSSIAN TABLE

◀ MAHOGANY
*c.*1790
The inspiration behind this oval table is clearly the French neoclassical style of the 1780s. Much Russian furniture followed designs from western Europe, although they were often given a national flavor. The top of finely figured mahogany, the extensive use of linear gilt bronze decoration and the unusual stretcher of this table are all Russian additions, although the basic shape, the pierced gallery and details on the legs are standard neoclassical features.

❧ STEEL FURNITURE ❧

The small-arms factory at Tula in central Russia, which was founded by Peter the Great, also produced steel furniture and ornaments from the early 18th century. Although few products of this early period have survived, there is a considerable quantity from the later 18th century, when steel furniture was made for Catherine the Great's palaces. Her own visit to Matthew Boulton's factory in Birmingham, England, probably influenced the style of much Russian cut-steel work, and it is possible that Birmingham craftsmen went to Russia and introduced Boulton's techniques.

Fireplaces, fenders, fire-irons, caskets, and other small ornamental furnishings of burnished steel were decorated with neoclassical motifs in faceted beads and are strongly reminiscent of Adam designs. Particularly elegant are the folding X-frame chairs, some with backs and sides filled with scrolling plant decoration, others with seat and back formed by straps of metal. A development of the cut-steel technique was the encrusting of other metals – silver, pewter, brass, and copper – on the steel surface.

boiseries into Peter the Great's study. The importation of fashionable French furniture and the published designs of other leading practitioners of rococo style were additional factors in the adoption of a highly developed form of the style. Later, Count Bartolommeo Francesco Rastrelli (*c.*1700–71), son of an Italian sculptor, became chief architect at the Russian court, and he introduced a florid, Germanic style of decoration to the imperial residence Tsarskoe Selo (1749–56) and the Winter Palace at St. Petersburg (1754–62).

Neoclassicism in Russia took an equally sumptuous form. It was introduced by the Scottish architect Charles Cameron (*c.*1743–1812), who worked for Catherine the Great (reigned 1762–96) from the late 1770s and provided decorations and furnishings for many of the royal residences. The furniture was supplied by the most fashionable Parisian *ébénistes*.

David Roentgen was also a major influence on the development of neoclassicism in Russia. He visited St. Petersburg several times and supplied Catherine with no fewer than seven consignments of furniture. Many of the most respected cabinet-makers working in Russia were German migrants imbued with the craftsmanship ideals of the Roentgens' workshop at Neuwied-am-Rhein. One of these was Christian Meyer; another was Heinrich Gambs (1765–1831), who designed furniture for Catherine's successor, Paul (reigned 1796–1801).

RUSSIAN TEA CADDY

◀ STEEL
18th century
This neoclassical tea caddy is decorated with Tula steel work.

SCANDINAVIA

Painted furniture – of birch, beech, or ash as well as pine – was characteristic of Scandinavian houses (even those of the rich), almost all of which were themselves of timber. Even so, Sweden and Norway were as open as any other country to stylistic developments in Europe. The English demand for timber to reconstruct London after the Great Fire of 1666 brought both prosperity and English furniture design to

▶ PAINTED WOOD
early 18th century
This cabinet, which is 4 feet 5 inches wide, is decorated with figures, landscapes, and buildings. The blue borders imitate oriental lacquer and the grounds imitate red marble. It has a remarkably shallow fall-front concealing a fitted interior, and behind the double doors of the upper cabinet are drawers and pigeonholes.

Scandinavia in the late 17th century, and because English design was itself affected by Dutch, Scandinavian furniture of the period is distinctly Anglo-Dutch.

The high-backed, cane-seated, or upholstered chair that was fashionable in late 17th-century England and the Netherlands was enthusiastically adopted in Scandinavia, and the style persisted well into the 18th century. The general conservatism of Scandinavian chair-makers – who were traditionally separated from the more progressive cabinet-makers – ensured the persistence of chair styles that were outmoded in other parts of Europe. The cabriole-legged, splat-backed chairs of the Queen Anne and early Georgian periods enjoyed an extended popularity in Scandinavia, where the chairs were fitted with turned stretchers long after these had been abandoned in England.

English styles, as purveyed in many books of designs for gentlemen's furniture, influenced bourgeois furniture in Scandinavia. The fall-front case and longcase clock were among the English forms that appealed to the Scandinavians, and they were made over a long period.

Because of its geographical proximity, Germany also strongly affected Scandinavian furniture types and styles. Many Scandinavian craftsmen learned their trade in Germany, while German cabinet-makers also practiced in Denmark, Norway, and Sweden.

ROCOCO

The rococo in Scandinavia, at first seen only at court, tended to be interpreted in its Germanic form, especially in Denmark and Norway. Sweden was more francophile, and Paris-trained architects dominated the introduction of the rococo style into the salons of Stockholm in the 1730s and 1740s. Enthusiasm for French art was not new. In the late 17th century, both the old royal castles of Copenhagen and Stockholm had been replaced by grand palaces in the spirit of Versailles, and much of the furniture for them had been imported from France and the rest copied by Danish craftsmen from French models.

NEOCLASSICISM

French influence on Denmark became strong in the neoclassical period, largely through the appointment of the French sculptor Jacques-François Saly (1717–96) as director of the new Copenhagen Academy, where he raised Danish artistic standards. In Sweden, where neoclassicism was adopted later than in Denmark, its interpretation included both French and English elements. Commodes followed French forms but were often veneered, English-style, in mahogany rather than in the decorative parquetry which was favored in France. Mahogany was also used in solid construction, especially for splat-back chairs of Hepplewhite and Sheraton derivation.

George Haupt (1741–84), the most important cabinet-maker working in Stockholm in the 1770s, had gained experience all over Europe and proved himself as capable of producing delicately crafted tables with a strong English flavor as of creating large-scale masterpieces, embellished with gilt bronze, in the Louis XVI style. Louis Adrien Masreliez (1748–1810) and his brother Jean Baptiste Edouard (1753–1801) continued to adopt French styles for Swedish court furniture. But Gotlob Iwersson, another major Swedish cabinet-maker working at the turn of the century, was mostly inspired by English models.

▼ MARQUETRY, MARBLE, AND GILT BRONZE
1780
This marble-topped neoclassical commode, with marquetry decoration and chiseled gilt bronze mounts, was made by George Haupt, the versatile Swedish cabinet-maker.

AMERICAN CHAIR

▶ WALNUT

*c.*1740

It is interesting to compare this American Queen Anne style chair with contemporary chairs from Britain – the shell carving, general shape, and cabriole legs are very similar. The scrolls on this chair from Philadelphia, however, have an extraordinarily sinuous effect, and the splat is finely figured to combine simplicity with decoration.

AMERICA

❀ The term "colonial furniture" is used broadly to refer to pieces made before 1775. Before the War of Independence, design influences came from England and from Europe generally. Each nationality of immigrant, especially the Dutch, brought not only pieces of furniture but also affection for a traditional national style. These influences combined to create a recognizably "American" style.

QUEEN ANNE STYLE

In the United States the term Queen Anne is generally used to describe pieces made between *c.*1715 and 1750. The graceful lines and elegant carving of this style were a revelation to Americans, who found that the appearance of the pieces fitted well with the new colonial sense of expansion and prosperity. No longer did furniture have to "look" solid. Hogarth's "line of beauty" (the ogee) took precedence over the

AMERICAN DAY-BED

▶ MAHOGANY

*c.*1740–50

The eight legs on this day-bed identify it as a transitional piece, part William and Mary style, part Queen Anne style – later examples have six legs. The bow back, with its flanking spindles, harks back to earlier influences, and a multi-arm stretcher connects the legs.

right angle, and chair backs, seats, and legs, the aprons of chests and highboys, the edges of tables were designed to incorporate the wave-like bend.

The style of chair and table legs soon developed from simply curved to fully fledged cabriole – that is, with an exaggerated double curve. They ended in a pad or a foot cleft in three, and the knees and the top rails of dining chairs were often decorated with single scallop shells. Stretchers, carried over from the William and Mary period, eventually disappeared. The development of chairs in the Queen Anne style clearly mark the development of an indigenous tradition. In New York, an elaborately baroque Dutch style tended to produce rather bulbous splats and an abundance of foliage carving, especially on the crests, but in New England, particularly Massachusetts, British conservatism favored a vertical look with higher backs and, occasionally, with a sturdy rear stretcher. Oriental lacquer became increasingly popular, and there are some notable chairs from this period with slightly elaborated European-oriental decoration. Thomas Johnson, who described himself as being "Japaner at the Golden Lyon in Anne Street, Boston," was notable for this kind of work.

Comfort was now established as a factor in chair design. The wing chair, with a tall back, face-level fire-protector and rolled arms, was introduced. On this, as on other upholstered furniture, the turkeywork and velvet of the previous century were supplanted by silk, damask, and wool. A small number of upholstered sofas in the Queen Anne style survive, but more popular were all-wood settees and day-beds with bowed top rails.

The American Windsor chair first appeared *c.*1725. This all-wood chair was characterized by the use of turned spindles, socketed into the seat, for both back and legs. American examples differ from the English versions in the lack of a back splat and the exaggerated angle at which the legs were set to the seat, which combined to make them lighter in feeling than the English chair. This effect was heightened in early

examples by the larger number of spindles used to form the back. Two styles were common – the bow back, in which the top rail was bent into a three-quarter hoop, and the comb back, in which the top rail was almost straight.

The popular gate-leg table gave way to the more elegant drop leaf, in which two of the four legs were movable, swinging in to let down the leaves of the round or oval top. Some of the best examples had an extra pair of legs, providing greater support when the leaves were down. Toward the end of the Queen Anne period, square or rectangular drop-leaf tables were made. Ball-and-claw feet began to replace pad feet, as they also did on chairs. Gaming tables were made, and small rectangular (later circular) occasional tables were adapted for use in serving the newly fashionable tea.

Perhaps the artistic high point of the Queen Anne style was the highboy, a chest of drawers with the upper, taller section standing on a lower section with legs. In its first incarnation, during the William and Mary period, the high-

▲ *c.*1750
Even more notably than in Britain, American chairs may be divided into rustic (used by most people) and formal (based on imported, popular styles). This Carver chair is a good example of what might be described as Jacobean American, and the design was based on a chair supposedly brought to America by John Carver, the first governor of the then British colony. The chair has a typically 17th-century English, slightly baroque look, and it is clearly related to its English counterparts.

◄ WALNUT AND BURR VENEER
*c.*1730–50
This piece from Massachusetts is a fine example of the Queen Anne highboy. The six turned legs of the William and Mary style have become four cabriole legs, with the two turned apron knops marking their departure. The top, however, has not yet developed the curved pediment that came into vogue 20 years later.

portions of the piece, and in the 1730s the curve of the apron became more pronounced, and eventually even the flat top acquired a curved pediment. The earlier walnut gave way in popularity to mahogany, except in Philadelphia.

Another tall piece to exploit the changes in cabinet making was the secretary (bureau) bookcase. Made of walnut, maple, or mahogany, it echoed the architectural lines of the Palladian architecture currently fashionable, particularly in the arched paneling of its doors and the details of its pilasters and cornices. A small relation of this large storage piece that first appeared at about this time was the corner cupboard, either in simple pine or in walnut, with a carved shell top.

AMERICAN HIGHBOY

▲ MAHOGANY
*c.*1760
The shell carving identifies this piece as a fine example of New England furniture-making.

AMERICAN CORNER CUPBOARD

▶ BLUE-PAINTED WOOD
early 18th century
Cupboards such as this, with glazed upper door and reeded columns in the early Federalist mode, are extremely desirable.

boy was usually made of walnut and had six, rarely four, spindle or ball-and-cone turned legs, connected by stretchers and terminating in ball feet. The highboy was soon joined by the lowboy – the lower section of the taller piece. Usually made of walnut or with a fine walnut veneer, the lowboy, like the highboy, was used in all rooms of the house. By 1710 japanning had come into vogue, and it was used to excellent effect on these pieces.

With Queen Anne style, the earlier six spindle or bell-and-cone legs developed into four cabriole legs, and turned pendant knops decorated the apron. The ogee suited the pro-

CHIPPENDALE STYLE

Some elements of the work of the English designer Thomas Chippendale (1718–79) had appeared in American pieces during the 1730s and 1740s, before the publication in 1754 of *The Gentleman and Cabinet-Maker's Director*, but it was not until the 1760s that the full force of his work struck the fashion-conscious inhabitants of American cities. Chippendale's French-influenced rococo style, flavored with elements of Chinese and gothic, was embraced in its entirety. The finest Santo Domingo mahogany

✿ THE PENNSYLVANIAN TRADITION ✿

*D*uring the mid-18th century the Quaker and other nonconformist groups who had settled in Pennsylvania turned their energies toward the creation of idiomatically made and decorated furniture. Among the national customs brought from Europe was the tradition of the dower chest, given by parents and friends to the daughter of the family. Made to contain homespun linens, quilts, hangings, and towels for a future marriage, the chests were painted to order in a background shade of soft blue – green, black or brown were sometimes used – and decorated with motifs from medieval myths and Christian legend. Symbols included unicorns (virginity), hearts (love), mermaids (sex), the tree of life (mortality), flowers (fertility), doves (peace), and the pelican and fish (Christ).

Several chests carry the owner's name or the initials and date it was made. Most of the artists were unknown, but two names have survived – Christian Selzer (1749–1831) of Jonestown and Heinrich Otto.

Other typical pieces included painted tables, chairs, and beds, wall-mounted cabinets, corner cabinets, and pie safes with pierced tin panels. The largest piece was the Schrank, a heavy wardrobe of thick planks and a rather medieval character, which was ornately painted or inlaid with the usual mythological symbols or more temporal motifs, such as crowns and swastikas. Chests, Schranks, and cupboards were usually supported on ball or bracket feet. By the early 19th century, such furniture had largely been assimilated in the wider American tradition.

◀ 1789
This painted, two-door blanket chest on bracket feet was made by Johannes Rank. All the painted motifs had symbolic meanings.

AMERICAN CHAIR

▶ *c.*1765
This chair, which was made in New York, clearly shows the influence of English Chippendale, and it does, in fact, have many of the characteristics shown in Chippendale's pattern-books. There is, however, that balance between decoration and plainness that had its roots in the designs of the original Dutch settlers in New York, even though it exhibits so many English traits. This chair was made for Elias Boudinout of New Jersey.

was used to embody his ideas, and walnut never recovered in popularity.

Philadelphia was the capital of furniture-making in the Chippendale style. Among its fine craftsmen were Thomas Affleck (*fl.*1763–95), Benjamin Randolph (*fl.*1762–92), John Folwell (*fl.*1775), James Gillingham (*fl.*1765–91), William Savery (*fl.*1742–87), and Thomas Tuft (*fl.*1765–93). The chairs, highboys, and bureau-book-cases made by these and other cabinet-makers were masterpieces of elegance. They are crisper in execution than their English equivalents, and the curves are less extravagant. The flame finials, frequently seen on the pediments of sec-retaries and highboys, and the peanut carving enlivening the top rails and aprons of chairs, mark these pieces out as uniquely American.

AMERICAN BUREAU

▶ MAHOGANY
*c.*1760–70
The vigorous lines of Queen Anne style are still evident in this elegant block-front bureau, which was probably made in Rhode Island. The blocking on the front is characteristic of work from Connecticut and Rhode Island, and it is a technique that emphasizes the quality of the wood as the undulating surface reflects every change in the light.

New York, Boston, and Salem followed the lead of Philadelphia. Fine cabinet-makers included Thomas Burling (New York, *fl.*1772–1800), Samuel Prince (New York, *fl.*1760–78), John Cogswell (Boston, *fl.*1769–1818), and Samuel McIntire (Salem, *fl.*1757–1811), whose rendition of the monumental chest-on-chest places him among the best of the late practitioners of the Chippendale style. In the work of these craftsmen, paneled doors continued to adorn bureau-bookcases, even though glass-fronted versions had become more fashionable in Britain. In Boston an idiosyncratic version, known as the kettle base or *bombé* appeared. The swollen base narrows toward the top, giving a distinctly feminine look to the piece.

Despite the outstanding output of New York, Boston, and Salem, it was the craftsmen of Rhode Island and Connecticut who offered more serious alternatives to Philadelphia's dominance. The vigorous forms of the Queen Anne style, which were still alive there, were effortlessly integrated into the new style. Deceptively simple yet majestic block-front desks, secretaries, and chests of drawers by such craftsmen as Benjamin Burham, John Goddard (*fl.*1750–85), and the Townsend family (*fl.*1777–90s) have become as distinctively American in character as the highboy. It was on such large pieces that blocking (the projecting, squared, flat-carved facing particular to this region) was seen to best advantage, often crowned with exquisite intaglio shells on the lower pediment or paneled doors.

A small number of chair-back settees and wing chairs with the new open-rolled arms (curling outwards, away from the seat) were also made.

Tea tables were, by this time, circular, with elaborately carved supports and tripod legs ending in claw-and-ball feet and with pie-crust or shell patterns rimming the top. A new "birdcage" mechanism made it possible for the top to fold flat against the support when the table was not in use.

Higher ceilings meant that bedposts were taller than ever, the most elegant being over-

topped by a straight oblong wooden canopy with hangings of wool, crewelwork, or linen. By the 1760s the curtains at the foot of the bed were being omitted, and the exposed posts were ornamentally turned and fluted. Chippendale-style beds were produced in mahogany, cherry, or maple, depending on the wood available locally.

◄ WALNUT
*c.*1760
The tilting top of this Chippendale-style tea table, which is similar to English pieces, is released by a "birdcage" mechanism – the latch is surrounded by tiny turned columns, like a cage. These are just visible at the top of the column support. The table, made of finely figured walnut, has a slight upturn around the edge of the top. The slender column has a knop known as a compressed ball, and there are sharply curving cabriole legs. The ball-and-claw feet have the pronounced shape that is characteristic of pieces made in Philadelphia, and the whole table has a refined, elegant look, typical of work from that city.

AMERICAN WING CHAIR

◄ MAHOGANY
*c.*1770
This chair in the Chippendale style could easily be English, although it was actually made in Newport, Rhode Island. The upholstered parts are the same shape as those on its English equivalents, and the cabriole legs have typically carved ball-and-claw feet and are joined by delicately turned stretchers ending in substantial blocks. The frame of a similar English chair is more likely to have been made of walnut than mahogany, however, and this style of chair was popular in England some 50 years before this example was made.

THE
19TH
CENTURY

The great mass of European furniture made during the last quarter of the 19th century and in the first decades of the 20th century is, at first glance, indistinguishable from pieces made in the preceding three centuries. A closer look, however, reveals such errors of proportion and debasement of materials and craftsmanship that it is impossible to confuse the imitation with the original. Some fine reproduction furniture was made, but the best pieces were almost always original in their design.

ENGLISH WORK TABLE

ENGLISH WORK TABLE

▶ MAHOGANY
*c.*1815
This small sewing table shows all the Regency attributes that might be expected of this date. Decorated with dot-and line brass inlay and its top cross-banded in rosewood, this practical table was fully equipped for its purpose. Its main drawer was sectioned into a sewing box, with compartments for cottons, needles, scissors and the like, and the "sliding well" drawer made of fabric that hangs beneath would have held bulkier items.

ENGLISH WRITING TABLE

▼ ROSEWOOD VENEER AND BOXWOOD STRINGING
*c.*1810
A particular feature of this piece is the use of finely cast and chased gilt bronze. Lion masks and ring handles were popular throughout the period, but more unusual are the *espagnolettes* on the corners.

BRITAIN

REGENCY

As a description of a period of English furniture design, the word Regency is an imprecise, modern term. Far from being confined to furniture made during the single decade of the historical Regency (1811–20), when the Prince of Wales (later George IV) took over the reins of monarchy from his ailing father George III, it includes furniture produced from *c.*1790 until the early 1840s.

The earliest pieces of furniture designated Regency are those of the late 18th century that cannot be categorized as a late flowering of the Adam style, such as those inspired by Louis XVI furniture that were included by Thomas Sheraton in *The Cabinet-Maker and Upholsterer's Drawing Book* (1791–3). At the other end of the period, the last Regency furniture is principally in a somewhat debase neoclassical style.

Neoclassicism, which had replaced rococo in the 1760s, was dominant throughout the Regency period, but this was an age of eclectic taste, and there were many other popular styles, including chinoiserie, gothic revival, Egyptian

revival, Louis XIV revival, and rococo revival. A single designer would often produce work inspired by a variety of stylistic traditions.

None of the styles current during the Regency period existed in isolation. They were related to similar trends in architecture, painting, sculpture, and the decorative arts. Nor did these styles appear out of the blue. They were the result of such influences as furniture imported from abroad, the presence in London of *émigré* cabinet-makers from Revolutionary France, articles brought back from the Grand Tour, and the availability of foreign pattern-books and other source materials.

The Regency period saw considerable demographic change. In 1780 the population of Great Britain was perhaps 7.5 million; by 1815 it was 13 million, and by the 1870s it had doubled again. From 1815 to 1840 there was a move away from the countryside and a vast increase in the urban middle class. Cities such as Birmingham and Glasgow at least doubled in size. Some furniture-makers adapted to these changes. While continuing to cater for wealthy, aristocratic patrons with expensive, and luxurious furnishings, at the same time they supplied the new market with solid, serviceable items. These remain as respectable and practical today as when they were first made.

🌿 SHERATON'S 🌿 CABINET DICTIONARY

*T*homas Sheraton (1751–1806) trained as a cabinet-maker, but from 1793 he supported his family by writing. His second book, The Cabinet Dictionary *(1803), is an important collection of furniture designs, and it illustrates many characteristic features and motifs associated with Regency furniture. Many of the 500 or so subscribers to the* Dictionary *were cabinet-makers, and this demonstrates how important such pattern-books were in disseminating styles.*

The 79 principal plates illustrate a wide range of furniture, including chairs, tables, bookcases, sofas, and mirrors. Sheraton's designs include caryatids, saber legs, lion masks, animal feet, and X-supports for chairs.

Notable among the manufacturers of the period are Gillow of Lancaster and London (active from *c.*1730 and throughout the 19th century), Seddon of London (1753–1868), Trotter of Edinburgh (*c.*1750–1852) and Blain of Liverpool (1830s). Less well known are Wilkinson of London (1808–40) and James Winter of London (1823–40). Their furniture tends to be not particularly distinguished in terms of design, and although it was well-executed, it might have escaped identification altogether had they not marked their pieces. During this period – as indeed throughout the 19th century – many firms stamped their name on the top of a drawer front, the door of a cupboard or on the underside of a chair or table.

🦋 BRASS INLAY 🦋

The British passion for collecting grand French furniture reached a high point during the first quarter of the 19th century. Massive dispersals of the collections of the French royal family and nobility occurred after the Revolution in 1789. The Prince Regent, the writer William Beckford, and the Duke of Wellington were among the notable figures who took advantage of the opportunities offered. These three collectors all owned examples of boulle furniture dating from the 17th and 18th centuries, and the appearance in England of pieces ornamented in this style had a profound effect on the decoration of early 19th-century domestic furniture.

Brass inlay was used for furniture decoration in four main ways. The simplest was a stringing (thin lines) or slightly broader strips. In 1803 Thomas Sheraton wrote: "Small lines of brass are now much in use in English furniture, and look very handsome in black rose and other dark wood grounds." The second use was to create decorative borders of anthemions, scrolls, Greek key patterns, and other motifs on various types of furniture, including sofas and chair backs.

The third use of brass inlay was as complete boulle panels on cabinet doors and table tops, usually on a wooden ground rather than on the tortoiseshell used by the French. Finally, brass inlay was used in French-style brass and tortoiseshell boulle marquetry on a small group of Louis XVI revival pieces made by Louis Le Gaigneur of London (c.1814–c.1821), Thomas Parker, also of London (1805–30) and some other cabinet-makers. These near-copies of French prototypes were doubtless produced to make up a shortfall in the supply of imported originals caused by excess demand. The only pieces of this description identified to date are some coffers on stands, writing tables, and inkstands.

ENGLISH TABLE

▶ EBONY

*c.*1815
This writing table was made in England by Louis Le Gaigneur in the French style. It has brass inlay and gilt bronze mounts.

Design is marked by an archaeological approach – diligent research was undertaken into all available sources of styles. Material drawn upon ranged from antique marbles to contemporary publications, such as Thomas Hope's *Household Furniture and Interior Design* (1807). The resulting furniture included both accurate reproductions of antique forms and stylization of them. In the work of an able designer, such as George Bullock (d.1818), furniture that thus revealed its sources of inspiration from the past was, nevertheless, characteristic of its own period.

Most furniture produced for the middle classes was not made by leading cabinet-makers, and it is therefore less distinguished than pieces made by some of the famous names. Even so, much of it shows great elegance in its use of typical Regency features derived from pattern-books, such as saber legs on chairs, turned or reeded legs on tables and chairs, stylized acanthus and lotus leaf carving, and inlaid brass borders. Kitchen and servants' furniture tended to be made with an emphasis on durability rather than style, but even so it, too, can have considerable charm.

The principal woods used in commercially produced furniture during the period were mahogany and rosewood. However, the grander early 19th-century pieces were often veneered with rare and exotic woods. Satinwood remained fashionable, as it had been at the end of the 18th century, and amboyna, calamander, ebony, and kingwood were also popular. Where appropriate, furniture was embellished with gilt gesso moldings and with gilt bronze and lacquered brass mounts. Brass inlay was widely used, both for inlaid lines and for decorative borders and panels. Also common was painted furniture with landscape vignettes on chair backs, and there was an increased use of native woods, such as oak, elm, and yew, not just for country-made pieces but also for sophisticated London-made furniture, such as that made by George Bullock.

A key figure in the introduction of late 18th-century French neoclassicism into English furniture design was the architect and designer Henry Holland (1745–1806). His major commissions during the 1780s and 1790s included work for the Prince of Wales at Carlton House,

ENGLISH CHAIR

◀ BEECH
*c.*1810
Painted seat furniture was popular throughout the Regency period, and the beech of this side chair has been painted to simulate maple. The lyre is an attribute of Apollo, the god of music and poetry, and it is likely that this lyre-backed chair was designed for a music room.

ENGLISH ARMCHAIR

▼ GILT WOOD
*c.*1800
This armchair is part of a suite made by Marsh and Tatham for Powderham Castle, Devon, and it clearly shows the influence of Louis XVI style on English design. The dolphin, an attribute of the god Neptune, is often found on Regency furniture; in this instance it represents part of the family crest.

▶ ROSEWOOD VENEER
*c.*1810
The form of this chaste and elegant *secrétaire* owes a debt to the work of the 18th-century French cabinet-makers such as Saunier and Weisweiler. The lattice grille of the superstructure, the scrolled surround above the frieze drawers, the handles, and the legs are all typical of the work of John McLean.

▽ ROSEWOOD VENEER
*c.*1800
This French-inspired, marble-topped and gilded dwarf cupboard, represents a furniture style associated with the architect Henry Holland and one that remained popular throughout the Regency period.

London, and at the Royal Pavilion, Brighton. He also worked for the 5th duke of Bedford at Woburn and for Samuel Whitebread at Southill, both in Bedfordshire, and for the 2nd earl Spencer at Althorp, Northamptonshire. Much of the contemporary furniture that survives from these commissions has a distinctly French flavor, and some of it was almost certainly designed by Holland himself. The few furniture designs definitely attributable to Holland, such as those at the Royal Institute of British Architects, London, and at the Pierpoint Morgan Library, New York, are very much in the late Louis XVI style of a French *ébéniste* such as the German-born Adam Weisweiler (1744–1820).

At Southill there are several low, marble-topped cupboards and bookcases, which were probably made from Holland's designs by the royal cabinet-makers Elward, Marsh, & Tatham of London (active 1774–1840). These pieces typify the Anglo-French style of early Regency furniture. The overall appearance of these so-called dwarf cabinets recalls commodes by Parisian *ébénistes* such as Claude-Charles Saunier (1735–1807), Jean-Henri Riesener (1734–1806) and Weisweiler. The richly figured veneers relieved by delicate gilt bronze mounts, the gilded columns and the marble tops are all French-inspired.

❧ JOHN McLEAN ❧

*O*n the evidence of surviving furniture, one of the London cabinet-making firms that most successfully adapted the late 18th-century French style was John McLean & Son. The company's documented furniture can be dated only to 1805–15, but it was probably active from 1770 to 1825. McLean has the distinction of having been singled out by Sheraton in his Cabinet Dictionary (1803), to which he was a subscriber.

McLean's debt to Louis XVI ébénistes is clear in the restrained, somewhat severe form of his small tables and cabinets. His furniture is usually veneered with finely figured rosewood, now faded to a mellow color. It is enriched by distinctive lacquered brass mounts, the design of which seems, in some instances, to be unique for McLean's workshop. There is an exquisite bonheur du jour in the Metropolitan Museum of Art, New York. This latter piece has typical partly gilded, turned legs, and the upper part, which is a book tray, has a fine lacquered brass grille.

English dwarf cabinets of this type often have doors lined with pleated silk, and sometimes the door frames contain wire grilles. The dwarf cabinet remained popular throughout the Regency period, becoming less and less elegant toward the middle of the century. The later examples lack the proportion and refinement of the earlier pieces.

A valuable source of ideas for Regency furniture-makers was *Etchings, Representing the Best Examples of Ancient Ornamental Architecture; Drawn from the Originals in Rome* (1799) by Charles Heathcote Tatham (1772–1842). One plate in his book, "Antique Sets of White Marble from Originals at Rome," included a representation of a marble stool, and this inspired the manufacture of a pair of similar-looking beech and mahogany stools painted to simulate marble. The type of "reproduction" furniture, based directly on classical exemplars, would probably have been intended for a formal sculpture gallery or an entrance hall.

Another influential figure who based his designs on models from the antique world was Thomas Hope (1769–1831). Hope studied architecture from an early age and, while he was traveling in Egypt, Greece, Sicily and Spain on the Grand Tour, he made sketches of architectural remains. He later bought an Adam house in London and installed in it his collection of antique vases and ancient and modern sculptures. The rooms were specially created by himself to display his collection. The furniture and other modern works of art that made up the ensemble were, to a large extent, also designed by Hope, and they were sophisticated interpretations of mainly Greek, Roman, and Egyptian styles, although French Empire was also an influence.

Hope's *Household Furniture and Interior Decoration* (1807), which illustrates his own collection, is perhaps the most significant set of furniture designs published during the Regency period, and it had an enormous influence on commercial cabinet-makers. Hope's furniture displays purity of line and appositeness in its use of embellishment – for example, he included

◄ AMBOYNA
*c.*1805
Regency furniture often drew directly on classical sources. The balanced form of this magnificent inkstand, which is of amboyna and ebony with inlaid brass and gilt bronze mounts, is based on a Roman tomb, and its use of materials is exceptionally fine.

ENGLISH TABLE

◄ CALAMANDER VENEER
*c.*1810
This center table, with its gilded decoration and gilt bronze mounts, was inspired by a design by Thomas Hope. The exotic veneer gives it great richness.

ENGLISH ARMCHAIR

▶ PAINTED AND PARTLY
GILT WOOD
*c.*1810
This piece is based
directly on a design for
"drawing room chairs" in
George Smith's *A
Collection of Designs ...*
(1805). Classically
inspired animal heads
and legs regularly appear
on Regency furniture.

ENGLISH STOOL

▶ MAHOGANY
*c.*1810
The design of this lion-
headed, X-frame, partly
gilt stool is taken directly
from one illustrated in
Thomas Hope's
Household Furniture
(1807). Hope also showed
a version with goats'
heads.

bacchanalian masks on an urn for a dining room
and a sleeping greyhound on a day-bed.

Hope's style set a standard that few commercial cabinet-makers could follow. A notable
exception is the early 19th-century work of
Thomas Chippendale the Younger (1749–1822)
for Sir Richard Colt Hoare at Stourhead, Wilt-
shire. This work has much of the tension and
confidence in design that is associated with
Hope's furniture. For example, the mahogany
library chairs, with their low curved backs
resting neatly on supports like Egyptian
caryatids for the front legs, are both elegant and
original. Apart from the brass castors, there is
no additional embellishment, and it is the
design and the quality of the timber alone that
make them outstanding. Equally fine is the large
library desk with free-standing sphinx-head
caryatids at the ends and similar pilasters at the
sides supporting heads of Greek philosophers.

The first designer truly to popularize contemporary Regency taste was George Smith
(*c.*1786–1826), whose book *A Collection of
Designs for Household Furniture and Interior
Decoration* first appeared in 1805. Little is known
about Smith, although he is recorded in contemporary trade directories as a cabinet-maker.
There is scant evidence of his activity in this
field, and no documented furniture has survived.

Nor has there ever been any substantiation of
his claim to be "Upholder [upholsterer]
Extraordinary" to the Prince of Wales, to whom,
with permission, he dedicated his book.

The furniture designs published by Smith
are an attractive collection that, if judged by the
considerable number of surviving pieces inspired by them, were highly successful in pro-
moting what he himself termed his "most
approved and elegant taste." The designs, far
less rigorous than those of Tatham and Hope,
are embellished with popular motifs in classical,
gothic, and Chinese style. Many of the 158
plates in the book reveal a delightful sense of
fantasy, although on occasion the furniture is
somewhat overladen with ornamentation. Beds
are covered with colorful and elaborate upholstery – one, for example, is constructed in
the form of Roman spears and banners, while
another has carvings of draped figures holding
up the canopy and standing on plinths in the
form of candelabra.

Chimeras (carved animals) and caryatids
support tables, desks, commodes, and wardrobes. A "dwarf library bookcase," which is
appropriately inscribed "Homer" and "Virgil,"
has ends in the form of antique cineraria (urns
containing cremation ashes). There are two
designs for tables "in the Chinese style" and a
scheme for the "decoration of a drawing room in
the Chinese taste," complete with painted walls,
pagoda fireplace, vases of bamboo shoots, and
hanging "Chinese" lanterns.

ENGLISH SOFA

◄ SIMULATED BAMBOO
*c.*1810
The ten legs of the Regency four-seater, chair-back sofa are united by plain and turned stretchers. An unusually complex piece, it is made of simulated bamboo. In 1803 Thomas Sheraton had described how beech was turned in imitation of bamboo, and the taste for such faux-bamboo continued to some extent throughout the 19th century. It was an especial favorite in Regency England, especially for the furnishing of interiors in the chinoiserie taste.

Smith's work in the gothic vein is typical of that of the early Regency period and, as with 18th-century gothic, is more concerned with the quaint appearance of its quatrefoils, crockets, and pointed arches than with historically accurate use of such motifs or with the original forms of medieval English furniture.

CHINOISERIE

The first chinoiserie – that is, objects in Chinese or pseudo-Chinese style – was the 17th century European furniture, ceramics, silver, and textiles influenced by imports from China via the trade routes. In the main (porcelain and pottery were exceptions), chinoiserie produced in England consisted of already fashionable European forms that were Chinese in decoration only. Regency chinoiserie reflected the continuing influence of the East, which developed in late 17th-century England and was later popular as part of the rococo style. In the late 18th and early 19th centuries, the style survived the onset of neoclassicism by the use of Chinese and Japanese lacquer panels, together with European imitation, to decorate desks and cabinets with gilt bronze mounts.

The most extraordinary chinoiserie interiors from the Regency period are, without doubt, those at the Royal Pavilion, Brighton. They re-flect the combined tastes of the architect John Nash (1752–1835), who rebuilt Henry Holland's original in 1815; of the decorators Frederick Crace (1779–1859) and Robert Jones; and of the Prince Regent.

Although now much restored, the Pavilion's ground floor has a variety of fantastic schemes. The walls in the principal corridor are decorated with painted bamboo branches and

ENGLISH TABLE

▼ LACQUER WITH BRASS BANDING
*c.*1815
This is one of a pair of center tables. It is a typical example of Regency chinoiserie – the top is of Chinese lacquer but the frieze and legs are "japanned" in imitation of oriental work.

ENGLISH TABLE

▶ HAND-COLORED
AQUATINT
February 1814
This design for a writing
and games table is from
Ackermann's *Repository*.
The table was: "intended
to serve the double
purpose of usefulness and
pleasure ... it is
convenient as a breakfast
or sofa table ... a
convenient writing table
... for the game of chess,
drafts, backgammon &c."

ENGLISH LIBRARY TABLE

▼ HAND-COLORED
AQUATINT
March 1826
This design for a gothic
library table appeared in
Ackermann's *Repository*
in 1826.

ACKERMANN'S REPOSITORY

*There is no better overview of design during
the central years of the Regency period
than the furniture designs that appeared in* The
Repository of Arts, Literature, Commerce,
Manufactures, Fashions and Politics
*(1809–28), a series of magazines published by
the German-born Rudolph Ackermann
(1764–1834).*

The first issue of The Repository *showed two
of George Smith's designs, a* chaise longue *and
a window seat. Throughout, Ackermann was
apparently able to persuade leading cabinet-
makers to provide him with designs.
Contributions were made by the London
cabinet-makers Morgan & Sanders (active
1802–20) and John Taylor (1821–9). Morgan
& Sanders are remembered for their
"metamorphic" furniture (adjustable dining
tables, portable chairs, collapsible beds, and the
like) and their patent furniture (pieces that
usually incorporated some mechanical device,
the invention of which was protected
by a patent).*

*Before setting up on his own, Taylor had
provided designs for the cabinet-maker George
Oakley (fl.1773–1840), recorded at various
London addresses. Oakley appears to have had*
*a significant business, but little of his work has
been identified. His best known commission,
from which a considerable amount of elegant
"Grecian-style" furniture has been recorded,
was in 1809 for Charles Madryll Cheere of
Papworth Hall, Cambridge.*

*Two other well-known firms of London
cabinet-makers who provided Ackermann with
designs were William and Edward Snell (c.1788–
1839) and Morel & Hughes (1790–1830).*

Year by year the designs that appeared in
The Repository *reflected the developing taste
for such revival styles as neoclassical, Egyptian,
French empire, and gothic. The magazine also
included designs for patent and metamorphic
furniture, as well as a wide range of designs for
window curtains, and it is a consistently useful
guide to the methods and materials used in
upholstery at this time.*

*In two instances Ackermann illustrated the
work of designers whose furniture was in the
forefront of fashion. Between 1816 and 1822
there were at least 12 designs by the cabinet-
maker George Bullock and from 1825 to 1827
the magazine published 27 plates of "gothic
furniture" by A.C. Pugin (1762–1832),
perhaps assisted by his son A.W.N. Pugin
(1812–52), one of the most influential of all
19th-century architect-designers.*

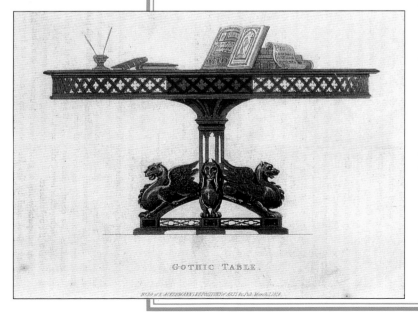

GOTHIC TABLE.

rocaille (shell and rock motifs) in blue on a pink ground, and the banqueting room has large Chinese figure groups, framed within painted bamboo borders. Both schemes are based on the original decoration. The music room has a gold and red ground decoration of Chinese landscapes and gilding. Throughout, columns turn into palm trees, a cast iron staircase appears to be made of bamboo and light fittings are adorned with Chinese dragons. Elward, Marsh, & Tatham supplied cabinets and chairs in beechwood, carved and painted to simulate bamboo.

Imitation bamboo furniture was popular throughout the period – and for the rest of the century – particular for bedrooms. There were also small cabinets and tables with fanciful polychrome chinoiserie scenes, sometimes with painted metal panels. Other typically Regency examples of popular chinoiserie as decoration can be found on tea caddies, occasional tables, coasters, hand screens, and work boxes. The decoration is most commonly in gold on a black ground, but other backgrounds include white, red, green, and brown. Another form of chinoiserie, found on the same range of articles, was penwork. In this technique the design was

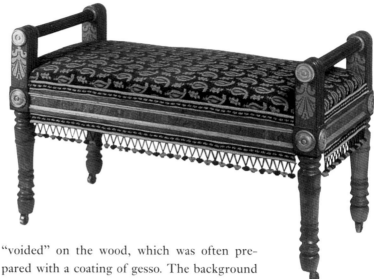

"voided" on the wood, which was often prepared with a coating of gesso. The background was inked in, usually in black, and ornamental details on the design were then carried out in fine line work with a pen.

No cabinet-maker embodies the eclecticism and vigor of Regency designs to a greater degree than George Bullock (d.1818). He is first recorded practicing as a cabinet-maker in Liverpool in 1804, when he was in partnership with William Stokes. In 1814 Bullock moved to London where, with the financial backing of Colonel Charles Fraser, he lived and worked in

ENGLISH WINDOW SEAT

▲ OAK AND HOLLY
*c.*1815
At first sight this seat, one of a pair, by George Bullock does not appear to be out of the ordinary, but it does, in fact, mark the beginning of the gothic revival. The woods, oak and holly, are both native British and the decoration is not typically Regency – there are no eagle's head, lion's paw or spears and helmets, there is no gilt bronze decoration, and the legs are turned horizontally rather than being fluted vertically.

ENGLISH SOFA

◀ OAK
*c.*1810
This partly gilt sofa is attributed to George Bullock. Deep fringes were often used in the early 19th century to decorate the lower edges of sofas. This sofa is of especially fine quality, and may, as was customary at the time, have been sold complete with a loose protective cover of damask chintz or brown calico.

▲ *c.*1815
This sofa table in the Regency style, which is attributed to George Bullock, is more substantial and impressive than its 18th-century forebears. The influences of George Smith, in the chunky lion's paw feet and substantial pedestal, and of Thomas Hope, in the brass inlay of exotic architectural pattern, are clearly visible. The table top is squarer than in earlier examples, but is lightened by the linear central column and gilt bronze mounts.

▶ PAPIER MACHE
*c.*1850
These lavishly decorated tables, with turned supports and gilded decoration on the legs and stretchers, were probably made in Birmingham or Wolverhampton. They have painted and gilded tops and inlays of mother-of-pearl.

a prestigious house in Tenterden Street. Modern workshops were erected at the end of his garden. Bullock's gregarious nature and artistic personality attracted a sophisticated patronage, including the novelist Sir Walter Scott. Perhaps his most famous commission was to provide the British government with furniture and household supplies for Napoleon's use in exile on St. Helena, and his reputation rests mainly on this brief period when he was in London before his death at the early age of 35.

Bullock was a designer of considerable talent, capable of working in many styles. The "Tracings by Thomas Wilkinson from the designs of the late Mr George Bullock 1820" provide ample evidence of his abilities. Most of his surviving designs and furniture are in the neoclassical style, but from 1804–5 he also worked in the gothic revival style, which was developing as the result of growing antiquarian research into Britain's past.

Throughout his career Bullock supplied furniture appropriate for "Old English Mansions," as he stated on the title page of *Furniture with Candelabra* (1826), which was published by his collaborator Richard Bridgens (1785–1846). This "Old English" style is exemplified by the oak and painted furniture that Bullock supplied to Battle Abbey, Sussex, in 1816–18. In its use of flat-pattern ornament based on British plant forms, Bullock's work has a vitality that anticipates later 19th-century designers such as A.W.N. Pugin, Owen Jones, and Christopher Dresser.

VICTORIAN REVIVALS

The seeds of a whole range of historical revivals in furniture had already taken root by the beginning of Queen Victoria's reign (1837–1901), chief among them being the gothic, Elizabethan, Louis XIV, and Renaissance. Most of these were stylistically mixed, borrowing elements from one another in a way that appalled contemporary purists but delighted the public, who had little interest in historical accuracy.

These revivals fitted in with the needs of an increasingly affluent middle class, who, anxious to display their wealth as conspicuously as possible, made novelty the only criterion for acquisition. In furniture the new was sought not only in design and ornamentation but in material, and exotic woods became increasingly favored and, through the growth of the overseas empire, increasingly available. Mahogany, satinwood, and rosewood continued to be used, but even more sought after were elaborately figured woods, such as walnut and the expensive amboyna, thuja, purplewood (amaranth), and calamander (coromandel). In many instances these were combined with other woods, both native and imported.

Marquetry became more popular than ever, and metals were increasingly used, both as decoration, in the form of inlaid brass or gilt bronze mounts, and, in their own right, as in cast iron garden and other mass-produced furniture and brass bedsteads.

Developments in papier mâché manufacture produced a material that was sufficiently strong to be used for tables, chairs, and even beds, as well as trays and boxes. Its decorative possibilities appealed to the exuberant Victorian taste, and it was inlaid with pearl shell, gilded, bronzed, and painted in brilliant colors on lustrous dark backgrounds.

The introduction of wafer-thin, machine-cut veneers and mechanically carved decoration also contributed to the extravagant Victorian style. The architectural and horticultural writer J.C. Loudon (1783–1843) noted that most people wanted "to get a display of rich workmanship at as cheap a rate as possible."

ELIZABETHAN REVIVAL

Mechanical carving was well suited to the production of furniture in the Elizabethan style, with its panels of open decoration and strapwork and profusion of knobs and bosses. This style was associated in the minds of early Victorians with the "Merrie England" and "Olden Times" that were romanticized in the books of, among others, Sir Walter Scott. Although some of its proponents, such as the architect Anthony Salvin, were serious antiquarians who paid attention to stylistic accuracy, most producers of Elizabethan revival furniture mixed genuine Tudor motifs with decorations typical of the 17th century.

ENGLISH TABLE

▲ CAST IRON
*c.*1855
This deerhound table was made by the Coalbrookdale Company, which had been established in the 18th century by Abraham Darby. It was designed by John Bell, a student at the Royal Academy in London. The arms on the dogs' collars are of the Hargreaves family in Lancashire, for whom the table was made.

ENGLISH BOOKCASE

◄ MAHOGANY
*c.*1840
The foliate decoration and "jewels" on the pilasters, the heavy twist-turned columns, the pierced strapwork, and the jeweled lower doors are typically hybrid on the Elizabethan revival bookcase.

ENGLISH TABLE

▲ ROSEWOOD
*c.*1835
The design for this table
appears in A.W.N.
Pugin's *Gothic Furniture*
(1835). Rosewood was an
unusual choice,
suggesting that the table
was made to an individual
commission – Pugin's
preferred wood was oak.

The strictly classical architect C.R. Cockerell
went so far as to criticize Elizabethan revival as
"an imperfect and incongruous imitation of
both Grecian and Gothic styles," but its popularity was bolstered by publications such as T.F.
Hunt's *Exemplars of Tudor Architecture adapted
to Modern Habitations* (1830), Henry Shaw's
Specimens of Ancient Furniture (1836), and
Joseph Nash's *Mansions of England in the Olden
Time* (1838–49), and it persisted into the 1840s.

GOTHIC REVIVAL

The Elizabethan style and the gothic had much
in common. Both were seen as particularly
English and therefore patriotic; both were

rooted in the cult of the picturesque; both were
adopted by romantics hungry for novelty; and
both used native woods such as oak or walnut.

Gothic architectural embellishments, such as
crockets, cusps, and pinnacles, were used in
Victorian furniture of standard manufacture,
but the revival of the gothic style pursued by the
English architect and interior designer A.W.N.
Pugin (1812–52) was much more radical. It was
a search for historical accuracy and aesthetic
purity, and in this respect had far more in common with neoclassicism than with the old
romantic associations of the gothic. In 1835
Pugin published *Gothic Furniture in the Style of
the 15th Century*, in which his assimilation of
medieval forms of construction is evident.
However, it was in the solidly simple furniture,
its decoration pared to an elegant minimum,
that he designed for the House of Lords and for
country houses during the 1840s that Pugin
most nearly attained his interior design ideals.

These pieces clearly exerted a considerable
influence on later furniture designers such as
William Burges (1827–81), William Morris
(1834–96), Charles Eastlake (1836–1906), and
Bruce Talbert (1838–81), and they encouraged a
movement in British furniture design toward
simple construction and restrained ornament
that was to become apparent later in the century.
At the Medieval Court, a feature of the Great

ENGLISH TABLE

▶ OAK
mid-19th century
This center table shows
clearly how the Victorian
revival of the medieval
gothic style penetrated
every area of design,
including tables, chairs,
and other items of
household furniture. The
stark simplicity of this
table is truly gothic, and
it would have fitted well
into an early fortified
manor house or the
refectory of a monastery.

ENGLISH SIDE CABINET

◀ EBONY
*c.*1855
Made by Jackson of London, this exhibition-quality side cabinet, is in the French style of Eugène Prignot. The ebony carcass is embellished with purpleheart, gilt bronze, lapis lazuli, and watercolor in the style of the conspicuously rich.

Exhibition of 1851 and the International Exhibition of 1862, such pieces were displayed by Pugin, John Pollard Seddon (1827–1906), Richard Norman Shaw (1831–1912) and Morris, Marshall, Faulkner & Co. Most of the work was decorated with painted ornament, incorporating scenes from medieval legends, and it had long strap hinges with large lock-plates and handles in chased iron or steel. The designers were trying to invoke, but not imitate, the furniture of the Middle Ages, and they consciously avoided forms and decoration introduced during or since the Renaissance.

LOUIS XIV REVIVAL
The label "Louis XIV" was given to the vast array of furniture of more or less French influence that filled the homes of the Victorian middle classes. It actually embraced the Louis XV, neo-rococo style as well, and this kind of furniture is, therefore, often simply referred to as Louis. In the more expensive examples, weighty baroque forms were overlaid with asymmetrically curvaceous rococo ornament, and gilding was often used. Even the relatively unostentatious pieces rarely escaped rococo flourishes, such as cabriole legs and C-scrolled

borders. Particularly sumptuous were literal copies of French 18th-century marquetry pieces by the finest English craftsmen.

Closely related to the neo-rococo style was the naturalistic style, which looked back to the early 18th-century *genre pittoresque*, which was characterized by a lavish use of plant and animal forms in the decorative motifs.

RENAISSANCE REVIVAL
During the 1840s classical forms re-emerged in a revived Renaissance or Italian style. This was another hodgepodge of ornamental ideas, as shown in a contemporary writer's view that Renaissance design "may contain the classical orders and ornaments combined with conventional Byzantine scrollwork, Moorish tracery and interlacings, scrolled shield, fiddle-shapes, and strapwork, natural imitations of animal or vegetable forms of every description, and grotesque arabesques."

OTHER REVIVALS
The furniture displayed at the Great Exhibition of 1851 was marked by dazzling craftsmanship and stupendous decorative excess. Most middle-class Victorians continued to feel

▶ WALNUT, EBONY, AND
BRASS
mid-19th century
The well-figured veneers
are contrasted with ebony
borders on the drawers
and a brass-galleried shelf
above. The fall-front is
disguised as two drawers
in this useful, well-made
piece, which is of a type
that would have been
seen in many a
comfortable Victorian
home.

Arts & Crafts aesthetic with Protestantism, but others, such as Pugin, saw a clear affinity between the revival of medievalism and the Catholic cause. Some members of the movements, such as designers William Morris (1834–96) and C.R. Ashbee (1863–1942) cherished handicraft and tended to reject the opportunity to produce for a mass market. Others, such as the architect Frank Lloyd Wright (1867–1959), positively welcomed the creative and social advantages of machine production.

The unifying factor was a belief that mid-19th-century design had gone astray. Members of the movement joined in condemning the shoddy workmanship, indiscriminate use of materials, inefficient forms, and elaborate ornamentation that characterized most mid-Victorian manufactured products. They strove to ensure that traditional methods of hand-

comfortable with lavishly decorated historical pastiches. During the following decade, however, the plainer "Old English" style came to be favored, and a little later the Queen Anne style, both much influenced by architects of the domestic revival such as Eden Nesfield (1835–88) and Richard Norman Shaw (1831–1912).

Good quality reproductions of French furniture continued to be made for the affluent by such firms as John Webb, Wright & Mansfield, and Edwards & Roberts. At the same time, almost all manufacturers purveyed furniture in the quintessentially English styles of Chippendale, Hepplewhite and, by the end of the century, Sheraton.

ARTS & CRAFTS

The Arts & Crafts movement developed in England during the second half of the 19th century as a protest against the character of mid-Victorian manufactured products. It incorporated a variety of artists, writers, and craftsmen, and it is difficult to define the limits of the movement. Some of its precursors were deeply conservative and looked wistfully back to a medieval past. Others were social reformers. Still others, such as John Ruskin, identified the

▶ RUSH SEATED
*c.*1865
The "Sussex" range of
chairs, known also as the
"Good Citizens"
furniture, was based on
vernacular, country
designs dating from the
18th century. Unlike
many of the products of
Morris & Co., this was a
range of furniture for
those of modest means.

🍃 THE CENTURY GUILD 🍃

Inspired by the example of John Ruskin, Arthur Heygate Mackmurdo's Century Guild was infinitely more successful than that of his mentor. A pupil in Ruskin's Oxford drawing class and a companion on his visits to Italy, Mackmurdo established the Guild on Ruskin's advice in 1882. His aim was to render "all branches of art the sphere no longer of the tradesman but of the artist." In the following year the Guild's workshops were opened in partnership with another of Ruskin's associates, Selwyn Image (1849–1930). Other members of the Guild included the potter William De Morgan (1839–1917), the designer Heywood Sumner (1859–1940), the sculptor Benjamin Creswick, the textile designer and metalworker H.P. Horne (1864–1916), and the metalworker Clement Heaton (1861–1940). Mackmurdo had trained as an architect but had also attempted to learn several crafts, trying his hand at brass-work, embroidery, and cabinet-making. The purpose of the Guild was to accommodate craftsmen active in a number of métiers and unite the traditionally separate disciplines of architecture, interior design, and decoration. While Morris had attempted to level the disciplines of painting and sculpture to the rank of democratic handicrafts, Mackmurdo's Century Guild aimed to raise the status of crafts such as building, fabric design, pottery, and metalworking so that they might take their place alongside the "fine" arts.

The work of the Guild tended to be more stylistically eclectic than that of Morris and his followers, although it aspired to the same ideal of artists, architects, and designers cooperatively undertaking the design of the home and its contents. Mackmurdo admired the Italian Renaissance and even baroque architecture. The furniture produced by the Guild was equally eclectic, ranging from the restrained and utilitarian to a style of decoration that anticipated the asymmetrical arabesques of the Aesthetic Movement and art nouveau.

craftsmanship would survive, and they wanted at the same time to ameliorate the conditions of artisans and craftsmen and to encourage artistic collaboration among workers.

Much of the furniture produced by Morris, Marshall, Faulkner & Co. (or Morris & Co., as it was from 1875) was designed by the architect Philip Webb (1831–1915), whose style was characterized by subtle manipulation of volumes and refined elaboration of structure. Gradually he liberated his work from the domination of the neo-gothic style and exploited a wide range of sources, including Japanese furniture forms.

AESTHETIC MOVEMENT

The ethos of simple, well-made furniture in the neo-gothic or vernacular style was widely disseminated by Charles Eastlake (1836–1906) in his book *Hints on Household Taste in Furniture, Upholstery and Other Details* (1868), which was

ENGLISH TABLE

◀ OAK
1880–90
The center table, made by Morris & Co., is believed to have been designed by Philip Webb and George Jack, a pupil of Webb's. It was designed for Clouds.

illustrated with many of the author's own designs. Eastlake's book assisted the transition from neo-gothic to Queen Anne revival, which became the style favored by many architects and designers during the 1870s and 1880s. Some, such as Bruce Talbert (1838–81), E.W. Godwin (1833–86), and Charles Bevan, worked happily in both styles, the main point of their furniture being that it was plainly constructed and generally free of carving and veneers. The Japanesque furniture designed by Godwin and others shared these features. It was loosely based on the architectural forms of Japan as shown in the woodblock prints that were arriving in the West.

All these various styles contributed to Aesthetic Movement furniture, which was characterized by the extensive use of ebonized wood and was sometimes decorated with painted panels or ceramic tiles. Furniture designs by Christopher Dresser (1834–1904) included pieces in a wide variety of styles, including Greek, Egyptian, gothic, and Japanese.

The furniture that the architect Arthur Heygate Mackmurdo (1851–1942) designed for the Century Guild, founded in 1882, was derived from Queen Anne and other 18th-century styles. Two pieces, however, had a profound influence on subsequent furniture design, and these may be counted as important precursors of art nouveau. One was a side chair, which was basically in early 18th-century style but whose fretwork back was decorated with a design of swirling submarine protozoa that looked to some French, Belgian and German furniture made towards the end of the century. The other influential piece was a desk by Mackmurdo, based on a Georgian original but formed into uncompromisingly geometrical shapes and the ancestor of many similar pieces designed over the next three decades in England, Scotland, Austria and the United States.

Furniture designed by George Jack (1855–1932) and W.A.S. Benson (1854–1924) for Morris & Co. during the late 1880s and 1890s was largely based on 18th-century forms, although Benson also created some pieces derived from country furniture. The Guild of Handi-

craft, founded in 1888 by Charles Robert Ashbee (1863–1942), produced furniture to his design. Loosely Queen Anne Revival, Ashbee's designs were often decorated with painted and gilt gesso.

Before setting up their own workshops in the Cotswolds, Ernest Gimson (1864–1919) and Sidney Barnsley (1865–1926) were both associated with Kenton & Co., an association of architects and craftsmen formed in 1890 to produce furniture of quality. Gimson's pieces were made up by skilled carpenters, but Barnsley constructed his own. The work of both is usually in a "farmhouse" style: massive, solidly built, with chamfered stretchers and supports, and occasionally decorated with inlay or simple gouged ornament.

FRANCE

RESTORATION

The restoration of the Bourbon monarchy after Napoleon's defeat at Waterloo led to the reigns of Louis XVIII (1815–24), Charles X (1824–30), and Louis-Philippe (1830–48). This coincided with the beginning of the industrial revolution in France, and the output of decorative furniture increased to cater to the aspirations of the newly prosperous middle classes. Antiquity ceased to be the sole source of artistic inspiration as interest in the arts of other nations was encouraged by improved means of

▶ BOULLE
*c.*1840
These chairs, made during the reign of Louis Philippe (1830–48), are loosely based on the style popular in the reign of Louis XIV (1643–1715), especially the tortoiseshell and brass inlay of André-Charles Boulle. In fact, the high, rounded backs and low seats are almost a caricature of the original styles, although the workmanship is of good quality.

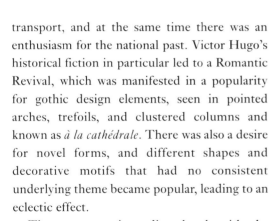

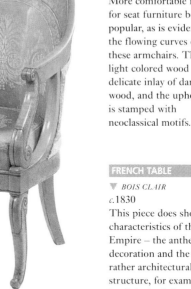

FRENCH FAUTEUILS

◀ *BOIS CLAIR*
*c.*1825
More comfortable forms for seat furniture became popular, as is evident in the flowing curves of these armchairs. The light colored wood has a delicate inlay of darker wood, and the upholstery is stamped with neoclassical motifs.

FRENCH TABLE

▼ *BOIS CLAIR*
*c.*1830
This piece does show characteristics of the Empire – the anthemion decoration and the heavy, rather architectural structure, for example – but it is the light wood, *bois clair*, that makes this table so strikingly different from Empire pieces. Furniture from this period of French history shares a number of characteristics with German Biedermeier furniture, notably the plain lines, a lack of decoration, and the use of native woods, all evident in this table.

transport, and at the same time there was an enthusiasm for the national past. Victor Hugo's historical fiction in particular led to a Romantic Revival, which was manifested in a popularity for gothic design elements, seen in pointed arches, trefoils, and clustered columns and known as *à la cathédrale*. There was also a desire for novel forms, and different shapes and decorative motifs that had no consistent underlying theme became popular, leading to an eclectic effect.

There was no immediate break with the Empire style – Louis XVIII retained Napoleon's furniture but replaced the imperial bees with the royal fleur-de-lis, for example – but gradually a less grandiose, more domestic style developed. Gilt bronze mounts were replaced by inlaid decoration and a greater use of wood carving. A fashion for *bois clair* (pale or light wood) encouraged the move away from bronze decoration, and inlays of darker woods, such as rosewood or ebony, or of pewter or plain brass were used to contrast with the wood. The popularity of *bois clair* was aided by the move towards mechanization, as machines were increasingly used to produce smooth, regular veneers, which brought out the best even in European woods and made hand-finishing less important.

In seat furniture comfort replaced pomp. Pieces became smaller, and curves reappeared in rounded seats and backs that swept down to legs decorated with scrolls. Turned legs were also used, and back legs were often saber-shaped. Sofas and *chaises longues* were made in a variety of shapes. The *pommier*, for example, was a hybrid piece, a cross between a sofa and a *chaise longue*, with one armrest the same height as the back and the other lower.

▼ EBONIZED WOOD AND ORMOLU

*c.*1860

Standing on four front and three back legs, one of the most unusual features of this sofa is its asymmetry. The high back is unusual for the period, and harks back to the 18th century while it also looks forward to art nouveau. Such a piece would have been made for a fashion-conscious customer, the ormolu mounts being especially popular at this time as embellishments for good quality pieces. The upholstery fabric is not original.

Case furniture became both more utilitarian and more fussy. Desks the shape of the *bonheur du jour*, often standing on clustered-column end supports, were made with many small drawers. *Etagères* (two- or three-tiered open cabinets used as bookcases or repositories for knick-knacks) were constructed with fretwork side panels and galleries, and in an astonishing range of shapes. Commodes and *secrétaires* abounded, but they were now outnumbered by a variety of new functional pieces, including jardinières, small screens, side tables, and, for the first time, the piano, as items of furnishing.

SECOND EMPIRE

The monarchy was replaced in 1848 by the Second Republic, but four years later its first president, Louis Napoleon, declared himself Emperor Napoleon III. The Second Empire lasted until 1871, when it was replaced by the Third Republic. This time no imperial style was imposed from above, and it is, in fact, difficult to discern any clear Second Empire style. Artists and craftsmen tended to interpret and adapt a wide range of styles from both the past and all over the world. Designers even sometimes used several styles for one piece. What was new, however, was the technical perfection made possible by modern mechanical processes.

The Renaissance style was especially popular with furniture-makers, and great cabinets, incorporating a profusion of carving, marquetry and other techniques, were produced. The 17th and 18th centuries also proved a source of inspiration. The Empress Eugénie, for example, felt nostalgic about Marie Antoinette, Louis XVI's queen consort, and many pieces were made in imitation of Louis XVI style. These were often in marquetry inlaid with fake Sèvres porcelain plaques or in ebony inlaid with panels of *pietra dura*.

The Louis XIV style was also copied. Boulle marquetry case furniture was made, often with a red tortoiseshell background, and Louis XIV

chairs, beds and other pieces were popular. The finest or most elaborate pieces were most likely to be copied, and the detail was exaggerated and painstakingly executed. Lacquer, usually black and decorated with painted or gilt detail or mother-of-pearl inlay, was extensively used, being applied to spindly chairs, tables, cabinets, screens, inkstands, caskets, and many other objects. Some of these articles were made of papier mâché, which was a cheap material that lent itself to mass-production.

It became fashionable to design whole rooms in a specific style, and often different rooms were furnished and decorated in a particular style – a Renaissance dining room, a gothic library, and a Louis XV drawing room, for example. Every available shape and technique in furniture-making was used, although the emphasis was on the intricate and lavish. Porcelain, marble, *pietra dura*, rare woods, patinated and gilt bronze, silver, cast and wrought iron, pewter and other metals, ivory, and tortoiseshell were used in profusion. Upholstery was equally complex, and stools, chairs, and settees were luxuriously and deeply padded.

NEO-GOTHIC

"We all cribbed from Viollet-le-Duc," stated the architect and designer William Burges (1827–81), referring to the neo-gothic school of English designers. Eugène Viollet-le-Duc

(1814–79) was a French architect, most of whose career was devoted to the restoration of gothic buildings. He also designed furniture in a gothic style for the châteaux of Pierrefonds and Roquetaillade, but his approach was archaeological and his furniture designs had neither strength nor originality. What impressed Burges and his friends were Viollet-le-Duc's books, especially his *Dictionnaire Mobilier Français* (1858–75), a comprehensive guide to the gothic decorative arts.

Viollet-le-Duc had considerable influence on the work of the graphic artist Eugène Grasset, who designed some furniture for Charles Gillot, the owner of the press where most of Grasset's work was printed. The oak and walnut suite, made between 1879 and 1885, was decorated with low-relief carving and elaborate iron fittings, but its most telling feature was the clearly indicated construction – stretchers, supports and brackets making a lively visual display.

In Paris, most cabinet-makers rested on their laurels, gained during the 18th century and the earlier part of the 19th century. They continued to make furniture that was richly decorated with gilding, silvering, boulle work, and metal mounts. Renaissance, Louis XV and Louis XVI styles were popular throughout the second half of the 19th century. Pieces in the Renaissance style were often decorated with sculpted figures.

◀ TULIP-WOOD AND BRASS
*c.*1870
One of the most popular vogues in 19th-century France was for Louis XV furniture, and this table is very much in the spirit of the mid-18th century. The tulip-wood is decorated with marquetry and the top is edge with brass. The stretcher and stand supporting the legs at each end are, however, clumsier than those elements would have been on a similar table made a hundred years before. The table, which is stamped with the name of its maker, Gardiennet, is well made.

◀ WALNUT AND FRUITWOOD
*c.*1895
This table, by Emile Gallé, is in the "organic" style of art nouveau, which is ornamented with swirling lines and a variety of natural motifs, including entomological and botanical themes. On its upper and lower tiers a fine inlay of many different woods appears in a natural surrounding. The figures on the table legs are similar to the neoclassical sphinx, but are depicted in a typical art nouveau manner.

▲ *c.*1900
This office suite,
consisting of a desk,
matching chair, and
sideboard, was designed
by Eugène Vallin in an
exaggerated art nouveau
style.

FRENCH ARMCHAIR

▶ MAHOGANY
*c.*1900
The cabinet-maker Louis
Majorelle was influenced
by the work of Emile
Gallé, but Majorelle's
version of art nouveau
was more abstract, with
an emphasis on long,
sweeping curves and
shallow carving. There is
an elegance about
Majorelle's furniture that
reveals his roots in the
19th-century rococo
revival.

ART NOUVEAU

Emile Gallé (1846–1904), already renowned for
his pottery and glassware, established furniture
workshops at Nancy in 1884. His early pieces
were in a variety of styles, including Japanese,
rococo, and Renaissance. Soon, however, he began to use natural forms, both for structural
members of his furniture – table legs carved as
dragonflies, chair backs shaped as blossoms –
and for marquetry decoration. When, in a
further stylistic development, Gallé adopted
curving supports and sinuous stretchers, he had
effectively arrived at art nouveau. His furniture
was generally made of oak or walnut.

Another Nancy cabinet-maker was Louis
Majorelle (1859–1929), whose furniture during
the 1890s was influenced by Gallé's work. Previously his output had been predominantly
rococo in style, and the lightness and elegance of
these Louis XV pieces persist in his art nouveau
furniture. The gilt bronze mounts which adorn
his pieces also recall the work of the 18th-

In the extraordinary furniture made by the
sculptor Rupert Carabin (1862–1932) there was
an element of parody in the carved female nude
figures which, with their physical flaws and in-
decorous poses, were far from the idealized
classical maidens and athletes usually associated
with Renaissance decoration.

Another escape from the straitjacket of
historical styles was achieved by the Paris
cabinet-maker Gabriel Viardot. Since the 18th
century there had been in France a taste for
chinoiserie, and cabinet-makers such as Giroux,
Sormani, and Duvinage, contemporaries of
Viardot, made pieces, usually of rosewood or
ebony, designed and decorated in an oriental
manner, with shelves turned up at the ends,
curled feet and ornament of ivory, lacquer, and
enamels. Viardot's oriental creations, however,
were original and fantastic, featuring complicated, asymmetrical arrangements of shelves,
sculpted bronze dragons and lacquer panels. His
sources included not only Chinese and Japanese
forms and ornament but also the art of Vietnam,
which had been colonized by the French.

same flowing forms as that of Vallin, and is far removed from Gallé's rococo touches.

Meanwhile, the art nouveau style had affected the furniture-makers of Paris. In 1895 Siegfried Bing (1838–1905) opened La Maison de l'Art Nouveau, where he sold furniture designed by Georges de Feure (1868–1943), Eugène Gaillard (1862–1933), and Edward Colonna (1862–1948). De Feure and Colonna created furniture of great lightness and simplicity. Narrow, tapering chair and table legs have no stretchers, giving the furniture an airy, floating appearance, curves are gentle and carving is shallow and minimal. Some pieces were gilt, others were sparsely decorated with marquetry. The furniture was constructed of walnut or occasionally ash.

Gaillard represents the functional side of art nouveau furniture. He studied the problem of

FRENCH SIDE CHAIR

◀ WALNUT
*c.*1900
The leather upholstery and simple lines of this chair by Eugène Gaillard show a concern for function above uncontrolled fantasy. Gaillard adopted furniture forms inspired by nature.

FRENCH TABLE

▼ PEARWOOD
1904
Hector Guimard designed this occasional table for the industrialist Léon Nozal. The waxed wood has been made into the same rather taut, sinuous shapes as his entrances for the Paris Métro.

century *ébénistes*, although Majorelle's are molded into botanical forms treated in the art nouveau manner.

In 1900 Jacques Gruber (1870–1936), who had designed furniture for Majorelle, set up his own workshop to make furniture and stained glass. Some of the latter was incorporated in the doors of cabinets designed by Eugène Vallin (1856–1922).

Other cabinet-makers in Nancy worked for either Majorelle or Gallé – occasionally both. Victor Prouvé (1858–1943) specialized in marquetry work for both masters as well as designing his own pieces. Eugène Vallin (1856–1925) worked for Gallé and produced pieces of far greater weight than those of his master. Vallin's work eschews intricate natural detail and instead concentrates on broad, swaying linear rhythms anticipating the end of his career, when he took up architecture and used cast concrete for his effects. Jacques Gruber (1870–1936) produced designs for Majorelle and was also professor of decorative arts at the Ecole des Beaux Arts in Nancy. His furniture shares the

▶ PEARWOOD
*c.*1900
The idiosyncratic inventiveness and sculpted, abstract, curvilinear lines of Hector Guimard's design seem to deny the nature of the material that he chose for this cabinet, which is characteristic of his high art nouveau phase.

function in design and produced designs of an increasingly light, almost classic simplicity. His chairs were concerned with comfort, had molded backs, sometimes with padding at the shoulder, and leather- or fabric-covered coil-sprung upholstered seats.

The art nouveau architect Hector Guimard (1867–1942), best known for designing the entrances to the Paris Métro stations, also designed furniture. For the Castel Béranger, a block of flats that he built between 1894 and 1898, he created furniture which reflects his adherence to the principles of rational design taught by Viollet-le-Duc. Its construction, although visually flamboyant, is always justifiable in terms of strength and utility. The linear decoration carved in low relief is abstract but clearly inspired by natural forms. All traces of the gothic that characterized his earlier work disappeared.

While the Castel Béranger was being built, Guimard visited Brussels, and his furniture was influenced by the work of the architects and designers Henri Van de Velde (1863–1957) and Victor Horta (1861–1947) whom he saw there. Guimard's chairs and sofas usually have seats and backs covered in leather incised with linear ornament. He furnished several of his subsequent buildings, including the Coillot house in Lille, the Castel Henriette outside Paris, the Castel Val near Auvers-sur-Oise, his own house in Paris and a house for his friend Paul Mezzara, also in Paris. He used oak and pearwood, but particularly favored eucalyptus.

LES SIX

In 1897 a group of artists calling themselves Les Six held an exhibition in Paris that included furniture designed by the architect Charles Plumet and the brothers Pierre and Tony Selmersheim. Their work was art nouveau in style, often with a strong flavor of rococo in its sinuous lines and gilt metal fittings. Like the Nancy designers, Plumet and the Selmersheims often alluded to natural forms in their work.

Another member of Les Six, the sculptor Alexandre Charpentier (1856–1909), designed furniture whose main effect was achieved by the treatment of the wood, its gilt bronze reliefs and

its colour. The wood was carved to give it a molten, sometimes almost liquid, appearance. The relief panels, handles and lock-plates represented female nudes, and the wood, usually hornbeam, was waxed to give it a yellow tint, somewhere between gold and honey.

Jean Dampt, another sculptor who belonged to the group, was a disciple of John Ruskin and an admirer of the English Arts & Crafts Movement. His furniture is art nouveau, often with neo-gothic touches.

ITALY

The full-blown Napoleonic Empire style was established in Italy by various members of the Bonaparte family, not least Napoleon's sister Eliza

▼ CARVED AND GILT WOOD
*c.*1800
There are no traces of the rococo in the two stylishly neoclassical chairs, which were made in Florence. These two examples are from a set of four.

▶ BLACK MARBLE ON GILT WOOD
*c.*1850

Justly famous for marble work since the 16th century, Italy was still considered a center of art and learning in the mid-19th century. The precise craftsmanship evident in the mosaic decoration on this table top – depictions of Roman ruins around a classical scene of doves – was admired throughout Europe. It was created by hundreds of chips of glass and marble to each square inch. The table is edged with a band of malachite. The large gilt stand has a structural, slightly baroque look, which is reminiscent of 17th-century work from Venice, but this table was made in Florence.

a tasteful restraint reminiscent of German Biedermeier furniture. He is, however, most celebrated for ingenious pieces such as a robust oval chest on legs, standing on a plinth that slides open to form an elegant writing desk with raised inkstand and a chair.

A little earlier, the Sienese architect Agostino Fantastici had designed similarly restrained neoclassical furniture, veneered in walnut with ebony bandings and with a minimum of decoration. Some of his most celebrated work, made for Giuliano Bianchi Bandinelli, an influential advocate of neoclassicism, shows a distinct quirkiness of style.

The Empire style endured in Italy long after the fall of Napoleon, especially for palatial decoration. In furniture it was interpreted in its most ponderously heroic form by Pelagio Palagi (1775–1860), who provided highly sculptural pieces for the Palazzo Reale in Turin in the 1830s. His work included candelabra, stools, sofas, chairs, and the gilt bronze table in the council chamber, with its massive winged caryatids supporting a deep frieze of anthemion and scrolls. Palagi worked in the gothic style, too, when he felt it was appropriate. Both gothic

Baciocchi, who, as a grand-duchess of Tuscany, employed the cabinet-maker Giovanni Socchi (*fl.*1809–15) to make furniture for the Palazzo Pitti in Florence. His style is exemplified in a series of drum-shaped cupboards with marble top, pine-cone feet, and gilded wood mounts, of

▶ *c.*1815

Many of the characteristic features of the Empire style in this table – the laurel leaves on the frieze, the heavy lion's paw feet, and the ornate horn-like fruiting legs – were, in fact, found in Italy before the end of the 18th century, but it was not until the French Empire style of Napoleon's reign became popular that Italian workmen employed these features coherently. The resulting style is known as Italian Empire.

GERMANY AND AUSTRIA

NEOCLASSICAL

The elegance of David Roentgen's late 18th-century tables and cabinets in the neoclassical style contrast strongly with the ostentation of his earlier, essentially rococo pieces. Marquetry now took the form of graceful flowers, leaves, beribboned festoons, or writing or musical instruments, rather than the earlier colorful elaborate architectural scenes. At the same time, furniture forms lost their curves and became elegant interpretations of Louis XVI style.

Other cabinet-makers in Germany were less eager to adopt the austere lines of neoclassicism, and in some transitional pieces, rococo curves co-exist with straight, tapered legs and rectangular carcass shapes. In other pieces neoclassical ornament is superimposed on old forms. By the end of the 18th century, however, classical straight-lined discipline of form and decorative motifs had been accepted in furniture that reflected both English and French in-

revival and Renaissance revival appeared in Italy, notably in a native manifestation known as Dantesque. This style was characterized by X-frame chairs, uncomfortable stools, and heavily carved tables.

SPAIN AND PORTUGAL

In 1808 Napoleon's invasion of Spain began a period of political tumult for the country that continued until the 1830s. Furniture tended to follow the French Empire style, while the sumptuous Fernandino style was marked by the use of applied ornament in gilded bronze of "antique" classical motifs in carved and gilded wood.

In Portugal in the 19th century, styles were governed by successive outside influences. Early in the century the French Empire style gave rise to some chunky classical interpretations. After the expulsion of Napoleon in 1811, furniture followed the English style. After 1820 the Biedermeier style came into fashion.

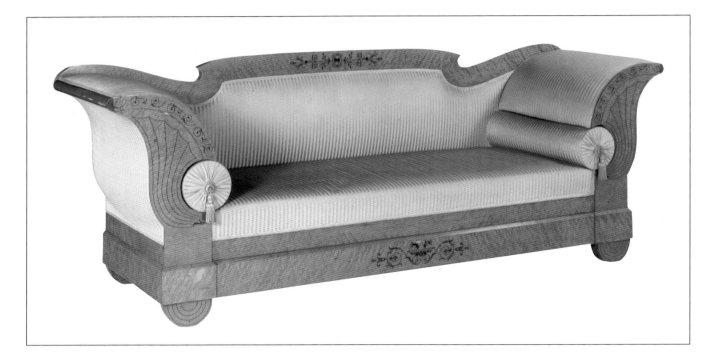

▲ MAPLE
early 19th century
This fine example of the
Biedermeier style is one
of a pair. The shaping of
the arms is both unusual
and skilful.

fluences. Nowhere was such elegant neo-classicism more successfully exhibited than in Vienna, at the court of the emperor, Joseph II (reigned 1765–90). Vienna became the focus of the new and distinctive Empire style of the Napoleonic years in the early 19th century.

The fully fledged Empire style was too short-lived – and perhaps too austerely academic – to become a style of the people. It was seen in the furniture of palaces, like that designed by Johann Valentin Raab for the Würzburg Residenz, Leon von Kelnze (1784–1864) in Munich and Karl Friedrich Schinkel (1781–1841) for the Prussian royal family in palaces in and around Berlin.

▶ MAHOGANY
early 19th century
This circular center table
has a swiveling top and
four spring-loaded
drawers. Its ebonized and
partly gilt decoration
includes neoclassical
motifs and masonic
symbols.

BIEDERMEIER

The most pervasive development of the classical influence was the Biedermeier style, which flourished in and around Vienna c.1815–48 and spread through German-speaking Europe. This plain but comfortable style evolved in response to the authoritarianism in Austria after the Congress of Vienna. Discouraged from political activity, people concentrated on commerce, home life, and a bourgeois culture of elegant simplicity. In furniture-making there was a new, comfort-led practicality, which was combined with the use of colorful textiles and figured woods. Different timbers – mahogany, rose-wood, walnut, fruitwoods, maple and sycamore – were used to great effect, and inlaid patterns of ebony or black-stained fruitwood were used as a concession to decoration. Lines were clean, but as often rounded as straight.

The ostentatiously large items of furniture of former years tended to give way to smaller pieces designed for specific functions. These included ladies' writing desks, sewing tables, cheval mirrors, and bookcases. Every well-

PORCELAIN FURNITURE

The Austrian fashion for porcelain furniture was inspired by the 19th-century passion for decoration. Porcelain furniture had a great advantage over wood in both carving and gilt work. Its harder surface could be modeled with far more detail, and gilt and other bright fired-on-glazes could be applied directly to its surface. (A coat of gesso had to be applied to wood before the gilt so that the polychrome was not absorbed into the wood.) Porcelain was obviously more fragile, however, and larger pieces were usually held together with internal metal rods and brackets.

furnished parlor now had a piano, and many had a china cabinet too. Emphasis was given to comfortable seating, and well-upholstered sofas with upswept sides were complemented by deep armchairs and a range of side chairs with upholstered seats and boldly shaped backs. These pieces stood on square tapered or turned legs. The demand for such pieces was met by increasing numbers of town-based cabinet-makers, of whom the most prolific was Josef Danhauser (1780–1829).

In northern Germany, the style was interpreted with less color and variety, most often in mahogany and upholstery of black horsehair. The shapes were similar to those seen in early 19th-century Britain.

The pure designs of Biedermeier were inevitably displaced by the anti-classical, romantic spirit that emerged in the 1830s and 1840s all over Europe, unleashing its historical hodge-podge. The epitome of the new extravagance was reached by Carl Leistler (1805–57) of Vienna, who not only completely refurnished the entertainment rooms of the Palais Liechtenstein with his carved neo-rococo splendors but also produced a monumental gothic bookcase for the 1851 Great Exhibition in London.

Although Biedermeier can be thought of as an artistic movement – its most famous exponent being the self-taught artist Carl Spitzweg (1808–85) – it mirrored a tendency throughout

▲ ASH
*c.*1835
The lines in Biedermeier pieces are always clear and simple, concentrating on the vertical and horizontal, and this often gives a feeling of neoclassical simplicity, although it can lead to heaviness. Here the deep frieze and heavy table top are balanced by the massive, cuboid feet ending the plain column legs.

◄ PORCELAIN
*c.*1860
This piece is made with porcelain from the Vienna factory, and it is decorated with gilt scrolls and precisely modeled fruiting vines on its stem. The hand-painted decoration on the top shows rustic scenes from the more exotic corners of the Austro-Hungarian Empire, including Dalmatia and Hungary. The scenes are labeled with the name of each area represented, and they are extremely precise in their detail.

Europe to return to an uncluttered but dignified form. The combination of elements from English Regency, French Louis XVI, and neo-classical styles led to a form that seemed to herald the concentration on line that characterized art deco.

BENTWOOD

Leistler did not completely fill the Palais Liechtenstein with his own work. The chairs in the ballroom were provided by the Prussian-born Michael Thonet (1796–1871), whose bentwood (steam-curved wood) style is famous not just for its elegance but also because it represents the first mass-produced, universally available furniture. Thonet subsequently exported all over the world. All types of furniture were sold, in parts, to be assembled with a few screws at their destination.

RUSSIA AND EASTERN EUROPE

By the early 19th century, French influence was once again more dominant in Russia, encouraged by the predilections of the francophile Alexander I (reigned 1810–25). He employed a Swiss artistic adviser, Thomas de Thomon (1754–1813), who designed furniture as well as carrying out architectural projects, and the tsar imported considerable quantities of French furniture for his palaces.

The two most important Russian designers of the early 19th century were Andrei Nikiforovich Voronkin (1760–1814), who had trained in Paris and interpreted the furniture designs of Charles Percier and Pierre-François-Léonard Fontaine with a muscular enthusiasm unknown in France, and the Italian Carlo Rossi (1775–1849) whose work is an elegant distillation of the Empire style.

Most Russian craftsmen tended to produce furniture in a style deriving from both French and English models – a compromise between the work of Jacob Desmalter and that of

Thomas Sheraton. This tendency to adopt the characteristics of European styles grew during the 19th century, and a great deal of mid-century Russian furniture is indistinguishable from European examples. A more distinct identity was conferred by the use of native woods, particularly Karelian birch, which was light in color and was interestingly figured.

RUSSIAN CONSOLE TABLE AND PIER GLASS

▶ MAHOGANY
*c.*1810
The beauty of this piece lies in its purity of line and spareseness of decoration. The combination of mahogany and gilt bronze is clearly influenced by French Empire style – the grain markings of the "flame" mahogany are featured around the mirror frame – as are the delicate winged-sphinx legs.

THE NETHERLANDS

In the early 19th century, the French neoclassical influence was reinforced by Louis Napoleon, whose conversion of the town hall in Amsterdam into a royal palace in 1808 gave employment to Dutch craftsmen such as Carel Breytspraak (*fl.c.*1795–1810) and Joseph Cuel, who supplied stylish furniture in the more severe Empire style exhibited by the French furniture designers Charles Percier and Pierre Fontaine in their pattern-book *Recueil de décorations intérieurs* (1801). This book, which has been described as the manifesto of a new archaeological classicism, was as influential in the Netherlands as elsewhere in Europe and did much to encourage the careful use of gilt bronze mounts as a contrast with the dark woods then favored. All-over gilding of grandly carved furniture was also a feature of the later Empire style, which persisted for some time after Napoleon's downfall.

BIEDERMEIER AND AFTER

In the second quarter of the 19th century, many Dutch people clearly preferred the restrained elegance of Biedermeier furniture, for which lighter woods such as amboyna, ash, and walnut were used as often as mahogany and fruitwoods. The well-made, gently curving but essentially "Grecian" designs were eminently well suited to the Dutch interior.

Before long, however, a demand for more ostentatious ornament developed. New factories, such as those of the Horrix Brothers in The Hague and M. Roule in Antwerp, were able to supply it, and the Netherlands shared in a general European stylistic eclecticism. Dutch cabinet-makers again made a specialty of floral marquetry, much of which was exported. In addition, plain old furniture was re-veneered with the Dutch flower-pieces of which the public all over Europe never seemed to tire.

The 19th-century revival of rococo style made the most of the Dutch passion for ebony or ebonized furniture. (Ebonized furniture consisted of black lacquer-painted furniture, made to resemble ebony.) Exotic materials, such as tortoiseshell, ivory, and marble, were extracted from the countries forming the Dutch overseas empire in the 17th century, and they were often combined with ebony to give the piece an overall lighter finish.

◀ KARELIAN BIRCH
early 19th century
Beneath a clock in the upper section is a cupboard with a classical figure in gilt bronze in a niche in the door. The cupboard is flanked by two pairs of white marble and gilt bronze columns, and beneath is a drawer with a fold-down front. Behind the leather-lined fall-front, the writing compartment is fitted with small drawers and pigeonholes built in the same style as the exterior, with white marble columns flanking a mirror-backed central niche.

▼ MARBLE INLAY
*c.*1860
The sculptural effect and apron carving of this table were to the Victorian taste, and a number of these were exported around Europe. The style of cabriole legs and pierced stretcher is in the style of the 1720s, and the top shows a variety of marble *pietra dura* work.

▶ MAHOGANY
*c.*1820
The deep drawer in the frieze gives a somewhat top-heavy look to the piece, especially as the legs are so slender. The legs themselves, with their in and out curves, are not a traditional form, and the stretcher supporting the whole piece bows in from the front and the back, creating a lower tier that might have been used to hold a bowl and jug. The mirror's arch pediment is decorated with a fan-shaped inlay.

▽ PINE
*c.*1815
Both French and English influences can be seen in much Swedish furniture, like this dolphin-supported console table. Native pine, available in plentiful supplies, provided an ideal base for gilding.

SCANDINAVIA

In the early 19th century, the French Empire style was favored for the most important Scandinavian furniture, and subsequently English furniture was no longer popular, largely because of the hostility that resulted from the British bombardment of Copenhagen during the Napoleonic Wars. Even so, the straightforward styles of early 19th-century English furniture were still favored, as were some of its forms. One of these was the sofa table, an all-purpose piece made in a range of designs, its flat top standing on either a central pillar support, lyre-shaped ends, or four tapered legs.

Most imported furniture now came from Germany, and in the stylish and idiosyncratic simplicity of the ensuing Danish Empire style there are strong echoes not only of English Regency but also of Biedermeier. Such classical elegance lingered on throughout Scandinavia until the second quarter of the 19th century, when it was overtaken, first in Sweden and later in Denmark and Norway, by the eclecticism that pervaded the rest of Europe.

AMERICA

The War of Independence brought an abrupt halt to the development of the decorative arts. When the war was over English design styles continued to be influential, but the craftsmen of the new republic were eager to make something specifically American.

FEDERAL AND DIRECTOIRE

The ideas of three English designers – Robert Adam, George Hepplewhite, and Thomas Sheraton – were largely amalgamated into a style usually known as Federal, which lasted from *c.*1790 to 1830. The term Federal is chronological rather than stylistic, and it derives from the period of Federalist Party rule in Washington.

AMERICAN SOFA

◀ MAHOGANY
*c.*1800
This elegant inlaid sofa in the Federal style was made in New York. The seat, which is covered with a loose cushion, is slightly bowed. It stands on line- and bellflower-inlaid square, tapering legs, which end in cross-banded cuffs.

At this time the rigid classicism of Adam played a minor role – furniture-makers preferred the more lyrical ideas of Hepplewhite and Sheraton as the nation became more self-confident and outward-looking. A key feature of Federal style was the use of fine mahogany, inlaid with satinwood, maple, and birch. Plain stringing was a specialty of New York makers. More decorative patterns – shells, flowers, and eagles, for example – are found on pieces from Philadelphia, Baltimore, Salem, and, to a lesser extent, Boston.

The period is also notable for the introduction of new pieces and the rediscovery of old ones. The charming little sewing-table, with its commodious pouch, made an appearance, as did the sideboard. The dining table assumed new dimensions, as French pedestal legs and the addition of supplementary leaves became fashionable. Later, dining tables were fitted with accordion-type mechanisms that made them easy to extend. The day-bed reappeared, this time as a Roman couch or *chaise longue*, with a high scroll back and inward-curved foot ends, all carved, often gilded and richly upholstered. After surviving briefly into the Federal period, highboys and lowboys fell from favor and cabriole legs gave way to straight, narrow legs.

The most important feature of the Federal period was, however, the stylistic treatment of established pieces – chairs, occasional tables, bureau-bookcases, chests of drawers, and bookcases. The Hepplewhite legacy could be seen in shield- and oval-backed chairs, often with carved central splats of plumes, wheat sheaves

AMERICAN WORK TABLE

◀ MAHOGANY
*c.*1805
It is possible that this work table was made by Duncan Phyfe or that it was made in his New York workshop. The beginnings of the preference for heavy carving that emerged in the early 19th century are clearly evident. The top part of the round section is plain, with finely figured veneer, but the bottom half shows a reeded tambour (sliding door) made of vertical slats that slide into the side panels. The texturing indicates that the fashion for plain surfaces was passing, and the deep top section gives the piece a somewhat heavy feel.

113

▶ CARVED AND PAINTED
WOOD
*c.*1825–50
This early example of a
Hitchcock chair
demonstrates the fine
carving and decorative
techniques used by
Hitchcock's factory. The
waterfall scene on the top
rail is complemented by
the marine motifs on the
back rest. Although they
were mass-produced,
these chairs have an
engaging individuality.
Some examples have
turned front stretchers
while on others the front
legs and top rail are
turned, with the floral
stenciled patterns
confined to the back rest.

or urns and with plain, tapering legs. Chairs with squarer backs, stronger lines, and spade feet showed the influence of Thomas Sheraton. A marriage of the two styles was apparent in the large sideboards, desks, and bookcases, in which, for example, the serpentine curves of Hepplewhite were combined with the inlaid vignettes of Sheraton.

After 1810, the fine lines of the Federal style gave way to the greater theatricality of the Directoire, which was based on the French style with the same name. Pieces had saber-shaped legs, animal-pawed feet, concavely arched chair backs, and serpentine fronts, and they were usually made in rosewood or heavy mahogany. The use of classical motifs on the legs of much seat furniture was typical of the fashion for Greek- and Roman-inspired motifs that was current, especially in New York, between 1805 and 1825.

The foremost exponent of Directoire style was Scottish-born Duncan Phyfe (1768–1854), who worked in New York from c.1792. His elegant sofas with their reeded legs, carved top rails, and striped brocade, together with lyre-backed chairs, monumental tables, and X-shaped *klismos* stools have a distinctive character. Phyfe specialized in light, elegant seat furniture, for which he usually used mahogany,

a wood that was strong and had a good, rich color. His workshops, where different craftsmen were responsible for different aspects of a piece's construction and assembly, were a kind of forerunner of later factory methods.

Phyfe's main competition came from French immigrants to America, who fled from Europe after the Revolution of 1789. Foremost among these was Charles-Honoré Lannuier (1779–1819), who arrived in New York in 1803 and who also worked in the classical mode. His furniture, which is usually more elaborate than Phyfe's, often has metal mounts in the French style.

VICTORIAN
The Federal period ended in neoclassical extravagances, such as ostentatious carving of acanthus leaves, pineapples, and tassels. This gave way to a gothic revival by the mid-1830s, and architectural motifs such as pointed arches, ogee moldings, and trefoils were widely used. In the 1840s, for example, the architect A.J. Davies (1803–92) built the gothic-revival house Lyndhurst in New York, which he furnished with pieces of his own design.

From the 1820s to the 1870s spool or bobbin-turned furniture was in fashion, and examples could be found in homes across the county.

AMERICAN SOFA

▼ MAHOGANY AND CANEWORK
*c.*1810
This elegant sofa has been attributed to Duncan Phyfe. The cornucopia design on the crest and arms and the reeded, X-shaped legs are characteristic Phyfe embellishments, betraying his fascination with the style of ancient Rome.

Between *c.*1825 and *c.*1850 the homely Hitchcock chair enjoyed immense popularity. These side chairs were made by Lambert Hitchcock (1795–1852), a Connecticut furniture-maker. The chairs, which were in a basically Sheraton style, were of inexpensive birch, maple, hickory, or ash and were painted black and decorated with hand-painted or stenciled floral motifs, often in gilt. The Hitchcock chair was made in other parts of New England, New York, Ohio, and elsewhere.

The middle years of the century saw a rococo revival, of which the most extreme expression was seen in the work of John Henry Belter (1804–63), a German *émigré* who worked in New York between 1844 and 1863. He exploited the idiom commercially by combining technology with fanciful designs, patenting a method of laminating thin layers of wood so that they could be steam-molded. His laminated rosewood or black walnut pieces are generally ornamented with floral carving on every available surface.

From the mid-1860s to the mid-1880s, there was a new eclecticism in furniture design, and styles ranged from Louis XVI and Renaissance revivals to oriental and bamboo.

SHAKER STYLE

The Shakers, a sect introduced to America in 1774 by Ann Lee, a dissident Quaker, valued industry, self-sufficiency, and communal spirit, and the principles won many followers. Their ethos determined the style of their furniture, which was marketed from the 1870s on.

Every piece of furniture made by the Shakers embodied their precepts, and the appearance of each piece was governed by its use – "utility is beauty." Once a design was achieved that was strong, easy to make, and served its purpose well, it became the accepted prototype for that piece among all Shaker communities, apart from a few regional differences in such features as chair finials and leg turnings. Respect for order

AMERICAN LOVE SEAT

▶ LAMINATED WOOD
*c.*1860
This rococo revival love seat, attributed to John Henry Belter, was a popular form in the United States, and variations on the theme were produced by many manufacturers. This example has Belter's characteristic cabriole legs and a serpentine front to the seat. The use of laminated wood with pierced work and hand carving are also typical of Belter's work.

decreed that drawers and standing cupboards provided the most effective storage space. Drop leaves on tables and chests catered for the need for extra working space and the lack of standing room. Nest boxes with fingered joints were for keeping odds and ends until they were required. Peg boards on the wall enabled chairs to be hung up when not in use. The sexes were segregated in the community, and each had its own type of furniture. Chairs for the women were lighter and smaller than those for the men – women's tables were lower, and their chests of drawers contained more compartments.

Fruitwoods, seasoned maple, pine, and birch were the favored materials, and soft reddish cherry has become especially linked with the uncluttered lines of Shaker tradition. The earlier the piece, the better the quality, and early examples are frequently dark red, painted or stained in pale colors. Towards the end of the century their individuality declined, and stains were used to simulate conventional hardwoods. Most of the Shaker pieces offered for sale today as antiques were made between 1815 and 1880; the rest are high-quality reproductions of a somewhat later date.

SPANISH SOUTHWESTERN STYLE

A distinctive style developed in the Spanish Southwest. Between about 1800 and 1880, the poorer ranchers and farmers of Arizona, New Mexico, Texas, and California obtained their furniture from peasant cabinet-makers and amateur carpenters, who used cheap yellow pine, mesquite, juniper, and cotton wood to produce copies of the fine Spanish pieces made by Mexican craftsmen. Planks were hand-hewn, ornament was cursory, and the finish was rough.

Sought-after pieces are pine chests with molded and carved panels; the *trasero*, a kind of food safe, with doors spindled or decorated with gesso; chairs with tooled leather backs or sawtooth carved horizontal back rails; and rustic tables. After 1840, traces of Empire and gothic styles from the East can be detected, although they are expressed with charming naiveté in the better pieces.

SHAKER ROCKING CHAIR

◀ CHERRYWOOD

*c.*1840

The Shaker sect, which spread to America from England in 1774 and flourished in the early 19th century, believed in the simple life. Their furniture, evoking a pre-industrial and vernacular craft tradition, possessed many of the qualities to which the pioneers of the British Arts & Crafts Movement aspired, and belief in the dignity of labor and the beauty of utility anticipated many of the aesthetic ideals of the American Arts & Crafts Movement. This chair is typical of the light, strong chairs produced by the Shakers in the area around New Lebanon. The slat back, mushroom finials on the arm ends and conical finials on the back are common to the area, although the plaited seat and rocker form are general to Shaker chairs from their communities in New England and the Midwest.

ARTS & CRAFTS STYLE

From about 1880, the ideas of the English Arts & Crafts Movement took hold in the United States. The movement held that mechanization was dehumanizing and inferior to individual craftsmanship, and the reaction against mass-production found one of its leading proponents in the Chicago architect and furniture designer Frank Lloyd Wright (1867–1956), whose work is considered in the next chapter. Among the major Chicago firms that brought the new aesthetic into the marketplace were the Tobey Furniture Co. (*fl.*1890s) and its subsidiary the Tobey & Christianson Cabinet Co. (opened 1888). These companies often relieved the straight lines and plain surfaces of their furniture with shallow relief carving suggesting the organic forms of stone or tree trunks.

THE
20th
CENTURY

ART DECO, MODERNISM, AND BEYOND

———————

The beginning of the 20th
century saw a great variety
of furniture styles vying for
fashionable acceptance in both
Europe and America. As we have
seen, art nouveau was one of the
most widely disseminated styles in
France in the late 19th century, but
its adoption in other countries was
more often seen in this century. It
was not suited to mass-production
however, and became one of the
many casualties of World War I.

Function rather than form was to be the springboard for 20th-century furniture design, but it was not until the 1920s that this concept was fully developed. Nevertheless, the years before World War I were a time for experiment. Designers such as Charles Rennie Mackintosh, Joseph Hoffmann, and Koloman Moser produced some highly individual furniture, which was stylistically influential without being functionally revolutionary.

Not all new furniture of the early 20th century was modern in styling. The Edwardians commissioned many fine pieces in Sheraton and Adam styles, and these fashionable revivals were reflected in commercially produced ranges.

New forms appeared at this time. The cocktail cabinet was one of the typical forms of the post World War I years, when the restrained, sleek look that had already been evident in some

of the work of Hoffmann and Moser in Austria came to the notice of a wider public. This new style has since come to be known as art deco, a name that derives from the Exposition des Arts Décoratifs et Industriels Modernes, which was held in Paris in 1925. The exposition promoted a sumptuous low-slung look in interior design, intensified by large expanses of gleaming veneer, exotic materials, and crackle lacquer, combined with bright chrome and steel. Art deco might be seen as the final chapter in the craft of cabinet-making. There were two trends: early experiments in modern furniture using metals and plastics in forms that would lead to mass-production; and high quality craftsmanship.

Functionalism had its philosophical roots in the 18th century, but it was in the 20th century that the idea that beauty could be directly equated with fitness for purpose began to have a dramatic effect on furniture design. It was first taken up by architects like Louis Sullivan and Frank Lloyd Wright in America before World War I and later in Europe by Le Corbusier, whose famous description of a house as "a machine for living in" automatically extended to the way in which it was furnished.

In Europe, one of the leading influences on functional design was the Bauhaus, a craft school founded by the German architect Walter Gropius at Weimar in 1919. The school survived only until 1933, but it established design standards that were adapted to machine production and that spawned a generation of utilitarian furniture that was obviously modern.

World War II set its own limitations on furniture design. In Britain, for example, it led to government intervention in the furniture industry so that only approved designs in the "Utility" range were manufactured.

After World War II, plastic became a commonplace material for furniture, and its effects on design have been crucial, moving the emphasis from decoration back to fluidity of line. More recent developments have shown a growing division between pieces of furniture designed and made for the mass market and items made specifically for collectors.

AMERICAN CHAIR

▶ OAK
1916–22
Frank Lloyd Wright designed the oak side chair for the Imperial Hotel, Tokyo. It is an essay in geometry – all angles and no curves – and like many of his creations it is attractive but not very comfortable.

BRITAIN

The designs of architect C.F.A. Voysey (1857–1941) are among the most innovative in the entire history of English furniture. Characteristic features of his work include tall, narrow uprights, broad, flat cornices, and large strap hinges with cut-out decoration. His furniture was made of oak, sometimes stained, and it was made by accomplished craftsmen, such as Arthur Simpson, who subsequently made furniture to his own designs in a style derived from Voysey's.

The furniture made by the Bedford firm of J.P. White to designs by M.H. Baillie Scott (1865–1945) was more elaborately decorated than Voysey's. Most pieces were inlaid with stylized flowers or birds. The forms, however, were quite simple. While some pieces designed by Baillie Scott for the grand ducal palace at Darmstadt were made up by cabinet-makers at the Guild of Handicraft, Ashbee's own furni-

ture became simpler. Its decoration, too, was influenced by Baillie Scott's work.

The designs of the Scots architect Charles Rennie Mackintosh (1868–1928) show a breathtaking virtuosity – even if they are sometimes self-indulgent. It is easy to understand why his furniture was not well received in England. Simplicity was sacrificed to sophistication, tradition was flouted, and scant respect was shown for materials. The furniture was made from various woods, including oak, cypress, pine and mahogany, which were rarely left untreated. They were either French polished, stained, ebonized, or painted.

Many of Mackintosh's designs were parodies of traditional types of furniture. For instance, his ladder-back chair has an exaggeratedly high back with its narrow uprights ridiculously close together. His belief was that furniture should fit its settings, and among his best known work are the pieces he designed for Miss Cranston's Tea Room, Argyle Street, Glasgow, when he aimed to create an intimate space in which people could converse over afternoon tea.

The designer George Walton (1867–1933), also based in Glasgow until 1898, when he moved to London, gave narrow, tapering legs to many of his pieces of furniture. One of his

◀ OAK
*c.*1900
The elaborate copper hinges of this desk, which was designed by C.F.A. Voysey, hark back to the medieval influence of the 1860s and 1870s, but the general freedom from ornament, the fold-out writing surface and the clean lines proclaim Voysey's defiance of Victorian conventions.

▽ WHITE PAINTED WOOD
*c.*1900
This table is quite unlike Mackintosh's atmospheric, medievalizing work. Among his more domestic pieces were several white chairs and tables with an enamel-like surface. This table has an enamel glass inset contrasting with the large flat surface. The legs broaden towards the floor, a form that emphasizes the vertical lines and complements the elliptical shape of the top.

▶ *c.*1897

Charles Rennie Mackintosh's designs for Miss Cranston's Tea Room, Glasgow, are among his most famous. This chair, which was exhibited at the Vienna Secession in 1900, is a highly original composition of geometric form that describes space in a very architectural way. Its proportions are perhaps closer to a throne than a normal chair – it is over 4 feet high – and the broad splat at the back gives it a massive appearance.

designs was an adaptation of a traditional, rush-seated chair that had arms curving forwards from a narrow back with a narrow splat back pierced with a heart-shaped opening. This design was widely imitated in both Britain and the rest of Europe.

Around the turn of the century several manufacturers produced furniture in a style often called "quaint" by contemporaries and loosely based on the work of Voysey, Mackintosh, and other designers of the Arts & Crafts Movement. Liberty & Co. made stained oak furniture often decorated with repoussé copper panels and fruitwood, metal, and mother-of-pearl inlay. Another firm, Wylie & Lochhead of Glasgow, produced furniture in a style influenced by idiosyncrasies. Like Liberty's furniture, it was often elaborately inlaid, and the wood was often stained unusual colors, such as gray or violet.

John Sollie Henry's firm in London made furniture in a similar style. Mahogany was generally used, and Henry himself did much of the designing. However, he also commissioned designs from Voysey, Benson, and Walton, and several of his pieces were designed by George Montague Ellwood (1875–*c.*1960). Other manufacturers producing similar furniture were the

Bath Cabinet-makers Company (for which Ellwood did some designs) and the London firm of Shapland & Petter.

One furnishing company, Heal & Son of London, produced a wide range of furniture in the Cotswold style created by Gimson and Barnsley. It was designed by Ambrose Heal (1872–1959) and was featured in a catalog of "Simple Furniture" issued by the firm in 1899. Oak was generally used, although chestnut or mahogany versions were also offered. The furniture was more modest in scale and less rustic in style than Gimson's and Barnsley's, intended as it was for suburban homes.

OMEGA WORKSHOPS

In 1913 Roger Fry (1866–1934) established the Omega Workshops in London to produce painted pottery and tin-glazed earthenware. Fry wanted to involve artists in the design of furniture, carpets, and textiles as well as ceramics, and the workshop produced furniture designed by, among others, Vanessa Bell and Duncan Grant (Fry's fellow directors), Wyndham Lewis, Nina Hammett, Edward Wadsworth, and William Roberts. The furniture was painted or decorated in marquetry, in aggressively modern styles based on Fauvism.

Fry himself was commissioned to design the furnishings for an entire apartment for the wife of the Belgian ambassador, Lalla Vandervelde, who liked the distinctive, brightly painted pieces produced by the young artists at the workshops. Among the pieces commissioned was a marquetry desk, whose badly fitting drawers and poor quality marquetry typify the workshops' output. Fry had founded Omega partly as a reaction against the serious craft-guild mentality of the post-Morris era, and he was more concerned with spontaneity and artistic expression than with craftsmanship and technique. Nevertheless, he provided many keen young artists with a means of earning a living and, by cultivating clients, managed to see the workshops through the difficult days of World War I. They closed in 1921.

Other influential designers included Edwin

Lutyens and Gerald Summers, who designed pieces of innovative furniture for the firm Makers of Simple Furniture. Lloyd Loom furniture achieved popular status, and some glass and chrome dining furniture, illuminated and inlaid with panels from Lalique, was produced by Asprey.

UTILITY

World War II set its own limitations on furniture design, just as World War I had, and in Britain it led to government intervention in the furniture industry in the form of the Utility Furniture Scheme in 1942, so that between 1943 and 1952 only approved designs could be manufactured. The Utility furniture that resulted – plain, unpretentious, but of guaranteed minimum quality – was intended to help the refurnishing of bombed homes, but it also helped to establish the idea that utility and good design are not mutually exclusive concepts. In that sense it was a combination of the spirit of the Arts & Crafts Movement and mass-production

techniques and materials – the forms would have found favor with Ernest Gimson or Ernest and Sidney Barnsley, although the materials would not. Some of the designs in the Utility range were produced by a design panel, chaired by Sir Gordon Russell (1892–1980).

MODERNISM AND POSTMODERNISM

War-time shortages in Europe saw a new generation of designers and, therefore, designs emerge. By the 1960s, however, the main technological changes, the use of plastics and new materials, had given a hitherto unknown freedom to structures, and designers such as Charles Eames and Vico Magistretti were not slow to exploit the possibilities.

The 1960s also saw a marketing revolution, which was represented, if not begun, by the Englishman Terence Conran with his Habitat shop. The notion of selling furniture in kit form to be assembled at home was not a new one. Gerrit Rietveld and Bauhaus designers had

ENGLISH BEDROOM SUITE

◀ 1912–18
This design by the Omega Workshops, is far removed from the opulent materials, techniques and tastes of French art deco. The furniture does, however, feature stylized flowers and leaves not unlike those found on contemporary pieces by, for example, the Swiss-born design Jean Dunand.

used this technique 50 years before. Mass-production was not new either – Giles Grendey and Thomas Chippendale, for instance, had employed vast workshops in the 18th century, and the Thonet Brothers produced many millions of bentwood chairs in the 19th century. However, the Conran combination of high-volume production sold in kit form by means of a catalogue soon became tremendously popular.

The first Habitat catalog appeared in 1971. It combined Habitat-designed wares with the work of other designers, including Eero Saarinen and Harry Bertoia. The mass-production kept prices down, and imaginative room settings in the catalog promoted the idea of more stylish households. Easy access by post or by visiting the rapidly growing chain of stores ensured Habitat's success. There is, in fact, little in the first catalogue of tremendous originality. It focused on the practical, clean lines of the 1960s, with bright colors and some up-market furniture classics, including Conran's own design line.

The Habitat range created a mean for bourgeois style that it then exploited with a chain of stores that were somehow very different from the traditional British quality stores, such as Heal's. Interestingly, the largest single feature in the catalog on chairs is taken up by photographs of Thonet's bentwood chair, number 14, which was designed in 1859.

FRANCE

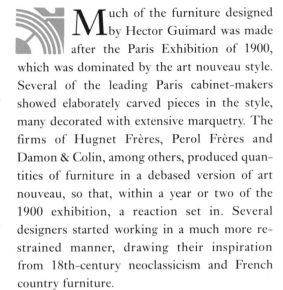

Much of the furniture designed by Hector Guimard was made after the Paris Exhibition of 1900, which was dominated by the art nouveau style. Several of the leading Paris cabinet-makers showed elaborately carved pieces in the style, many decorated with extensive marquetry. The firms of Hugnet Frères, Perol Frères and Damon & Colin, among others, produced quantities of furniture in a debased version of art nouveau, so that, within a year or two of the 1900 exhibition, a reaction set in. Several designers started working in a much more restrained manner, drawing their inspiration from 18th-century neoclassicism and French country furniture.

Paul Follot, formerly one of Eugène Grasset's pupils, exhibited at the 1909 Salon of the Société des Artistes-Décorateurs an interior furnished with pieces in a style of muted elegance, which reflected the current taste for the neoclassical. Léon Jallo, once director of Siegfried Bing's workshops, designed furniture with strong vertical and horizontal accents. It was decorated with ornament that, although based on natural forms, was arranged in small areas of geometrical patterns.

From about 1910, the painter André Mare designed furniture in a style that owed some-

FRENCH TABLE

▶ BRONZE AND MARBLE
*c.*1925
Armand-Albert Rateau was one of the most celebrated and eccentric of art deco designers, and his tables were especially striking. This example in bronze has a marble top in the form of a large tray, and its legs are the stylized forms of a bird.

thing to traditional country pieces and something to Cubism. In 1912 he exhibited the Maison Cubiste, an interior complete with furniture and decoration in the style pioneered by Picasso and Braque.

ART DECO

The elegance and opulence of Parisian art deco were best expressed in the stunning interiors of the 1920s and 1930s, often the collaboration between furniture and textile designers, sculptors, painters, lacquer-workers, and other talented artists and artisans. The *ensemblier* came to the fore with such names as Ruhlmann, the architect-designer Robert Mallet-Stevens (1886–1945), Francis Jourdain (1876–1958), Eileen Gray (1878–1976), and Louis Süe (1875–1968) and André Mare (1887–1932), who founded the Compagnie des Arts Français, taking on the formidable task of creating a total design, or *ensemble*, for a room, including the wall, window and floor coverings, furniture, and other co-ordinating accessories.

Art deco designers often paid homage to the heritage of the Louis XV, Louis XVI and Empire periods, as well as creating entirely new forms of their own. They used both innovative and traditional materials, although their techniques were usually subsidiary to the overall aesthetic effect. Colors were often bright and vibrant, but subtle pastel shades and deep, dark grays, browns, and blacks were also in evidence. The high style art deco interiors and furnishings in Paris were, above all, luxurious and lavish, and wealthy clients such as the couturiers Jacques Doucet, Jeanne Lanvin, and Madeleine Vionnet commissioned furniture, *objets*, and even whole rooms.

In 1920, for example, Jeanne Lanvin commissioned Armand-Albert Rateau (1882–1938) to design the interior of her Paris house. His patinated bronze, wood, and marble furnishings abounded with elaborate floral and animals motifs – birds supporting a bronze coffee table, deer and foliage on a bathroom bas relief, marguerites entwining a dressing-table, and fire-dogs in the shape of cats.

FRENCH CHAIR

◄ BRONZE
*c.*1925
This exotic bronze chair with its leopardskin cushions was designed by Rateau. It features marine motifs – scallop shells at the top and along the back and tentacle-like legs.

Rateau's furniture and overall vision are among the most figurative and truly sculptural of the period, but the heavily veneered, embellished, and often lacquered pieces of many of the other designers are more handsome and restrained, often deriving from such classical shapes as scrolls, and using stylized wings, animals, birds and human figures. Pierre Legrain (1889–1929), for example, was influenced by African and Egyptian forms, and he created a variety of innovative furniture, including chairs of carved wood similar to those used in ancient Egypt.

Furniture was embellished and sometimes even completely covered with such materials as mother-of-pearl, shagreen (sharkskin), snakeskin, gold and silver leaf, crushed eggshell lacquer, and ivory. These might be formed into patterns – usually stylized flowers or geometric motifs – or they might simply be used to show the natural texture of the material itself. The shapes of furniture ranged from the overtly traditional – 18th-century *bureaux plats*, ladies' desks or *bergère* chairs, for example – to the strikingly *moderne*, severely rectilinear, with not a curve in sight.

► LACQUER
*c.*1925
This table by Jean Dunand is clearly based on the traditional two-tiered circular table form of the 18th century. Dunand's tables and chairs tend to have basic geometric shapes, with an emphasis on decoration rather than form, and he specialized in lacquer work, experimenting by adding gold and silver dust, mother-of-pearl, and ivory to his lacquers in the traditional Japanese style.

► ROSEWOOD
1916–22
The furniture designed by Rulhmann marks a radical departure from art nouveau. The exotic materials that he used on this *armoire* – it is veneered in amaranth, with a marquetry floral urn in ivory and Macassar ebony – make this an especially luxurious piece, which, in its use of neoclassical motifs, looks forward to art deco style.

The greatest *ébéniste* of art deco France was Emile-Jacques Ruhlmann. His furniture is often compared with that of the great 18th-century French cabinet-makers: it is of excellent quality and made at great expense. Constructed in exotic wood, such as amboyna, it was decorated with neoclassical motifs and geometrical patterns inlaid in ebony and ivory. These were a far cry from art nouveau. Ruhlmann wrote that it was "the elite that launches fashion and determines its direction," and it is not surprising to learn that he was supported through much of his working life by wealthy patrons. He stated that the proportions of his furniture as a whole were far more important than their detail of ornamentation, but the luxury and style of his work – especially the applied decoration – are outstanding.

Jean Dunand (1877–1942) also designed and decorated elaborate furniture, including cabinets, panels, and screens, which were often covered with figural or animal designs. Irish-born Eileen Gray, another great Parisian furniture designer and *ensemblier*, started out fashioning exquisite hand-made objects such as screens, tables, and chairs, which were often embellished with

Japanese lacquer. She eventually moved on to more rectilinear and functional furniture.

The best known pieces by Le Corbusier (1887–1965) are the chairs he designed in collaboration with his cousin Pierre Jeanneret (1896–1967) and Charlotte Perriand (b.1903). His *chaises longues* and armchairs, often fashioned of tubular steel frames and simple but comfortable and functional leather seats, were slightly more inviting than the spare, minimal designs of the Bauhaus. These, especially the designs of Marcel Breuer and Mies van der Rohe, were even further removed from the plush, upholstered chairs of André Groult (1884–1867) and Maurice Dufrène (1876–1955), which recalled a luxuriant past. Theirs instead clearly signaled a new era in design that still reigns today.

MODERNISM AND POSTMODERNISM

From the very start, art deco had comprised two extremes of style. In France, where the movement had evolved, high style art deco manifested itself emotionally, with exuberance, color, and playfulness. Elsewhere in Europe and in America it was interpreted more intellectually, with designers basing their work on theories of functionalism and economy.

By 1926 a loosely knit band of French Modernists – Francis Jourdain, Pierre Chareau, Le Corbusier, Robert Mallet-Stevens, and René Herbst – had become increasingly outspoken in their criticism of art deco designers, who catered to select clients by creating elaborately crafted unique pieces. The Modernists argued that the new age required excellent design for everyone and that quality and mass-production were not mutually exclusive concepts. Modernism made rapid progress in the late 1920s, although most designers took a stance somewhat short of the severe functionalism espoused by its most ardent adherents.

The partnership of Jean-Michel Frank (1895–1941) and Adolphe Chanaux (1887–1965) produced some original work from their design studio in Paris. In 1927 Frank commissioned Chanaux to decorate his apartment to his own design, and so began a professional association that ended only with Frank's suicide in New York shortly after the outbreak of World War II. The two sometimes collaborated with their immediate neighbors, including Salvador Dali, Alberto and Diego Giacometti, and Pablo Picasso, and among their well-known patrons were Mr and Mrs Nelson Rockefeller, Elsa Schiaparelli, and Templeton Crocker. The partnership's furniture was known for its sparseness and simplicity of line and function. On visiting Frank's apartment, Jean Cocteau remarked that Frank was a nice young man and it was a pity that burglars had taken everything.

Raymond Subes (1893–1970), who was born in Paris, studied metal engraving at the Parisian school of metalwork, the Ecole Boulle, before working for the influential architects Borderel and Robert. In 1919, he became the director of their metal workshop, and he was responsible for many important architectural projects. He usually worked in wrought iron, but also used bronze, copper, and aluminum. Subes's work followed on from that of Emile Robert, who was responsible for the revival of metal work as an Arts & Crafts interest in the 19th century, and of the great art deco metalworker Edgar Brandt (1880–1960). Brandt and Subes both worked for the top designers of the time and exhibited under their own names.

René Herbot of Paris produced a variety of minimalist designs that are still being reproduced by Ecart. Other important French designers included Jean Lele.

▼ WROUGHT IRON AND GRANITE
1925
This center table by Raymond Subes makes full use of the flexible strength and malleability of the wrought iron. The image on the surface of the gray granite, a nude with fruit bowl, is highlighted in reverse in red ochre.

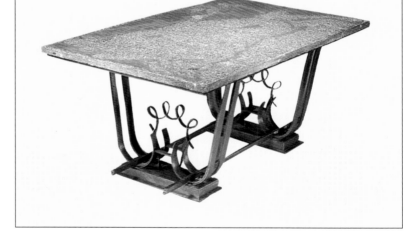

FRENCH CHAIR

◀ 1928
The famous chaise-longue by Le Corbusier was the ultimate in luxury and comfort and influenced many designers. This particular piece is a reproductioin by Cassina.

BELGIUM

▼ WOOD
*c.*1900
The Belgian architect
Victor Horta revealed his
debt to rococo forms in
this piece that he
designed for his own
home.

The Belgian architect Victor Horta (1861–1947) created wild and flamboyant art nouveau for the house he designed in 1892 for the engineer Emile Tassel. It was marked by whiplash lines and scrolling, curved ironwork, and stained glass; woodwork and wall decoration also abounded. Some of the furniture designed by Horta for the Tassel House was, however less innovative than the building itself. A buffet, for example, with glazed cupboards at each end surmounted by S-shaped scroll pediments and carrying a pair of

candelabra with several curling arms, would scarcely have looked out of place in a rococo setting. On the other hand, the profusion of curved stretchers and supports under chairs and tables was pure art novueau.

Horta's style moderated progressively throughout the 1890s, and by 1905 he had virtually abandoned the art nouveau style. His furniture is characterized by its abstract forms derived from nature and by its rather thin, spindly structural members. Horta created the idea of built-in furniture, which became such a typical feature of the art nouveau interior that the French writer Edmond Goncourt invented for it the sobriquet "yachting style" – for example, a banquette would run along one wall, turn a corner and finish as a display case.

Like Horta, Gustave Serrurier-Bovy (1858–1910) was influenced both by Viollet-le-Duc's drawings and by William Morris, the leader of Britain's Arts & Crafts Movement. In 1884, he had visited England and had been deeply impressed by the theory and practice that Morris propounded. Serrurier-Bovy's earliest furniture was based on designs published in the London magazines *Cabinet Maker* and *British Architect*. The pieces that he showed in 1894 at the Salon de la Libre Esthétique, an exhibiting society formed by Belgian artists and designers, were still oriented towards the English Arts & Crafts style. However, those he showed at the Salon in the following year, although made of plain wood with iron mounts, acknowledged the art nouveau of Continental Europe with the strongly curved elements of their design.

For the next decade Serrurier-Bovy's furniture reflected both the influence of Morris, in simple panel-and-plank construction, and his enthusiasm for Belgian and French flamboyance. His furniture was enormously popular, and he was soon running a large factory in Liège. In 1899 he opened a retail outlet in Paris called L'Art dans l'Habitation, and his furniture was seen at the 1900 Paris Exhibition in Le Pavillon Bleu. Like the English craftsmen he so much admired, Serrurier-Bovy generally used oak for his furniture. Shortly before his death he

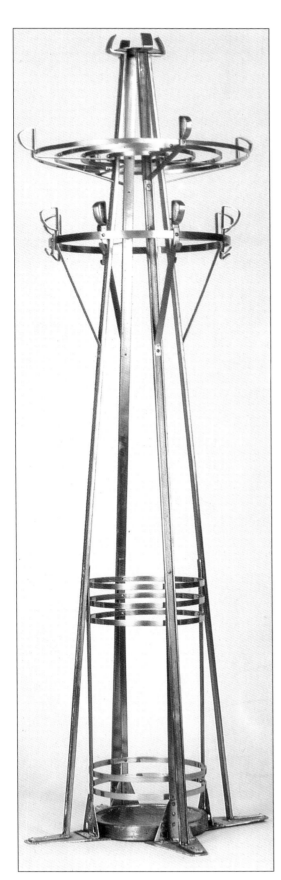

started to design furniture that featured strong geometrical elements in both structure and decoration.

The furniture of a third Belgian designer is also worthy of note. Henri Van de Velde (1863–1957) began his career as a painter, but in 1892 he gave up painting and devoted himself to the applied arts. In 1895 he built himself a house, Bloemenwerg, in Uccle, near Brussels, for which he designed all the furniture. Like Serrurier-Bovy's work, it incorporates features derived both from the English Arts & Crafts ethos and Horta's curvilinear style. It was made of oak, and some simply constructed side chairs were rush-seated. More elaborate pieces were decorated with carved ornament in a forceful art nouveau idiom.

Van de Velde had absorbed from the French neo-Impressionist painters the notion of using lines to express psychological moods, and he attempted to impart emotional power to his abstract ornament. This intellectual approach seems to have appealed to the Germans, and he designed office furniture for Julius Meier-Graefe, the German art critic who opened a shop in Paris to sell modern furniture and decoration. In 1899 he designed pieces for the German firm of Löffler, and in the following year he moved to Berlin, after which his career belongs to the history of design in Germany.

ITALY

Italy made a unique contribution to the history of furniture through the work of the eccentric designer Carlo Bugatti (1856–1940), the father of the sports car designer. Bugatti originally trained as an architect before opening his first furniture workshop and outlet in Milan in the 1880s. He also produced silver jewelry and other goods. His chairs and designs for interiors are wonderfully idiosyncratic and difficult to categorize. They drew heavily on the Near East (especially Syria and Egypt) for inspiration in their use of applied and worked metals, such as copper, and the extensive inlay of many different materials,

BELGIAN COAT STAND

◄ METAL
*c.*1905
The Belgian designer Gustave Serrurier-Bovy started an extremely successful furniture-manufacturing business with his own retail outlets in Liège, Brussels, Paris, Nice, and The Hague. This coat stand represents the transitional phase of late art nouveau, when its elongated forms became straighter and less ornate, and points toward the geometrical style that he adopted toward the end of his career.

ITALIAN DRAWING ROOM
FURNITURE

▲ WOOD, METAL, AND
VELLUM
c.1900
The Moorish style of this
furniture, designed by
Carlo Bugatti exhibits the
eclectic approach to styles
and materials employed
by this idiosyncratic
designer.

ITALIAN TABLE

▶ GLASS AND WOOD
c.1950
The combination of wood
and glass is typical of the
work of Carlo Graffi. The
wood of this card table is
cut into a shape that is
not inherently strong,
and it is stressed by
tensioning bars. It is
stylish, with straight legs
and a severe outline, and
trays for the counters
slide out from each
corner.

including pewter, ivory, and other woods. He
had no qualms about mixing different materials
and methods. Vellum, painted with Arabian
scenes, was used for seats and backs of his chairs
and became one of his trademarks, as did the
circle or half-finished circle. His work often has
a chunky, geometric look, and he often hung
cords and tassels from the extended uprights. At
the 1902 Turin Exhibition in Italy the wood of
some of his furniture was completely covered in
vellum, and sporadically decorated with
abstract and naturalistic designs such as insects
and birds.

STILE LIBERTY

Around 1900, Italian architect Ernesto Basile
(1857–1932) created furniture in the art
nouveau style, which was known in Italy as *stile
Liberty* or *stile floreale*. The elegant forms of
Basile's furniture are decorated with carved
foliate ornament. Basile, who was primarily an
architect, became chief designer for Vittorio

Ducrot's firm, a sizable interior design workshop in Palermo, Sicily. They designed extensively in art nouveau style as well as in more
organic styles, completing some prestigious
projects and exhibiting at Italian fairs in the
early years of the century. Overall, however, the
firm's work was commercial, and it produced
good quality, stylish furniture, such as that of
the Grand Hotel, Palermo, for general use.

Also influential in this style was cabinet-maker Carlo Zen, whose art nouveau furniture, which often has a dual function, is elaborately carved with floral decoration.

MODERNISM AND POSTMODERNISM

Although the Milan school was responsible for countless innovative ideas, many have not endured well. The influence of the Milan school, particularly its premier exponent, the innovative designer, Carlo Mollino, can be seen in the work of Carlo Graffi, especially his juxtaposition of materials, such as wood and glass.

Alberto Giacometti (1901–66) was a Swiss-born sculptor, painter, and poet who trained in Italy in the 1920s. While he was there he was greatly influenced by the Romanian-born sculptor Constantin Brancusi (1876–1957). In the 1930s Giacometti produced mainly surreal work, with mythological and mysterious elements, and he later went on to concentrate on

ITALIAN COFFEE TABLE

◀ CAST BRONZE
*c.*1955
This table comes from a series of bronze and glass furniture based on skeletal human and organic forms designed by Alberto Giacometti.

ITALIAN SUITE

▼ WOOD
*c.*1900
The combination of elegance and function is typical of the work of Ernesto Basile and Vittorio Ducrot. This suite was designed by Basile, and reveals his characteristically restrained approach to art nouveau.

▷ 1980s
This beautifully
structured sofa, known as
Eastside, was designed by
Ettore Sottsass for
Memphis. The headrests
are a pleasing feature of
the overall shape, and are
emphasized by the use of
a contrasting color.

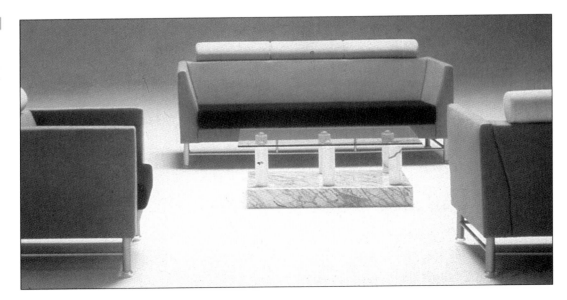

the stick-like, emaciated figures, made from wire frames applied with plaster of Paris, for which he is, perhaps, best known. His furniture is generally fairly light-hearted, and it is highly prized by collectors of 20th-century works.

Ettore Sottsass (b.1917), who was born in Austria but became an Italian citizen, is widely regarded as the most outstanding Italian designer of his generation. He was a pioneer of the postwar *ricostruzione*. He is an architect, industrial designer, and furniture designer, as well as an artist. For a short period in the 1970s, he was involved with an avant-garde Milanese group, Studio Alchymia, designing some curious pieces for their collections. However, his most important work was produced in the 1980s by the Milanese group known as Memphis, which Sottsass was instrumental in establishing and of which he has become a leading light.

SPAIN

The Spanish architect Antoni Gaudí (1852–1926) created furniture for some of the buildings he designed. He was influenced by Viollet-le-Duc, and much of his early work was in a neo-gothic style. Between 1885 and 1890 he built a palace in Barcelona for the Güell family, for which he designed asymmetrical furniture in an organic style that prefigures art novueau.

GERMANY

ART NOUVEAU

The German term for art nouveau was *Jugendstil* (youth style). In Munich during the 1890s, a number of architects, painters, and sculptors, including Hermann Obrist (1863–1927), August Endell (1871–1921), Richard Riemerschmid (1868–1957), Bernhard Pankok (1872–1943), and Bruno Paul (1874–1968), turned their attention to the applied arts. In 1897, these five, among others, founded the Vereinigte Werkstätten für Kunst im Handwerk (United Workshops for Art in the Handicrafts). Obrist and Endell designed furniture in flowing, natural forms that were determined by a theory of interaction between physical appearances and psychological reactions. Obrist's furniture was made of oak, and Endell's of elm. Pankok's designs were also based on natural forms. He used oak, pearwood, walnut, and spruce.

Richard Riemerschmid's earliest experiments in furniture were some pieces he designed for his own apartment in 1895. They were in the neo-gothic style, made of stained and painted pine, and decorated with elaborate wrought-iron hinges and foliate ornament carved in low relief. However, Riemerschmid's style was to change as a result of seeing in 1897 an exhibition in Dresden of Henri Van de Velde's furniture, whose abstract art nouveau style had a considerable impact on all the Munich artists. The following year Riemerschmid designed an oak side chair, its backrest carried on supports that descend in a sweeping curve to the feet of the front legs. A slightly altered version was soon being sold by Liberty's in London.

Another Munich designer, Bruno Paul (1874–1968), also created furniture that was influenced by Van de Velde. Paul's work was characterized by elegant curved lines and was free of any ornament.

DRESDEN WORKSHOPS

One of the intentions underlying the work of the Munich artists was to create furniture cheap enough for a far larger public than could afford the hand-built furniture produced by the leading avant-garde designers of Paris, Nancy, and Brussels. When selecting the forms that their furniture would take, the Germans took into account the new woodworking machines that were being developed. The leader of this tendency was the cabinet-maker Karl Schmidt (1873–1948), Riemerschmid's brother-in-law,

who in 1898 opened the Dresdner Werkstätten (Dresden Workshops). At an exhibition of industrial art held in Dresden in 1899–1900, Schmidt showed an apartment of two living rooms, bedroom and kitchen that were inexpensively furnished with simple, modern furniture. Five years later, the Dresdner Werkstätten produced a range of machine-made furniture designed by Riemerschmid.

GERMAN WORKSHOPS

In 1902 the artist Adelbert Niemeyer and the upholsterer Karl Bertsch founded a workshop in Munich for the manufacture of furniture and other items of interior decoration. In 1907, the workshop merged with the Dresdner Werkstätten, and the two became known as the Deutsche Werkstätten (German Workshops). The Werkstätten should not be confused with the Deutsche Werkbund, an association of designers, craftsmen, manufacturers, and retailers promoted by the German government and founded in the same year.

Niemeyer continued to design furniture for the Deutsche Werkstätten until his death. Other

GERMAN SIDEBOARD

▼ OAK

*c.*1900

August Endell based his designs on the psychological effects of line and proportion, and he believed that shape alone could induce feelings of serenity and satisfaction. His decorative motifs were derived from illustrations in scientific books dealing with primitive life forms.

GERMAN CABINET AND CHAIR

▶ WOOD
c.1900
These pieces were designed at Darmstadt by Josef Maria Olbrich, an Austrian who settled in Darmstadt. The marquetry on the cabinet doors shows the influence of the British Arts & Crafts designer M.H. Baillie Scott.

GERMAN CHAIR

▼ 1925
It is said that Marcel Breuer bought an Adler bicycle and was inspired by the chrome steel handlebars to design this chair, which was intended for Wassily Kandinsky's studio at the Bauhaus. The chair, one of the most famous of 20th-century designs, has been in continual production since 1925.

designers who occasionally worked for the Dresden concern were Baillie Scott and the Austrians Josef Hoffmann (1870–1956) and Koloman Moser (1868–1918).

DARMSTADT DESIGNERS

Baillie Scott's work was well known on the Continent of Europe, having been frequently illustrated in the magazine *The Studio*. The illustrations had caught the eye of the grand-duke Ernst Ludwig of Hesse-Darmstadt, who in 1897 had had a drawing room and a dining room in his palace at Darmstadt furnished and decorated by Baillie Scott and Ashbee. He encouraged the establishment of an artists' colony at Matildenhohe on the outskirts of Darmstadt and gave some land for the project. Seven artists were invited to join the colony, and by 1900 their homes were being built. For his house Peter Behrens (1868–1940), a painter and architect who had been working in Munich during the 1890s, designed furniture that was close in style to the work of Henri Van de Velde. Hans Christiansen (1866–1945) designed pieces in a geometrical style, decorated with inlaid patterns, marquetry or low-relief silver plaques.

Josef Maria Olbrich (1867–1908) was an Austrian architect who started his career in Vienna and became one of the leading figures of the Secession. In 1899, however, he took up the grand-duke's offer to settle at Darmstadt. There he created furniture for his own and other artists' houses in a style that was a successful blend of organic shapes and geometrical ornament. Olbrich died at Darmstadt at the age of only 41 after a prolific career. His furniture was mostly for the houses he built, although, perhaps as a result of his early departure from Vienna, it has a timeless, universally applicable restraint, especially when compared with the creations of his fellow Secessionists Josef Hoffman, Otto Wagner, and Joseph Urban.

NEOCLASSICAL REVIVAL

Christiansen's furniture had a neoclassical character that became prevalent in German design during the years before World War I. Two rooms displaying work in this style were exhibited by the Deutsche Werkstätten at the 1910 Salon d'Automne in Paris and had a powerful impact on French design. They were the work of Nieymeyer and Bertsch, who, with many

other German designers, had responded to a government call for conformity to the principles of classicism.

ART DECO

Art deco has come to be so closely associated with France and, to a lesser degree Britain and America, that it is easy to overlook the fact that the decorative arts were thriving in Weimar Germany. Germany may have suffered economically under the harsh conditions laid down by the Treaty of Versailles (1914), which led to the financial collapse of 1926 and the great depression of the 1930s, but the demand for basic items for the home continued – the German porcelain and ceramic industries were the largest in Europe in this period, for instance. Companies like Villeroy and Boch in Dresden flourished by meeting the realities of the economic situation. Good cheap design did not have

to be a luxury, and until 1933 it would be true to say that France's position as the center of the art world was challenged by Germany. After 1933, with Hitler's rise to power, the leading lights of German culture emigrated to America, mostly via London.

BAUHAUS

The work of the Bauhaus (founded by Walter Gropius in 1919) helped to create the Modern Movement. Influential designers included Marcel Breuer (1902–81), who designed the important Wassily chair, and Mies van der Rohe (1886–1969). The Bauhaus was the laboratory of the avant-garde. The design of a chair, for example, would be broken down into its most basic components.

Breuer left Hungary to study painting in Vienna, and in 1924 he took charge of the Bauhaus workshop concerned with interior

GERMAN *CHAISE LONGUE*

▼ LAMINATED BEECH AND PLYWOOD
1935
This *chaise longue* was designed by Marcel Breuer for the Isokon furniture company of London, and it reveals how modern furniture-making methods can be used to create a structure in which perfection of form is paramount. Breuer designed his furniture both in steel and woods, to provide maximum comfort with a minimum use of material and labor. The *chaise longue* was originally fitted with a continuous cushion, which did not detract from the concept of unity.

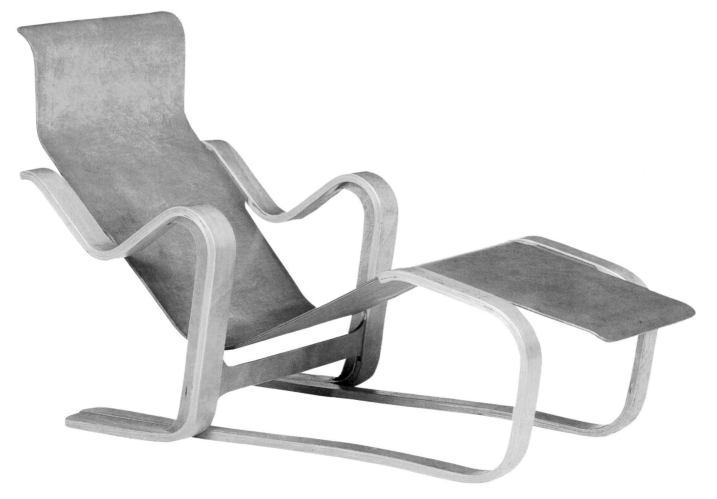

▶ WALNUT AND COPPER
*c.*1902
This table, which is
known as the Elephant
Trunk table or the Spider
table, was designed by
Adolf Loos. Although it
is not functional, the
table's intriguing design
includes legs that are
supported on semicircles
that appear to combine
oriental inspiration, an
interest in geometric
design, and cabriole legs.
The table is finished with
copper around the lobed
top and copper feet on
the legs.

design. He encouraged the students to produce
in simple materials, in keeping with the broad
principles of originality and function. The
Wassily chair, which was designed at the
Bauhaus in 1925, has become an icon of
Modernism, but its form is not simply the result
of the designer's vision. It is equally the result of
the properties of the materials from which it was
made. The strength of tubular steel allowed for
a lightweight design with flat leather surfaces
intersecting to make an innovatory and comfortable chair. The fact that Breuer named the chair
after the Russian Constructivist painter Wassily
Kandinsky hints at the interaction between
those at the cutting edge of art and design at this
time. Indeed, Constructivist art reveals its influence in the intersection of the flat leather surfaces of the chair.

As political difficulties dogged the Bauhaus,
Breuer moved to Britain, where he helped
Isokon to develop designs using sculptured plywood, which again sparked off an entirely new
generation of furniture. Breuer's laminated
wood designs for Isokon included nesting tables,
a dining table, a square table, dining chairs, and

a *chaise longue*. In his work for Isokon Breuer
perpetuated many of the ideals of the Bauhaus,
notably economy combined with up-to-date
construction methods, to create highly sculptural, Modernist furniture. Remarkably, Breuer
was considered much more important as an
architect and was invited to the US by Gropius
to teach at Harvard University, where he was a
professor of architecture from 1937 to 1947.

▶ BENTWOOD AND BRASS
*c.*1900
The Viennese
manufacturers Jacob and
Joseph Kohn
commissioned the
Secession designer
Koloman Moser to
design several pieces of
bentwood furniture. The
upholstery of these chairs
is covered with fabric in a
contemporary pattern.
The great restraint of the
style was partly inspired
by Charles Rennie
Mackintosh.

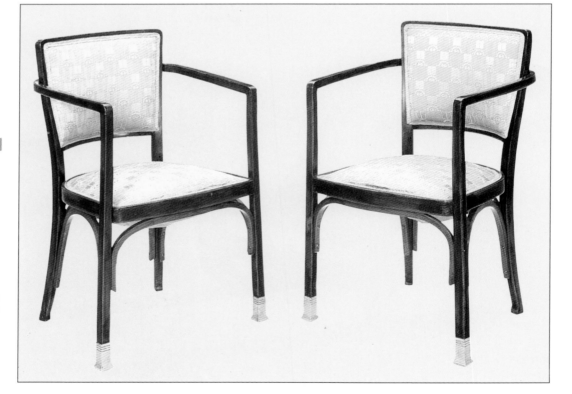

AUSTRIA

In Austria the art nouveau style was called *Secessionstil*, after the Vienna Secession, which was formed in 1897. A group of architects, painters, and sculptors seceded from the official artists' organization and held their own exhibitions in the Secessionhaus. One of the older Secessionists was the architect Otto Wagner (1841–1918), who designed some very plain furniture for his buildings. It was manufactured by the firm of Thonet Brothers, which had pioneered the technology of bentwood furniture.

Another Viennese architect Adolf Loos (1870–1933) designed bentwood chairs manufactured by Thonet for the Café Museum. Loos had been impressed by the work of the English Arts & Crafts Movement, and several of the pieces he designed were of simple, paneled construction. His work is marked by elegant proportions and a judicious disposition of simple reeding and metal fittings. Loos himself did not join the Secession, and he criticized its members for the ornament and deliberate "artiness" of much of the furniture they designed.

WIENER WERKSTÄTTE

The principal Secession designers were two young architects, Joseph Hoffmann (1870–1956) and Koloman Moser (1868–1918), who produced furniture that later became severely rectangular. In 1903 Hoffmann and Moser founded the Wiener Werkstätte (Vienna Workshops), which were financed by Fritz Waerndorfer and Otto Primavesi. Many members of the Secession were also active in the Werkstätte, which produced a range of decorative objects, including furniture. Some of the pieces designed by Moser were richly decorated with marquetry or inlaid metals, while others were simply painted white.

Many of Hoffmann's furniture designs show the influence of Charles Rennie Mackintosh, but he maintained a high level of personal inventiveness. Characteristics of his furniture are lattice-like chair backs and table aprons, and

small spheres of wood for decoration at points of structural significance. Hoffmann's style gradually became more retrospective, using some neo-classical and Biedermeier forms.

AUSTRIAN CHAIR
WOOD
*c.*1910
Josef Urban designed and furnished a number of apartments in Vienna before he was asked by Wiener Werkstätte to decorate its New York branch.

AUSTRIAN DESK
ELM
*c.*1910
Koloman Moser designed this luxurious desk as a special commission for a wealthy client. The basic elm carcass is decorated with ivory, mother-of-pearl, ebony, and jacaranda. Its rigidly geometric form and decoration are typical of the products of the Wiener Werkstätte.

▲ BENTWOOD
*c.*1905
These chairs are a good
example of Josef
Hoffmann's bentwood
designs, which were
executed by the factory of
Kohn & Kohn.
Characteristic of his
designs are the lobes or
spheres that support the
joints on the front legs.
The backs of these chairs
are a pastiche of a
Sheraton tea tray,
decorated with an inlaid
fan in the center.

RED-BLUE CHAIR

▶ *c.*1918
Gerrit Rietveld's striking
chair represents a clear
break with the organic,
curving art novueau style.
The straight lines yet
complex shape formed
out of the simplest
techniques are coupled
with strong, clear colors.
Rietveld used lines to
produce form by
enclosing space. The
structure has simple
components, and the
chair's colors are
reminiscent of the
geometric painting of Piet
Mondrian, whose squares
of color are concerned
with proportion.

The same influence is evident in the furniture created by Otto Prutscher (1880–1949) and Josef Urban (1872–1933), two other Wiener Werkstätte designers. Prutscher also designed for Thonet. Other Viennese manufacturers that employed Wiener Werkstätte designers included Jacob & Joseph Kohn, Portois & Fix, Franz Gloser, and Richard Ludwig.

THE NETHERLANDS

Most Dutch furniture of this period was simple, although the work of K.P.C. de Bazel and J.L.M. Lauweriks was sometimes decorated with carved motifs derived from Egyptian or Assyrian art. Their pieces often had copper mounts. Theo Nieuwenhuis, C.A. Lion Cachet and G.W. Gijsselhof all designed simply constructed furniture, and a line of plain, functional furniture descends from the architect H.P. Berlage, through the work of Jacob van den Bosch.

The best known designer of the time was Gerrit Rietveld (1888–1964). Rietveld, the son of a cabinet-maker, established his own furniture workshop in 1911. His early work was simply and carefully hand-crafted, in keeping with the Dutch Arts & Crafts tradition. In 1916, however, he was introduced to the painter Bart van der Leck, at that time a member of the De Stijl group, and to the architect Robert van t'Hoff, who asked him to copy, from photo-

graphs, furniture by Frank Lloyd Wright for the Huis ter Heide. The Red-Blue chair was designed a few months after this, its formal and spatial innovations no doubt inspired by Rietveld's recent encounters with new attitudes to materials and form. The chair was, in fact, designed as a personal experiment to demonstrate that: "a thing of beauty, e.g., a spatial object, could be made of nothing but straight machined materials." Following its illustration in *De Stijl* magazine, it became widely known in avant-garde circles throughout Europe. Its place in the history of modern art cannot be underestimated.

The Berlin chair (1923) is, in some ways, an even more exaggerated demonstration of Rietveld's belief in the principles of De Stijl: it is much simpler and uses only tones of black and white. In 1927 Rietveld designed the Beugel Fauteuil, which appears to resemble the Red-Blue chair in plywood and tube, but which in fact takes its strength from the integral triangles from which it is formed. Rietveld produced an extraordinary variety of innovative chair designs, typically planned with mass-production in mind. His concern for the method as well as the results of design led him to create the Birza chair, which was cut from a single piece of fiber that was then folded and fixed into a rigid shape.

SCANDINAVIA

Reflecting the contemporary Scandinavian interest in traditional folk culture, the furniture was simply constructed and often painted or carved with animal and floral motifs.

In Sweden J.A.G. Acke and Carl Westman designed pieces that featured the curving, rhythmic lines of Van de Velde, while Carl Bergsten's designs were influenced by the Wiener Werkstätte.

During the first two decades of the 20th century the Norwegian Gabriel Kielland, the Dane Kaare Klint (1888–1954) and the Swede Carl Malmsten designed elegant, good quality furniture. The Finnish designers Louis Sparre, Eliel Saarinen (1873–1950), and Eero Saarinen (1910–61) were pioneers of the international Modern Movement, and their work reflects a preoccupation with construction and function.

As a furniture designer the Finnish Alvar Aalto (1898–1976), one of the most prolific designers of modern times, rejected new materials, such as metal and plastic. Convinced that the human body should come into contact only with natural materials, he utilized laminated birch plywood, molded to follow human contours. His designs fell between the traditional craft approach of Scandinavia and the new forms developing in central Europe. His bentwood forms echo those of the Thonet Brothers in the 19th century, but belong unmistakably to his own time. In 1933 Aalto founded the firm Artek to produce inexpensive, well-designed textiles, light fixtures, and furnishings.

Comparisons have been drawn between Aalto's laminated birch furniture and the molded plywood furniture produced in the 1930s by, for example, Summers and Eames. The difference is that Aalto makes the structure work in the design, producing an integrated whole that is also elegant. His designs have a classic appeal that remains popular today.

AMERICA

The influence of many of the Chicago-based architect-teachers who had taught the young Frank Lloyd Wright can be detected in the writings and work of the Prairie School. George Grant

◀ 1927
A chair sculpted from a sheet of fabric showed Rietveld's concern for the method as well as the result of the design. It was designed for the Birza Room, an interior taking the name of its patron Dr W. Birza.

NORWEGIAN CHAIRS

▼ PAINTED WOOD
*c.*1911
Designed by Gerhard Munthe, these chairs are a virtuoso indulgence of decoration. The sculptural, carved mask heads clearly derive from Scandinavian folkloric tradition, and the interlacing strapwork has a Gaelic look to it.

▶ LAMINATED WOOD
*c.*1937
This is one piece of an original series of laminated wood furniture designed by Alvar Aalto. In an attempt to get away from tubular metal, Aalto devised the laminated frame with a veneer seat. Not only does it have a delightfully bizarre shape, but it is quite unlike anything being produced in the rest of Europe. The self-sprung seat depends on the natural flexibility of the wood.

Elmslie (1872–1952) and George Washington Maher drew heavily on medieval and Renaissance traditions, using the scrolls, carvings of animal heads, and deep arm- and backrests of 16th-century European designs but in combination with the sturdy woods and rugged individualism of the Midwest.

MISSION FURNITURE

The impact of the British Arts & Crafts ideas on American designers is perhaps best seen in the work and philosophy of Gustav Stickley (1857–1946), editor of the magazine *The Craftsman* from 1901 to 1916. Although he trained as a stonemason, Stickley began working in a relative's chair factory in 1876. He had seen Shaker furniture at the Philadelphia Centennial Exhibition in 1876 and set up his own workshops at Binghampton, New York, to emulate Shaker simplicity. It was not until 1899, when he formed the Gustav Stickley Co. in Eastwood, outside Syracuse, New York, that he was able to put his philosophy into practice. He was already a convert to the ideals of Ruskin and Morris, having visited Britain where he met Voysey and

Lethaby, who was involved with Kenton & Co. Stickley's strong, sturdy furniture was made in native hardwoods, often oak, sometimes inlaid with pewter, iron, or copper or upholstered in leather or canvas, and it was intended to evoke the "simple life" of the early pioneers. The success of his furniture and its adaptability to machine production meant that he had many competitors, including two of his brothers, who founded a rival company in 1902.

Nevertheless, Stickley continued to follow his personal ideals. In 1900, he had established the United Craftsmen in the Craftsman Building in Syracuse. The workshops were reorganized on cooperative lines, although they were abandoned in 1904. During this period, Stickley used *The Craftsman* to promote his ideas about architecture and design. Success encouraged him to open a 12-story Craftsman Building, but his uncompromising devotion to quality made him bankrupt by 1915, for by then "craft" furniture was being mass-produced by rival entrepreneurs and tastes were changing.

New York state was also the home of the community of craftsmen headed by Elbert

Hubbard (1856–1915) and working in East Aurora. Known as Roycrofters, they concentrated on the simplest pieces – oak benches, tables, chairs, and bookcases. The dark, austere work of the two New York groups has become known as Mission furniture because it was designed "with a mission to perform."

ART DECO

Furniture ran the gamut from variations on both the high-style French and functionalist Le Corbusier schools to small-scale architectonic essays and blatant neoclassical designs. Paul T. Frankl, whose 1930 cry "Ornament – crime" was taken up by many American designers, created distinctive skyscraper bookcases and cabinets, with stepped sections and intricate compartments. Kem Weber and J.B. Peters, two Los Angeles designers, also adapted the skyscraper style to their tall pieces, and Chicago-based Abel Faidy produced a leather settee with a whimsical design derived from architecture for a private apartment that could have been custom-built for Radio City.

The metal and wood furniture of Frank Lloyd Wright was not as severe as that of the Bauhaus. For instance, he enameled in warm russet-brown the steel frames of his renowned desk and chair from 1936–9, known as Cherokee Red and designed for the S.C. Johnson & Son building in Racine, Wisconsin, so that the color would complement the American walnut of the chair arms and desk top and the brown upholstery. The two pieces are an essay on the circle, oval, and line – and undoubtedly more inviting to an office-worker than, for example, the shiny chrome and black leather pieces of Breuer *et al*.

Eliel Saarinen, Eugene Schoen, Wolfgang Hoffman, Gilbert Rohde, and Joseph Urban were among the many designers who applied their talents to creating furniture for the American market. On the whole, their pieces were sturdy, mass-produced, and distinctly Modernist, some with echoes of French, German, and Viennese design, others uniquely American in form, color, and materials. Aluminum, chromium, and other metal furniture was

AMERICAN HALL BENCH
◀ OAK
c.1910
This bench is typical of Stickley's work, for which locally available woods were used in order to make it cheap enough for middle-class Americans to own. Its rather austere lines reflect Stickley's debt to Shaker furniture – he described his own pieces as "structural" – and exemplify the maker's belief that when art was brought into the homes of ordinary people they would be encouraged to adopt a plain-living, high-thinking philosophy.

ELBERT HUBBARD AND THE ROYCROFTERS

The Arts & Crafts ideal was applied with enthusiasm by Elbert Hubbard, who was born in Bloomington, Illinois. Until 1893 Hubbard sold soap, but in 1894 he visited Britain and came in contact with William Morris and John Ruskin. On his return to the U.S. Hubbard established the Roycroft Press (named for two English 17th-century bookbinders) at East Aurora, near Buffalo, New York, and he began to publish a magazine, The Philistine. *East Aurora became the center of a thriving artistic community.*

In 1901, Roycroft began producing Mission-style furniture, similar to that produced at United Craftsmen, together with equally simple ceramics and household objects in metal. The furniture, usually in oak, was known as Aurora Colonial Furniture by 1905. Examples of Roycroft furniture tended to be individually made by one craftsman, and apprentices, having mastered one craft, were encouraged to move to another to develop their skills.

Like United Craftsmen, Roycroft had democratic pretensions. Its catalog declared that beautiful objects should be available to everyone. Hubbard had hoped to encourage his craftsmen to work without the aid of machinery, although, like countless other craftsmen, he found that the well-intentioned aim of pricing household goods within the reach of the average income was incompatible with the aim of respecting the creative integrity of the artisan. Hubbard, like others active in the Arts & Crafts Movement in the U.S., compromised by using mechanized processes. However, despite such "heresies," he paid great attention to the working practices and conditions at East Aurora. Whenever possible, individual craftsmen maintained a considerable degree of autonomy in their daily work, while Hubbard, who extended the medieval guild system to extreme limits, called himself "Fra Elbertus." His enthusiasm for Arts & Crafts ideals was condemned by some as naively populist, one critic noting: "He popularized the Arts and Crafts to the point of vulgarity."

---

in the ascendancy, but wooden pieces continued to be popular, with veneers of native woods such as holly, birch, burr maple, and walnut handsomely covering large surface areas. Such synthetic materials as Formica and Lucite were already being used in furniture design, with an armchair by Elsie de Wolfe, its traditional scrolled-backed design of molded Lucite, demonstrating a strange but witty meeting of old and new.

Companies and studios producing metal furniture included the Herman Miller Furniture Co. in Michigan, and Warren McArthur, Kantack & Co. and Deskey-Vollmer in New York. The large makers of wooden furniture included Heywood-Wakefield in Boston, with several companies in Grand Rapids, Michigan, most notably Johnson-Handley-Johnson Co. At the far end of the spectrum was T.H. Robsjohn-Gibbings in California, which worked in a luxurious, fiercely anachronistic neoclassical style that greatly appealed to wealthy clients. Classical motifs such as scrolls, palmettes, lyres, rams' heads, and hoof feet adorned tables, mirrors, and chairs, which were mostly made of partly gilt carved wood and gilt bronze.

MODERNISM AND POSTMODERNISM

After World War II American design flourished with an influx of talented craftsmen and designers such as Walter Gropius and Eliel Saarinen before and during the World Wars. Saarinen's son, Eero, and Charles Eames (1907–78) worked with plastics, fiberglass, and molds in ways that have since been imitated and adapted throughout the world.

In southern California, the architect-designer Charles Sumner Greene (1868–1957) and his brother, Henry Mather (1870–1954), created furniture to complement their grand Spanish-style mansions, producing pieces in rich woods, such as walnut, cedar, and Honduras mahogany, inlaid with fruitwood and precious stones.

From the 1930s, Charles Eames (1907–78) was perhaps the most important 20th-century designer. The streamlined school of the art deco period was exemplified by industrial designers such as Raymond Loewy (1893–1987), Walter Dorwin Teague (1883–1960) and Walter von Nessen, who helped to define modern culture with their tableware, hardware and household appliances.

Important designers of recent years have included George Nelson (b.1907), Harry Bertoia (b.1915), Danny Lane, Floris van den Broecke, Eric de Graffe, and Philippe Starcke.

AMERICAN CHESTS OF DRAWERS

◄ WALNUT
c.1928
These chests of drawers, which have ebony trim and green-lacquered interiors, were designed by Paul T. Frankl in the skyscraper style – architectonic pieces that were intended to be at home in high-rise urban apartments.

FURTHER READING

PATTERN-BOOKS

Books of engraved patterns and ornament have been available since the 16th century. Listed here is a selection of publications that were influential on furniture-makers and designers.

Adam, Robert and James, *Works in Architecture*, 1773–1778 (2nd volume 1779, 3rd volume 1822)

Blondel, Jacques-François, *De la Distribution des Maisons de Plaisance*, 1737

Chippendale, Thomas, *The Gentleman and Cabinet-Maker's Director*, 1754 (2nd edition 1755, 3rd edition 1762)

Eastlake, Charles, *Hints on Household Taste*, 1868

Ince, William, and Mayhew, John, *The Universal System of Household Furniture*, 1759–1762

Hepplewhite, George, *The Cabinet-Maker and Upholsterer's Guide*, 1788

Hope, Thomas, *Household Furniture and Interior Decoration*, 1807

Johnson, Thomas, *Twelve Gerandoles*, 1755

—, —, *A New Book of Ornaments*, 1756–8

—, —, *One Hundred and Fifty New Designs*, 1761

Lock, Matthias, *Six Sconces*, 1744

—, —, *Six Tables*, 1746

—, —, *A Book of Shields*, undated

—, —, A *New Drawing Book of Ornaments, Shields, Compartments, Masks, &c.*, undated

—, —, *A New Book of Ornaments ... in the Chinese Taste*, undated

—, —, *The Principles of Ornament*, undated

Lock, Matthias, and Copland, Henry, *A New Book of Ornaments*, 1752

Loudon, John C., *Encyclopedia of Cottage, Farm and Villa Furniture*, 1833

Manwaring, Robert, *The Cabinet and Chair-Maker's Real Friend and Companion*, 1765

Passe II, Crispin de, *Oficina Arcularia*, 1621

Percier and Fontaine, *Receuil des décorations intérieurs*, 1801 (2nd edition 1812)

Pugin, Augustus, W.N., *Gothic Furniture in the Style of the 15th Century*, 1835

—, —, *The True Principle of Pointed or Christian Architecture*, 1841

Shearer, Thomas, Hepplewhite and others, *The Cabinet-Maker's London Book of Prices*, 1788

Sheraton, Thomas, *The Cabinet-Maker and Upholsterer's Drawing Book*, 1791–3

—, —, *Cabinet Dictionary*, 1803

Smith, George, *Collection of Designs for Household Furniture and Interior Decoration*, 1808

—, —, *Collection of Ornamental Designs after the Antique*, 1812

—, —, *Cabinet Maker and Upholsterer's Guide*, 1826

Stalker, J., and Parker, G., *A Treatise of Japanning and Varnishing*, 1688

Stuart, James, *The Antiquities of Athens*, 1762

Talbert, Bruce, *Gothic Forms Applied to Furniture*, 1867

Vredeman de Vries, Hans, *Différents Pourtraicts de Menuiserie*, c.1588

REFERENCE BOOKS

Adams, Steven, *The Arts & Crafts Movement*, Tiger Books, London, 1982

Agius, Pauline, *British Furniture, 1880–1915*, London, 1978

Agius, Pauline, and Jones, Stephen (introduction), *Ackermann's Regency Furniture & Interiors*, Marlborough, 1984

Bayer, Patricia, *Art Deco Source Book*, Phaidon Press, London, 1988

Bazin, Germain, *Baroque and Rococo*, London, 1964

Beard, G., *Grinling Gibbons*, London, 1989

Beard, G., and Gilbert, Christopher (eds.), *Dictionary of English Furniture Makers 1660–1840*, Leeds, 1986

Bridge, Mark, *An Encyclopedia of Desks*, Wellfleet Press, New Jersey, 1988

Burr, Grace H., *Hispanic Furniture*, New York, 1964

Cathers, David M., *Furniture of the American Arts and Crafts Movement*, New York, 1981

Chinnery, Victory, *Oak Furniture – The British Tradition*, Woodbridge, 1979

Collard, Frances, *Regency Furniture*, Woodbridge, 1985

Collins, Michael, *Towards Post-Modernism: Design Since 1851*, British Museum Press, London, 1987 (rev. ed. 1994)

Comstock, Helen, *American Furniture*, New York, 1962

Cooper, Jeremy, *Victorian and Edwardian Furniture and Interiors*, London, 1987

Cornelius, Charles A., *Early American Furniture*, New York, 1926

Downs, Joseph, *American Furniture in the Henry Francis du Point Winterthur Museum: Queen Anne and Chippendale Periods*, New York, 1952

Dubrow, Eileen and Richard, *American Furniture of the 19th Century, 1840–1880*, New York, 1983

Eames, Penelope, "Furniture in England, France and the Netherlands, 12th-15th Centuries," *Furniture History Society Journal*, Victoria & Albert Museum, London, 1975

Edwards, Ralph, *The Shorter Dictionary of English Furniture*, London, 1964

Erikson, Svend, *Early Neoclassicism in France*, London, 1974

Fairbanks, Jonathan L., and Trent, Robert F. (eds.), *New England Begins* (exhibition catalog, 3 vols), Boston, 1982

Flannagan, J. Michael, *American Furniture from the Kaufman Collection*, New York, 1986

Furniture of Charles and Henry Greene: An Introductory Booklet, Huntington Museum, San Marino, California, 1987

George Bullock Cabinet-Maker (exhibition catalog), London, 1988

Green, D., *Grinling Gibbons: His Work as a Carver and Statuary*, London, 1964

de Groer, Léon, *Les Arts Décoratifs de 1790 à 1850*, Fribourg, 1985

Hardy, William, *A Guide to Art Nouveau Style*, Magna Books, Leicester, 1986

Hayward, Helena (ed.), *World Furniture*, London, 1990

Heskett, John, *Industrial Design*, Thames and Hudson, London, 1980

Horsham, Michael, *'20s & '30s Style*, Grange Books, London, 1994

Janneau, Guillaume, *Le Meuble Bourgeois en France*, Editions Garnier

Jervis, S. (ed.), *Printed Furniture Designs before 1650*, London, 1974

Jourdain, Margaret, *English Decoration & Furniture of the Early Renaissance*, London, 1924

Joy, Edward, *A Pictorial Dictionary of Nineteenth Century Furniture Design*, Woodbridge, 1977

Kaplan, Wendy (consultant), *Encyclopedia of Arts and Crafts: The International Arts Movement 1850–1920*, Doubleday, New York and London, 1989

King, Constance, *An Encyclopedia of Sofas*, Wellfleet Press, New Jersey, 1989

Ledoux-Lebard, Denise, *Les Ébénistes Parisiens (1795–1830)*, Paris, 1951

Lucie-Smith, Edward, *Furniture: A Concise History*, Thames and Hudson, London, 1979

MacGregor, A., *The Late King's Goods*, London and Oxford, 1989

Macquoid, Percy, *The Age of Walnut*, London, 1905

Mallalieu, Huon (ed.), *The Illustrated History of Antiques*, Aurum Press, London, 1991

Mercer, Eric, *Furniture 700–1700*, London, 1969

Miller Jr, Edgar G., *Standard Book of American Antique Furniture*, New York, 1950

Montgomery, Charles F., *American Furniture: The Federal Period in the Henry Francis du Pont Winterthur Museum*, New York, 1966

Morrazzoni, Giuseppe, *Il Mobilio Italiano*, Florence, 1940

Nagel, Charles, *American Furniture*, New York, 1949

O'Neill, Amanda (ed.), *Introduction to the Decorative Arts: 1890 to the Present Day*, Gallery Books, New York, 1990

Ormsbee, Thomas H., *Field Guide to American Victorian Furniture*, Boston, 1951

Payne, Christopher, *19th Century European Furniture*, London, 1985

Schweiger, Werner J., *Wiener Werkstätte: Design in Vienna, 1903–1932*, New York, 1984

Thornton, Peter, *Authentic Decor 1620–1920*

—, —, *Seventeenth Century Interior Decoration in England, France and Holland*, London and New Haven, 1978

Trent, Robert (ed.), *Pilgrim Century Furniture*, New York 1980

van de Lemme, Arie, *A Guide to Art Deco Style*, New Burlington Books, London, 1986

Viaux, Jacqueline, *Le Meuble en France*, Paris, 1962

Ward, Gerald W.R., *American Case Furniture in the Mabel Brady Garvan and Other Collections at Yale University*, New Haven, 1988

Wilhide, Elizabeth, *The Mackintosh Style: Decor & Design*, Pavilion Books, London, 1995

Wills, Geoffrey, *English Furniture 1550–1760*, London, 1971

—, —, *English Furniture 1760–1900*, London, 1971

Yates, Simon, *An Encyclopedia of Chairs*, Wellfleet Press, New Jersey, 1988

—, —, *An Encyclopedia of Tables*, New Burlington Books, London, 1989

GLOSSARY

Words in SMALL CAPITALS have their own entries.

acanthus A classical ornamental device based on the prickly, indented leaves of the acanthus plant, used especially in the CAPITALS of Corinthian and Composite columns. Used especially on the late 17th- and 18th-century furniture.

Adirondack rustic/hickory Summer furniture made of hickory at several factories in Indiana between 1898 and 1940. Hicory saplings were bent into shape on metal frames, and the inner bark was cut into strips for the woven sections.

amorini Cupids carved on post-1660 furniture, especially chairs. *See also* PUTTO.

anthemion A classical ornament consisting of a band of alternating floral forms based on the honeysuckle flower. A single motif based on the honeysuckle is called an anthemion. Often found carved, inlaid, or painted on English Adam and Regency furniture.

apron An ornamental projection below a RAIL, often shaped and carved.

apron piece An ornamental rail on the underframe of chests of drawers, etc., and between the tops of legs of tables and chairs.

arabesque An ornament of scrolls, leaves, or geometric patterns, representing Islamic designs. Found in "Seaweed" MARQUETRY from *c.*1690 and on GESSO tables between *c.*1690 and 1730.

arcading A series of round-topped arches, frequantly used decoratively, especially in early carved furniture.

art deco A term deriving from the Exposition Internationale des Arts Décoratifs et Industriels Modernes held in Paris in 1925. It is generally used today to describe progressive designs from *c.*1910 to 1940, ranging from luxurious and expensive Parisian pieces to Modernist examples created by industrial designers.

art nouveau (*Jugendstil* in Germany; *stile Liberty* in Italy) The French term for an essentially curvilinear style, which was often asymmetrical and derived from organic forms, especially stems and leaves. Developed in the 19th century, its influence extended into the 1920s.

Arts & Crafts Movement A design movement of the second half of the 19th century. British and American exponents attempted to create beautiful, well-designed artifacts that would improve the quality of life through their daily use.

astragal (1) A small, convex MOLDING; (2) glazing bars in the form of meaning (1).

ball-and-claw foot Sometimes claw-and-ball foot. A foot in the form of a claw clutching a ball, often used in conjunction with a CABRIOLE LEG. Popular in England and America in the 18th century.

ball foot The spherical base of a turned leg. Found on late 17th-century furniture.

► OAK
1916–22
Frank Lloyd Wright designed the oak side chair for the Imperial Hotel, Tokyo. It is an essay in geometry – all angles and no curves – and like many of his creations it is attractive but not very comfortable.

baluster or **banister** A short supporting column, bulbous near the base, that is used in series to form a balustrade.

baluster-turned *See* TURNED LEG.

banding A decorative border. Veneer was often used in bands to form decorative borders to the main surface. Cross-banding was cut across the grain, while feather or herringbone banding was cut with the grain at an angle so that two strips, laid side by side, resembled a feather.

banister *See* BALUSTER.

barley-sugar turned *See* TURNED LEG.

barley-twist turned *See* TURNED LEG.

baroque A decorative style that originated in Italy and reached its height in the 17th century. It was characterized by heavy and exuberant forms. Its influence varied from country to country, but baroque furniture tends to be sculptural and often architectural in form and is frequently gilded, with human figures, scrolls, and shells much in evidence. It was seen in England between *c.*1725 and 1750, particularly in the gilt, carved furniture of William Kent.

Bauhaus A school of architecture and industrial arts, established at Weimar, Germany, in 1919 by Walter Gropius. At first artist/craftsman pieces were made, but after the move to Desau in 1925 their main focus of interest was in industrial design with an emphasis on functionalism.

beading A three-dimensional decorative motif in the form of a series of round beads in a single line or a very fine half-round MOLDING. *See also* COCK BEADING.

bentwood Wood that is bent by steam or boiling water in special molds. Developed in the 1830s in Austria by Michael Thonet (1796–1871), his Vienna factory used mainly beech. It was a popular material for chairs and for light sofas or *chaises longues* with wicker seats and backs.

Biedermeier (German) A term used to denote: (1) the period 1815–48; (2) the decorative style, popular in Germany, Austria and Scandinavia in the 1820s, 1830s and 1840s, characterized by solid, unpretentious furniture in light-colored woods. Biedermeier was a newspaper caricature symbolizing the uncultured bourgeoisie.

bird's eye maple Maple with a regular burr pattern resembling a bird's eye. It was very popular in the 19th century.

blind fret A cut-work design against a flat background.

bobbin-turned *See* TURNED LEG.

bolection molding MOLDING of OGEE section projecting around the edges of panels.

bombé An exaggeratedly curved and swollen form characteristic of the ROCOCO style.

boulle A distinctive form of marquetry decoration making use of metal and other veneers, usually brass and tortoiseshell, to form a rich

GERMAN SOFA

▼ MAPLE
early 19th century
This fine example of the Biedermeier style is one of a pair. The shaping of the arms is both unusual and skilful.

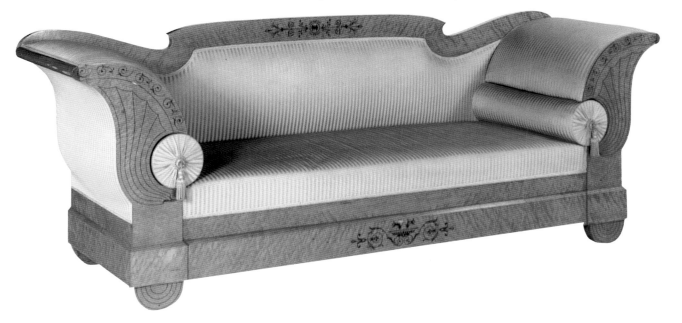

ENGLISH DINING CHAIR

▶ WALNUT
*c.*1730
The shape of this chair's seat, as well as the vigorously carved lion masks on the knees of the cabriole legs are characteristic of the best examples of early Georgian seat furniture. The chair has carved front legs and a vase-shaped splat. The upholstery is embroidered.

AMERICAN TEA TABLE

▶ MAHOGANY
*c.*1765
This Chippendale-style table, which is very similar to tea tables made in England *c.*1750, has a simple, dignified shape, a plain circular top, a turned column and tripod base – all features of European pieces. It is also made of the favored English wood of this period, mahogany, but it was probably made in Boston, Massachusetts.

pattern. It takes its name from André-Charles Boulle (1642–1732), ÉBÉNISTE to Louis XIV, who perfected but did not invent the technique, which was known in Italy since the late 17th century. The method of production, cutting the design from layers of brass and tortoiseshell glued together, resulted in two sets of veneer. One, known as *première partie*, has the pattern in brass against tortoiseshell; the other, known as *contre partie*, is the other way round. It was first produced in England by Gerrit Jensen at the end of the 17th century and revived during the Regency.

bracket foot A square foot, used on case furniture from *c.*1690.

breakfast table A snap-top table. The top tilts vertically on the pedestal for storage. "Snap" refers to the sound made by the catch (which is like a cylinder lock) when the table is tilted down for use.

breakfront A word used to describe a piece of furniture in which one section or more projects from the main body.

brown furniture A word used in the antique trade to refer to the plain mahogany furniture

made in England during the Georgian period.

bulb-turned *See* TURNED LEG.

bun foot A flattened form of BALL FOOT.

bureau The French word for all kinds of writing desks, often further defined – e.g., *bureau plat* or *bureau à cylindre*. The word is derived from *bure*, a coarse cloth used to cover the writing tables of clerks and secretaries in the Middle Ages. In Britain "bureau" has come to mean a slope-front writing desk of traditional pattern; in America it is used to describe a dressing chest, often with a mirror.

burl The American term for burr. *See* VENEER.

burr The British term for burl. *See* VENEER.

C-scroll A scroll in the shape of a letter C, a favorite ROCOCO motif.

cabochon An oval or round boss used decoratively, usually in conjunction with other motifs.

cabriole leg A sinuous tapering leg, curving at the knee, in toward the ankle and out again at the foot.

canapé (French) A sofa with arms.

canted When legs or projected members are set at an angle to the corner of a piece, they are known as canted legs or canted corners.

capital The head of a column, usually decorated according to the different architectural orders – i.e., Doric (plain, disc-like), Ionic (with four scroll corners), Corinthian (bell-shaped with bands of ACANTHUS leaves), Tuscan

(circular and plain), or Composite (a combination of Ionic and Corinthian).

cartouche A lozenge- or shield-shaped ornamental panel, which is decorative in its own right but may also carry an inscription, monogram, crest, etc.

caryatid An architectural motif consisting of a column in the form of a female figure, which is also often found on carved furniture as a bronze mount. (A male figure is known as a telamon; plural, telamones.)

cassapanca (Italian) A SETTLE with arms and back. The finest examples were made in the late 16th century.

cassone (Italian) A form of richly carved low chest, made as a formal piece of furniture.

cavetto Concave cornice MOLDING, especially on walnut pieces.

chair-back sofa A sofa whose backrest gives the appearance of from two to four chairs set side by side.

chaise longue (French) A term for a long, upholstered seat with a backrest, intended for only one person to recline on.

chamfer A narrow, flat surface formed by cutting away the apex of an angle between two surfaces, thus removing the sharp corner. Hence, chamfered leg, chamfered STRETCHER, etc.

channeling Fluting or grooves cut in the STILES of oak furniture and in the frames of Hepplewhite chairs.

chasing The tooling of a metal's surface. Bronze furniture mounts were chased after casting to remove blemishes and sharpen the detail before gilding.

chesterfield An upholstered sofa with the arms and back forming a low, unbroken line. Deeply padded and often buttoned.

chinoiserie A European imitation of Chinese decoration, usually more fanciful than accurate and frequently used to give an exotic touch to a basically European design.

chintz Cotton or calico with a printed pattern and sometimes glazed. First versions were exported to Europe from India in the 17th century.

chip carving Shallow ornamentation on oak

furniture, worked with chisel and gouge.

cipher A monogram or symbol.

ciseleur (French) A craftsman who used a variety of chisels and other tools to finish bronze mounts once they had been cast by a *fondeur* (founder). After finishing, they were usually gilded by a *doreur*. Under the guild system operating in Paris in the 18th century, *fondeurs-ciseleurs* and *doreurs* had separate corporations.

classical A word usually used to refer to the work of ancient Greece and Rome.

classicism The interpretation of the classical traditions.

club foot The foot seen most often on a cabriole leg. Known as a pad foot when set on a disc.

cock beading A very fine, half-round MOLDING applied around the edges of drawer fronts, used especially between *c.*1730 and 1800.

confident A sofa with attached chairs set at either end. Sometimes two sofas were set back to back with a chair set between them at each end.

console (1) a bracket, normally scrolled; (2) a table, originally French, introduced to England in the early 18th century, that was supported against the wall by its front legs or by a single support.

Consulate The period of government in France between 1799 and 1804.

contre partie See BOULLE.

conversation A sofa with seats arranged back to

▲ SIMULATED BAMBOO
*c.*1810
The ten legs of the Regency four-seater, chair-back sofa are united by plain and turned stretchers. An unusually complex piece, it is made of simulated bamboo. In 1803 Thomas Sheraton had described how beech was turned in imitation of bamboo, and the taste for such faux-bamboo continued to some extent throughout the 19th century. It was an especial favorite in Regency England, especially for the furnishing of interiors in the chinoiserie taste.

back or facing, so that sitters could converse discreetly. In some Victorian pattern-books these are described as ottomans.

cornice An architectural term used in the description of furniture for the top MOLDING of bookcases, cabinets, and other large pieces, many of which were conceived along architectural lines.

cornucopia A horn of plenty, used decoratively as a shell-like horn overflowing with fruit.

cresting The carved ornament on the TOP RAIL of a chair back.

cresting rail *See* TOP RAIL.

cretonne Strong, unglazed cotton with a printed pattern.

crinoline stretcher An inward-curving STRETCHER designed to accommodate a full skirt.

crocket A leaf-like projection, frequently placed on angles, arches, and pinnacles in gothic architecture and found as a decorative device on gothic-style furniture.

cross-banding *See* BANDING.

crosspiece A MEMBER that stretches across a piece of furniture.

cross-stretcher A STRETCHER, sometimes decorated, that runs across a piece of furniture.

cut-card work A form of slightly raised decoration, mainly found on silverware, consisting of thin sheets cut into patterns and soldered on to the surface.

day-bed A sofa on which one person can recline during the day, sometimes for the formal reception of visitors.

demi-lune (French) Half-moon shape.

dentil MOLDING of small rectangular blocks, often found on the cornices of mahogany furniture.

doreur *See* CISELEUR.

dowel A wooden peg used for joining timer, especially oak.

drop-in seat A removable, upholstered or caned seat that rests on clocks inside the SEAT RAILS of a chair.

ébéniste (French) A term for a cabinet-maker, a specialist in veneered furniture, as distinct from a *menuisier* (joiner), who specialized in carved pieces like chairs or beds. A MAITRE of the Paris furniture-makers' guild (*Corporation des Menuisiers-ébénistes*) was not bound to specialize, but the distinction was generally observed until the end of the 18th century.

ebonized wood Cheap woods such as beech were stained black to imitate ebony and used as stringing in the late Georgian period.

egg and dart A classical ornament, often carved on ovolo MOLDINGS.

escutcheon (1) A plate surrounding and protecting a keyhole; (2) a shield-shaped mount or armorial shield used as the central ornament of a pediment.

espagnolette A decorative motif in the form of a female head surrounded by a stylized lace ruff, much favored as mounts during the RÉGENCE period.

estampille The stamp with the name and initials of a *maître-ébéniste* that was obligatory on French furniture from about 1750 until the Revolution. The mark was struck with a cold punch rather than branded, although delicate pieces could be signed in ink. Long names were sometimes shortened – e.g., BVRB for Bernard van Risenburgh – and the marks were usually in

ITALIAN COMMODE

▼ WALNUT
mid-18th century
The exuberant inlays and decorations of ivory, mother-of-pearl, and gilt metal on this north Italian *bombé* commode belong to a style already popular in the late 17th century. Together with the elaborate handles and escutcheons, the inlaid flowers and other motifs illustrate the enthusiasm for decorative effects.

an inconspicuous place, often accompanied by the mark of the *Corporation des Jurés Menuisiers-ébénistes* – JME conjoined – a quality control mark. Furniture made for the crown did not have to be stamped, and royal craftsmen were exempt.

fauteuil (French) An upholstered chair with open arms, sometimes with armrests. The word was in use from the late 17th century.

feather banding *See* BANDING.

festoon A NEOCLASSICAL decorative motif in the form of a looped garland of flowers, fruit, and foliage.

figure The natural grain patterns of a veneer are known as figuring.

finial An ornamental projection from the top of a piece of furniture, often a knob, ball, acorn, urn, or flame.

fluting A decoration in the form of shallow, parallel grooves, especially on columns and pilasters or on the legs of furniture. Used from the 16th century onwards.

fondeur See CISELEUR.

fretwork Carved geometrical patterns, either in relief or pierced, or sawn with a fretsaw.

frieze An architectural term for the flat surface beneath a CORNICE, used loosely to describe flat, horizontal members in furniture, especially below table tops and the cornices of case furniture. Also used to describe a band of decoration usually found on the TOP RAIL of a sofa.

gadroon A form of decorative edging, usually in the form of a series of convex curved lobes or repeated spiral ribs resembling rope-twist.

gallery A miniature railing, often of brass, placed around the edge of a table or desk top to prevent papers and other small objects from slipping off.

gesso A mixture of powdered chalk and parchment size, used as the basis for GILDING.

gilding The application of gold to the surface of another material. Bronze mounts were frequently gilded to prevent tarnishing, especially in France. Wood was also gilded for decorative effect.

◄ *BOIS CLAIR*
*c.*1825
More comfortable forms for seat furniture became popular, as is evident in the flowing curves of this armchair. The light colored wood has a delicate inlay of darker wood, and the upholstery is stamped with neoclassical motifs.

gilt *See* GILDING.

gimp Simple silk or cotton braid used to conceal joins.

gothic A decorative style based on the pointed arches, cluster columns, spires, and other elements of late medieval architecture. Gothic revivals have influenced furniture design at several periods, particularly in Britain in the mid-18th century and again in the mid-19th century.

grisaille Monochromatic decoration in tones of gray.

gros point (French) A term for stitched work on canvas. The regular stitches are laid over two threads so that the effect is coarser than that of PETIT POINT.

guilloche A form of decoration consisting of interlaced bands or ribbons, circles or ovals, sometimes enclosing motifs, used as a border on 16th-century and late Georgian furniture.

herringbone banding *See* BANDING.

hump-back A sofa with a sudden sweeping curve.

inlay Although it is often used to mean mar-

ENGLISH WRITING CABINET

▼ WALNUT WITH FLORAL MARQUETRY
*c.*1690
The base of this William and Mary piece is made of two short and two long drawers beneath a fall-front writing compartment containing drawers and pigeonholes arranged around a central cupboard. There is a further concealed drawer with a cushion-shaped marquetry front in the frieze just below the overhanging cornice.

quetry, the word inlay strictly refers to decorative materials, such as ivory or ebony, set into the surface of solid wood, as distinct from VENEER, which covers the whole surface.

japanning The term used in America and Britain for techniques imitating the oriental lacquer-work that began to arrive in Europe, via the Dutch East India Company, in the 17th century.

joinery The word used to describe furniture formed of vertical and horizontal members, united by mortise-and-tenon joints and supporting panels.

Jugendstil See ART NOUVEAU.

lancet An arch with a pointed top.

lattice-work A pattern or structure of regularly crossed lines.

lion paw foot A foot carved in the form of a lion's paw.

lit de repos (French) A day-bed, intended for one person, introduced in the early 17th century.

love seat A small sofa introduced in the mid-17th century. Sometimes called a courting chair because two people needed to sit close together in it.

lowboy A late 17th- or 18th-century American dressing-table on legs, sometimes found combined with a slope-front desk.

maître Under the Paris guild system a master-craftsman who, having served an apprenticeship and paid a fee, was entitled to own a workshop and to stamp his pieces. *See also* ESTAMPILLE.

marchand-mercier Under the Paris guild system *marchands-merciers* combined the roles of furniture dealers and interior decorators. They were not allowed to run their own workshops but often exerted considerable influence on fashion by acting as intermediaries between customer and craftsman.

marquetry The use of VENEERS (woods of different colors, bone, ivory, mother-of-pearl, tortoiseshell, etc.) to form decorative designs, such as scrolls, flowers, and landscapes. Abstract geometrical patterns formed in the same manner are known as parquetry.

member Any of the structural components – RAILS, UPRIGHTS, STRETCHERS, etc. – of a piece of joined furniture.

menuisier See ÉBÉNISTE.

méridienne (French) An 18th-century day-bed, curving upwards at one end or both ends.

miter A joint in which the two pieces connect after being cut at half the angle of the joint – i.e., two pieces cut at 45° to form a right angle.

modular seating A type of seating in which complementary units, built to standard sizes, can be linked or placed against one another to form a variety of arrangements.

monopodium A term, derived from the

ITALIAN CABINET

◀ *SCAGIOLA* WITH
EBONIZED
AND PARTLY GILT
MOLDINGS
mid-17th century
In the 16th century the
grand-dukes of Tuscany
revived the Roman art of
making *scagliola*, a
composition material of
ground marble, gypsum,
plaster of Paris, and glue.
This was applied like
paint, allowed to dry,
then polished. It was so
like marble and *pietra
dura* that it was known as
counterfeit marble. The
architectural treatment of
this cabinet, with the
pediment over the central
cupboard and ripple
moldings, is similar to
contemporary work from
other areas, but the
scagliola decoration of
birds and flowers and the
geometric pattern on the
sides have their origins in
the distinctively Italian
craft of *pietra dura*.

Greek, to describe a piece of furniture with a single foot – e.g., a table that stands on a single column.

moquette Fabric with a wool pile. Some varieties are cut in imitation of cut silk velvet.

mortise-and-tenon joints The basic method of joining the framework of a piece of furniture. the basic method of joining the framework of a piece of furniture. The tenon is a projection (usually a slim rectangle) at the end of a RAIL, and it fits exactly into the mortise, a cavity cut in the side of an UPRIGHT. The tenon is normally secured by dowels.

molding A length of wood or other material applied to the surface of a piece of furniture. The shaped section of a molding is usually made up from a number of curves, and there are various standard types (ASTRAGAL, cavetto, OGEE, ovolo, etc.), mostly of architectural origin.

mounts Decorative motifs, usually of brass or gilt bronze, fixed to cabinet-work.

neoclassicism The predominant decorative style of the second half of the 18th century. Based on the restrained use of Greek and Roman architectural form and ornament, it is characterized by a sober, rectilinear emphasis, which was a conscious reaction to the exuberance of the ROCOCO.

ogee An arch with a slender, S-shaped line with two molded curves meeting at the apex.

ormolu Gilt bronze. A term derived from the French phrase *dorure d'or moulu* (literally, gilding with gold paste).

out-scrolled Curving outwards in a nearly horizontal plane.

outward-splayed At a significant angle from perpendicular, the distance at the bottom between the legs being greater than that at the top.

over-stuffed A type of furniture in which the stuffing and upholstery cover the frame.

panel A flat surface supported by RAILS and STILES in joined furniture.

parcel gilt Gilded in part only.

parquetry *See* MARQUETRY.

patera A neoclassical decorative motif, either oval or round, resembling a stylized flower or rosette.

petit point (French) The term used for embroidery in small stitches on canvas, worked to, at most, 15 stitches an inch. *See also* GROS POINT.

pierced Carved ornamentation is described as pierced when the design is cut right through the piece, as in FRETWORK.

pietra dura (Italian) Ornamental work in hard stone, such as jasper or agate, widely used for table tops and decorative cabinets in the late

▶ WALNUT WITH CANE BACK AND SEAT

*c.*1670

The wide mesh of the cane seat would have been covered by a cushion. The spiral turned supports of the legs and back later gave way to scroll legs and carved decoration. The cresting, back panel frame, and front stretcher of this transitional chair are treated as decorative areas.

▼ KINGWOOD AND GILT BRONZE

*c.*1735

This commode is a fine example of the bold gilt bronze mounts favored by its maker, Charles Cressent (1685–1768), who was France's most talented cabinet-maker of the Régence period.

16th century.

pilaster A shallow column attached to a piece of furniture.

première partie See BOULLE.

punch-work Decoration achieved by the use of punches struck by a hammer.

putto (plural, putti) A naked infant, often winged, used as a decorative motif. Also sometimes known as a cherub, cupid, amorino, or amoretto.

rail A horizontal MEMBER used in the construction of jointed furniture.

ratchet A toothed wheel that engages with a catch to prevent motion in one direction while allowing it in the other.

reeding Decoration in the form of parallel ribbing, especially on columns and pilasters or on the legs of furniture.

Régence The regency of the duc d'Orléans in France, 1715–24, while Louis XV was a minor.

Renaissance The rebirth of ancient Roman values in the arts that began in Italy in the 14th century and gradually replaced the gothic style in most of Europe during the following 250 years. Renaissance designers were inspired by the sculpture and architectural remains of the ancient world, and their furniture reflects this.

repoussé work A form of embossed decoration

produced by hammering sheet metal from the underside.

ribbon-back Wood carved in imitation of ribbons and bows on chair and sofa backs. A style popularized by Chippendale.

rocaille Stylized and fanciful rock and shell decoration, used by extension to refer to many of the decorative forms of ROCOCO.

rococo A decorative style that spread from France during the first half of the 18th century. It was characterized by delicate curved outlines, C-scrolls, fantastic organic forms and a tendency towards symmetry in ornamental details.

romayne work A form of ornamental motif, originally Italian but found on early Renaissance furniture from the Netherlands and England, consisting of low-relief ROUNDELS containing profiles of human heads.

roundel A circular form of decoration.

saver leg A leg of a chair, table, etc. that is curved and tapered, in the manner of a cavalry saber.

salon (French) A reception room.

saloon A large, formal reception room in a large country mansion in Britain.

scroll couch A couch with a scrolled end.

seat rail The horizontal framework that supports the seat of a jointed chair.

serpentine In the form of an undulating curve, convex at the center and concave at the sides.

settee An upholstered sofa.

settle A wooden bench-like seat with a back and arms, sometimes also with a box base for storage.

sgabelle (Italian) A Renaissance chair without arms. Early examples had three legs, with a solid seat and board back. The carving on the back became very elaborate.

show-wood The wood, often polished, that is revealed on a piece of furniture.

side rail A wooden connecting strut at the side of a chair or sofa.

spindle A slim, turned rod, frequently used as an UPRIGHT in chair backs.

splat The central upright member of a chair back that joins the seat to the top RAIL.

spoon-back The back of a chair or sofa that is curved like a spoon.

squab cushion A stuffed cushion with straight sides. Originally used in 17th-century day-beds, it is primarily connected today with MODULAR SEATING, which uses rubber or foam cushions.

square-section leg A leg that would be square if cut at right angles but that may also be tapering or shaped in some other way.

stile A vertical MEMBER used in the construction of joined furniture.

Stile Liberty See ART NOUVEAU.

strap-work A form of decoration, particularly popular in northern Europe in the 16th and 17th centuries, resembling interlaced, pierced, and scrolled bands of leather.

stretcher A horizontal cross-piece used to join and strengthen the legs of a piece of furniture.

stringing Thin strips of wood or metal inlay, used to decorate furniture.

strung border A border decorated with STRINGING.

stuff-over A term used when the upholstery of a chair covers the framework rather than being a panel within it. Hence, stuff-over seat.

swag A decorative motif in the form of a cloth; similar to a FESTOON.

table en chiffonnier A small 18th-century French work table with a high GALLERY around the top and several drawers in the FRIEZE, often fitted with a writing drawer or slide.

tempera Powder color mixed with thinned egg yolk. The paint work dries quickly and gives a tough surface.

tête-â-tête (French) A term used to describe various constructions in which the seats are angled towards one another. *See also* CONFIDENT.

timbers Another name for the heavy wooden framework of a piece of furniture.

top rail The topmost horizontal member that joins the UPRIGHTS of a chair back. Also known as a cresting rail or yoke rail.

torchère A flat-topped stand, usually ornamented with gilding and carving, designed to hold a candelabrum.

tracery Ornamental open-work.

triglyph A three-grooved tablet in the Doric

FRENCH *TORCHÈRES*

▼ GILT WOOD
*c.*1725
Torchères such as these were used to augment the main lighting of a room whose chief source of light would have been a chandelier or sconces. This substantial pair is cream painted, heightened with gilt, and features sculptural carving. They are probably made of a softwood such as beech, and they are in Régence style, which was popular in both France and England in the early 18th century. The blackamoor *guéridon* is a 19th-century copy of a late 17th- or early 18th-century Italian or French figure.

frieze, used in neoclassical ornamentation.

turned leg A leg shaped on a lathe, usually circular in section, mainly fashionable before the beginning of the 18th century. Turned legs are found in many traditional styles – for example, baluster (bulbous at the base and slim toward the top); barley-sugar or barley-twist (a double spiral resembling a piece of the confectionery of the same name); bobbin (a series of small bulbs or bobbins); bobbin and ring (small bulbs interspersed with rings); bulb (a large bulbous swelling of elongated, melon form, often carved and used with a base and capital to form a leg); and vase (in the shape of a vase, usually slim at the base and gradually increasing in diameter towards the top).

underframe The supporting structure of a piece of furniture, including legs, STRETCHERS, and other braces.

uprights The vertical parts of a chair back, formed as a continuation of the rear legs.

vase-turned *See* TURNED LEG.

veneer A very thin sheet, usually of wood, applied to the surface of a piece of furniture. Veneers cut from knotty areas of the tree are particularly decorative and known as burrs, hence burr walnut, for example.

vernis Martin A generic term for varnish and lacquer (japanning) used in France in imitatioin of oriental lacquer; specifically referring to the four Martin brothers, who were granted a monopoly for imitation relief lacquer in 1730, which was renewed in 1744. Their specialty was painted furniture, to which *vernis Martin* most often refers.

vitruvian scroll A classically derived ornamental device in the form of a series of scrolls resembling waves.

woods Although some woods are distinctive, the majority have so many species that it is hard to identify each separate type. Ebony, for example, comes in 90 different tree types, all of which have different grains and characteristics, such as hardness and color. Zebrawood, for example, closely resembles calamander (from Sri Lanka) and coromandel (from India) and can be difficult to distinguish from black rosewood and striped ebony.

X-frame An arrangement of diagonal STRETCHERS joining the front and back legs of a piece of furniture and crossing to form an X.
X-stretcher *See* X-FRAME.

yoke rail *See* TOP RAIL.

ENGLISH TABLE

▼ OAK
mid-19th century
This center table shows clearly how the Victorian revival of the medieval gothic style penetrated every area of design, including tables, chairs, and other items of household furniture. The stark simplicity of this table is truly gothic, and it would have fitted well into an early fortified manor house or the refectory of a monastery.

INDEX

A

Aalto, Alvar 139, *140*
Acke, J.A.G. 139
Ackermann's *Repository* 90
Adam, Robert 50–1
Adam style 87, 112–13, 120
Aesthetic movement 97–8
Affleck, Thomas 78
Anglo-Dutch style 44, 67–9, 73
ancient furniture 12, *12, 13*
architectural style 19, 20, 23, 32, 33, 47, 52, 54, 57, 115
armchairs 26, 29, *29, 33,* 34, *37, 39, 48, 50,* 53, *54, 55, 85, 88, 99, 102,* 109, 126, 142
art deco 110, 120
    American 141–2, *143*
    French *124,* 125, 126, 127
    German 135
art nouveau 132
    Austrian 137
    Belgian 128, 129, *129*
    English 98
    French *101,* 102–4, *102, 103, 104,* 124, 126
    German 132–3
    Italian 130–1, *131*
Arts & Crafts Movement 9, 96–7, *96, 97,* 105, 117, 122, 123, 126, 128, 129, 137, 140, 142
    Dutch 138
Ashbee, Charles Robert 96, 98, 121, 134
auricular style 39

B

Baillie Scott, M.H. 121
Barnsley, Sidney 98, 122, 123
baroque 7
    Dutch 69
    English 46
    German 38–9, 63, 64, 66
    Italian 37, 59
Basile, Ernesto 130, *131*
Bazel, K.P.C. de 138
Bauhaus style 120, 123, 126, 135–6, 141
bed canopies 15, 18, 31, 32, 79, 88
bed hangings 8, 9, 15, 44, *46*
beds
    American 17thC 41; 18thC 77, 79
    box 22
    Dutch 18thC 69
    English 15–16thC 18–19;

17thC 26, 27, 31–2; 18thC *46;* 19thC 88, 90, 92, 93
    French Renaissance 20; 17thC 32; 18thC 55, 57, 58; 19thC 101
    Italian Renaissance 20, 22; 17thC 37;
    medieval 15, *15*
    Melville 32
    Portuguese 18thC 63
    Sparver 15
    tent 15
Belter, John Henry 116, *116*
benches 14, 18, 40, 141, *141*
Benson, W.A.S. 98, 122
bentwood furniture 110, 124, *136,* 137, *138,* 139
bergère 53, 124
Bergsten, Carl 139
Bertsch, Karl 133, 134
Bertoia, Harry, 124, 143
Bevan, Charles 98
Biedermeier style 106, 107, 108–10, *108, 109,* 111, 112, 137–8
Bing, Siegfried 103, 124
Bonzanigo, Giuseppe Maria 62
bookcases 27, 30, *30,* 46, 48, 51, 57, *93,* 109, 113, 115
    bureau 59, 68, 76, 78, 79, 113
    dwarf library 88
    marble-topped 86
    skyscraper 141
Boulle, André Charles 35, 36, 38, 46
boulle marquetry 35, 36, *36,* 37, 39, 52, 55, 84, 85, *98,* 100, 101
Brandt, Edgar 127
brass bedsteads 92
brass inlay *see* boulle marquetry
Breuer, Marcel 126, 135–6, *135*
Breytspaak, Carel 111
Brustolon, Andrea 37, *37*
buffets *19,* 20, 33, 58, 128, *128*
buffet-commode 70
Bugatti, Carlo 129, *130*
Bullock, George 85, 90, 91–2
bureaus 69, *78*
bureau-bookcases 59, 68, 76, 78, 79, 113
bureau cabinets 44, *65,* 67, 69, *70, 72*
bureau Mazarin 35–6
Burges, William 94, 101
Burgundy style 20
Burham, Benjamin 79
Burling, Thomas 79

C

cabinets
    bureau 44, 67, 69
    display 67, *68*
    Dutch 17thC *39,* 40; 18thC 67, *68,* 69
    dwarf 86–7
    English 16thC 30; 17thC 27, 30, *31;* 18thC 44, 45, 46, 48, 51; 19thC 89, 91, *95,* 100
    French 17thC 31, 32–3, *33,* 34, *34,* 35; 18thC 55, 56; 19thC 101; 20thC *104,* 126
    German 16thC 23; 18thC 64, *64;* 19thC 107, 109; 20thC *134*
    Italian regional 61; 17thC *22,* 31
    japanned 31
    lacquered 31, 56
    Russian 19thC *111*
    skyscraper 141
    Spanish 16thC 22; 17thC 38
    writing *28,* 64, *111*
cabinets on stands 30, *31, 33,* 34, 38, 39, *39,* 44
Cameron, Charles 71
Carabin, Rupert 102
case furniture 46, 52, 53, 55, 100
cassone 21, *21*
Century Guild 97, 98
chairs
    American 17thC 40; 18thC 77, 78, *78, 79;* 19thC 113–15, *114,* 116, *116,* 117, *117;* 20thC 120, 141
    ancient 12
    Austrian 20thC *136, 137, 138*
    barrel 13
    bentwood 110, 124, *136, 138*
    Berlin 138
    Birza 138
    box 13
    Brewster 40
    British 19thC 9, *50, 85,* 88, *88,* 90, 91, 93, *96,* 98, *122;* 20thC *10,* 121, 122, 124
    burgomaster 68
    caned 11, 29, 45, 67, 68, 73
    Carver 40
    coronation 13
    dining *45,* 136
    Dutch 17thC 40; 18thC 67, 68, 69
    English 15–16thC 13; 17thC 26, 27, 29, *29;* 18thC 11, 44, 45, *45, 46,* 47, 48, *48,* 49, *50,* 51
    farthingale 10, 11, 29

French Renaissance 19, 20, *20;* 17thC 33, *33,* 34; 18thC 11, 52, 54–5, *55,* 57; 19thC 9, 99, 101, 103, *103,* 104; 20thC *10, 125,* 126, 129
Gainsborough 48, *48*
German 17thC 39; 18thC 63, 66, 67; 19thC 110; 20thC 133, *134*
gossip 13, 20, *20*
hall 48
Hitchcock *114,* 116
Italian Renaissance 21; 17thC 37, *37;* 18thC 59, 60; 19thC *105,* 106, 107; 20thC 130
japanned 45, 51
ladderback 121
library 88
medieval 10, 11, 12, 13
Muldbjerg 12
painted 51, 66
Portuguese 18thC 63, *63*
Red-Blue 138, *138*
roundabout 68
rush-seated 13, *96,* 126, 129
Russian 18thC 71
St Augustine's 12
Savonarola 13
Scandinavian 18thC *8,* 73; 20thC *139, 140*
sgabello 21, 29
Shaker 117, *117*
side 98, *103, 120,* 129, 133
Spanish 19thC *107*
Spanish Southwestern 117
upholstered 29, 39, 40, 45, 48, 51, 73, 104
wainscot 40
Wassily *134,* 135, 136
Windsor 50, *50*
wing 11, 29, 45, *45, 79*
X-frame 12, 13, 18, 40, 71, 107
chaise-longue 57, 99, 113, 126, *127, 135,* 136
Chambers, Sir William 50
Chanaux, Adolphe 127
Channon, John 48
Charpentier, Alexandre 105
Chareau, Pierre 126
chest-on-chest 44–5, 79
chests
    American 17thC 41, *41;* 18thC 77, *77;* 19thC 117
    bachelor's 45
    dower 77
    English 15–16thC 18; 17thC 26,

PICTURE CREDITS

a = above, c = center, l = left, r = right, f = far

Every effort has been made to trace and acknowledge all copyright holders. Quintet would like to
apologise if any omissions have been made.

Pg 7, b Sotheby's, New York; Pg 8, b Angelo Hornak; Pg 9, b Jonathan Harris; Pg 10, l Bridgeman
Art Library; Pg 13, Metropolitan Museum of Art; Pg 14, Private Collection; Pg 15, Musée de Cluny,
Paris; Pg 19, b Sotheby's; Pg 20, a Bresset; b Louvre, Paris; Pg 21, Martin Saunders; Pg 22, Phillips
Fine Art Auctioneers; Pg 23, Sotheby's; Pg 29, a Christie's Colour Library; b Temple Newsan House,
Leeds; Pg 30–32, Christie's Colour Library; Pg 33 a Christie's Colour Library; b Prudence
Cumming; Pg 34, Jonathan Harris; Pg 35, Raymond Fortt; Pg 37, Sotheby's; Pg 39, Christie's,
Amsterdam; Pg 41, Bernard and S. Dean Levy, Inc. New York; Pg 44, Christie's Colour Library;
Pg 46, Pilgrim Press; Pg 49, b National Trust, Waddesdon Manor; Pg 50, b Christie's Colour Library;
Pg 53 b © Christie's, New York; Pg 54 Christie's, Monaco; Pg 55, b Minneapolis Institute of Arts;
Pg 56, Christie's Colour Library; Pg 57 b © Christie's, New York; Pg 58, Gloucester House Antiques;
Pg 59 a Christie's Colour Library; Pg 60, Angelo Hornak; Pg 61, b Christie's, Rome; Pg 62,
Sotheby's; Pg 63, Sotheby's; Pg 64, Christie's Colour Library; Pg 65, Partridge Fine Art; Pg 66, a
Angelo Hornak; b Partridge Fine Art; Pg 68, a Sotheby's; b Christie's Colour Library; Pg 47 a
© Christie's, London; b Christie's Colour Library; Pg 70 Sotheby's; Pg 71 b Mallett & Son
(Antiques) Ltd; Pg 72, Wallace Collection; Pg 73, Bukowskis, Sweden; Pg 74, b American Museum
In Britain, Bath; Pg 75 b Robert O. Stuart; Pg 76 a Wayne Pratt and Company; b Colonial
Williamsburg Foundation; Pg 77, Metropolitan Museum of Art, New York; Pg 78, b Quarto
Publishing plc; Pg 82, b Christie's Colour Library; Pg 83 a Temple Newsam House/Christopher
Hutchinson; b *c Christie's, London; Pg 84, Blairman's; Pg 85, a Blairman's; b Christie's Colour
Library; Pg 86 a Blairman's; b Christie's Colour Library; Pg 87, a Christie's Colour Library; b
Blairman's; Pg 88 a Christie's Colour Library; Pg 89, a © Christie's, London; b Christie's Colour
Library; Pg 90, Quarto Publishing plc/Blairman's; Pg 91 b © Christie's, London; Pg 92, b Sotheby's;
Pg 93, b Sotheby's; Pg 94, a Blairman's; b Christie's Colour Library; Pg 95, Sotheby's; Pg 96, b

Design Council; Pg 97, Philips, London; Pg 99 a Phillip de Bay, Fine Art & Archival Photography;
Pg 100 Sotheby's; Pg 101 b Angelo Hornak; Pg 102 b Victoria and Albert Museum, London; Pg 103,
a Musée des Arts Décoratifs; Pg 104, Philippe Garner; Pg 105 Christie's Colour Library; Pg 108 a
Sotheby's; b Christies Colour Library; Pg 110, Partridge Fine Art; Pg 113 a Christie's, New York;
Pg 114 Abby Aldrich Rockerfeller Folk Art Center; Pg 115, Metropolitan Museum of Art, New York;
Pg 116–117 American Museum in Britain, Bath; Pg 120, Christie's; Pg 121, a Victoria and Albert
Museum, London; Pg 123, Angelo Hornak; Pg 127 a Bettman Archive/BBC Hulton Picture Library;
Pg 128, John Vaughn; Pg 129, Hubert Josse, Paris; Pg 130, a Christie's Colour Library; Pg 132, Knoll
International; Pg 133 Sotheby's/Musée des Arts Décoratifs; Pg 134, a Victoria and Albert Museum,
London; b Design Council; Pg 135, Sotheby's; Pg 136, b Victoria and Albert Museum, London;
Pg 137 Sotheby's; Pg 141, Museum of Art, Atlanta; Pg 143, Alistair Duncan/collection John P. Axelrod;
Pg 146, Christie's; Pg 147, Sotheby's; Pg 149, © Christie's, London; Pg 150, Christie's Colour Library;
Pg 151, Philips de Bay, Fine Art & Archival Photography; Pg 153, Phillips Fine Art Auctioneers;
Pg 154, a Christie's Colour Library; b Christie's, Monaco; Pg 156, Christie's Colour Library.

In addition the Publishers would like to thank the following for the use of copyright material:

Alias SRL, Milan; Annely Juda Fine Art, London; Architectural Association; Artek, Finland;
Artemide GB, London; The Australian National Gallery, Canberra; The Bridgeman Art Library;
Jeremy Broun, Bath; Rupert Cavendish; The Crafts Council, London, and the craftsmen they
represent; Christie's Colour Library; Christie Manson and Woods Ltd; Dover Publications; Ecart
International, Paris; The Edinburgh Photographic Library; E T Archive; Barry Friedman Ltd, New
York; Collection Galerie De Windt; Angelo Hornak; Toby Jellinek Private Collections; Knoll
International, London; Danny Lane, London; Bernard and S Dean Levy Inc, New York City; Lusty
Lloyd Loom, Chipping Camden, Gloucestershire, England; Lusty and Sons, London; Lutyens
Design Associates, London; Mallett and Son London Ltd; Musée des Arts Décoratifs; MW United,
London, on behalf of Mssrs Franz Wittman KG; The Octopus Group Ltd; Partridge Fine Arts Ltd,
London; Phillips Auctioneers, London, New York, and Bath; Sotheby's, London and New York;
Spink and Son, London; Stair and Co, London; Steelcase Strafor (UK) Ltd; The Storehouse Group,
London; Swiss National Museum, Zurich; Vitra Ltd, London; Private Collections.

Willow

start and finish line

no-man's
land

Vera Lake

THE JUNIOR
IDITAROD
TRAIL

Painter and Ugly were best friends. Through winter, spring,

summer, and fall, they were always together.

Nothing could keep them apart.

Painter and Ugly

Robert J. Blake

Philomel Books
An Imprint of Penguin Group (USA) Inc.

after every sled-racing season, the boy called Jake always left his dog team to run free on an island on the Yukon River. He was good to the team and every day returned with fresh water, food, and hugs for each dog.

Jake prized every one of his dogs, especially the two that were always together. He named one Painter when he knocked over a can of paint.

He named the other Ugly because most of the paint spilled on him.

Wherever you saw Painter, there you saw Ugly. If Painter went to fetch a stick, Ugly brought it back with him. If Ugly howled at the moon, Painter sang harmony. And when Jake built Painter's house too far away from Ugly's, the dog pushed it all the way down the hill and set it next to his best friend's.

Through the warm days of summer, right into fall, Painter and Ugly ran together, swam together, and even ate out of each other's dinner bowls together. And if for any reason they were apart, one dog would call out *yip*, the other would answer *yip*, and soon the two friends were running side by side as fast as they could.

But one day, Jake did not come with food, water, or hugs. Instead, there came a man with a voice like a chainsaw who herded the dogs onto a boat. Painter was happy to go on the boat because it meant that the team was going to the mainland. And going to the mainland meant that race training was about to begin. And race training meant that

Painter and Ugly, the fastest of all the local dogs, would soon be leading Jake and the team in the Junior Iditarod race.

Yip! Painter called, and Ugly ran to join him at the front of the boat.

But when the team reached the mainland, there was still no
Jake. There were only people shouting and waving papers. Big
Tonka cried out when he was hauled off by a woman in a beaver
coat. Keeneye growled as he was taken by a hairy man who
smelled of bacon.

Painter tried to slip out of his collar when a red-haired boy pulled him away from Ugly.

Ugly jumped from side to side when a black-haired boy rushed him away from his friend.

Each dog was placed into a different dog box on a different truck. Every truck drove each dog to a different home.

On his new dog lot, Painter peeked out of his
doghouse at the other dogs. They all knew each other.
Painter knew none of them.

Yip! he called out to Ugly. But no answer came.
Painter was surrounded by dogs, but he felt alone.

On his first training run, Painter was distracted as he looked for his best friend. He yipped at every team they passed, hoping Ugly would yip back. He missed commands, took wrong turns, and even ran the team up over a snowbank when he thought he caught his friend's scent in the woods.

The red-haired boy had to wade into the thigh-high snow to untangle the team. Then he took Painter's face in his hands and said, YOUGOTTOEARNYOURPLACEONTHETEAM. Painter did not understand the words, but he felt the tone in the boy's voice. He settled down then and easily impressed the musher.

By the time they went on their third practice run, Painter had earned the lead position.

Then came Junior Iditarod race day—two hundred dogs on twenty teams. Every dog was barking, rolling in the snow, and leaping high in the air. All except one. Painter stood still, with his nose tasting the air.

Rushing across the frozen river and through the race grounds, the wind delivered the sounds and smells of every team. And it brought Painter one familiar scent—Ugly.

Eight teams had already left when it was Painter's team's turn in the starting chute. The dogs barked and howled, screamed and cried—and then, suddenly, the whole team went silent. They were ready to take off. Soon the only sounds that could be heard were the jingling of the dogs' tags, *jing-jing-jing,* and the hiss of the sled runners on the snow.

After eighty miles of racing, Painter's team arrived at the halfway checkpoint just fifteen minutes behind the first-place team. Here the teams were required to stop and rest for ten hours. The red-haired boy gave the dogs food, water, and soft hay bedding to sleep on. As his team slept, Painter sat looking, sniffing, listening . . . hoping for a sign of his friend.

Then across the chill night came a familiar call—*Yip!*

Yip! Painter called back.

QUIET! yelled a musher. The dogs went silent.

But all through the night, just every once in a while, a soft yip ran across the night air. And another yip chased it back.

At dawn a great chorus of howls arose from a team behind a nearby snowdrift. They got louder and louder until suddenly they went silent. Painter knew this meant the first-place team had hit the trail. He cocked his ears and listened to the *jing-jing-jing* of the team's tags.

Painter leaped into the air when the team sprinted into view—Ugly was the lead dog! Ugly signaled to Painter by flicking his ears and letting out three quick yips. Painter answered with three quick yips of his own.

Then Ugly and his team were gone.

Up ahead, Ugly brought his team across the frozen Yentna River. When they reached the other side, his musher gave the command to turn left. HAW!

But Ugly did not turn his team. Instead he called out *Yip! Yip! Yip!* and jumped off the trail into the low brush.

When Painter reached the same turn, he called out *Yip! Yip! Yip!* and jumped into the woods, too.

A mile into the woods, Painter's team came upon the black-haired boy, alone in the snow. Ugly had led his team under some low branches, forcing the musher to jump from his sled. The red-haired boy ran to him as soon as he could slow his team. AREYOUALLRIGHT he called.

Painter called, too. *Yip! Yip! Yip!* Then he howled *Oooorrooo-ooo-oooo!*

From below the ridge came the answer, *Yip! Yip! Yip! Oooorrooo-ooo-oooo!*

Before the boys could stop them, Painter and his team ran off.

Soon the only sound that could be heard was that of a lonely raven calling in the chill air.

Until the wind brought the sound of something approaching from under the ridge:

jing-*jing*-*jing*.

Together at last, Painter and Ugly waited for no one. The teams ran hard to keep up with their leaders, and the boys ran hard to catch up with their sleds. Just as the dogs reached the frozen river, the two mushers jumped on the sled runners and called FASTER to their teams. Painter and Ugly knew they had to run full-out to catch up to the teams that had gotten ahead of them while they were off the trail. But running full-out together is what they liked best.

Once they reached the zone called no-man's land, Painter and Ugly passed every dog in sight.

Painter and Ugly crossed the finish line at exactly the same time together. Not a nose, not even one whisker stood out farther in front of one dog than the other.

People will talk about that race forever—what happened, how it happened, and why it happened—in the way that people do.

But Painter and Ugly, they never cared about people's talk.

Painter and Ugly only cared about being together—because nothing can keep two real friends apart.

AUTHOR'S NOTE

To create this book, I moved in with the Holt family in the town of North Pole, Alaska. Two of the Holt children were going to race in the Junior Iditarod. While with the family, I had the opportunity to help build a dog transport box, feed their sled dogs, and even mush a team in preparation for the race. My favorite dog on the team was a dog named Painter. Mr. Holt told me that Painter had come from another team that had been split up and sold. It seemed like Painter missed his friend from that team, a dog named Ugly. "Where is Ugly now?" I asked. But he did not know.

Whenever I write a story, I think, *What if*.

What if Ugly wound up on another sled-dog team? *What if* Ugly raced in the upcoming Junior Iditarod? *What if* Painter could tell that his friend Ugly was at the race start? *What if* the two dogs smelled each other, talked to each other, and then saw each other during the race? *What if* they made a plan to get together—because nothing could keep them apart?

The Junior Iditarod is a challenging race of speed, weather, and cooperation between mushers fourteen to seventeen years old and their dogs. On the first day, each musher must travel the trail approximately eighty miles with their ten dogs. Then they must sleep outside with them and return eighty miles the next day.

To my longtime loyal and dedicated friends
Alfred, Gary, Janet, and Lynn.

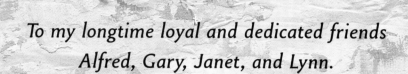 *A special dedication—*
To Patricia Lee Gauch—
in appreciation of your longstanding loyalty
and belief in your authors and artists.
We are proud to call you friend.

PHILOMEL BOOKS
A division of Penguin Young Readers Group.
Published by The Penguin Group. Penguin Group (USA) Inc., 375 Hudson Street, New York, NY 10014, U.S.A.
Penguin Group (Canada), 90 Eglinton Avenue East, Suite 700, Toronto, Ontario M4P 2Y3, Canada (a division of Pearson Penguin Canada Inc.).
Penguin Books Ltd, 80 Strand, London WC2R 0RL, England.
Penguin Ireland, 25 St. Stephen's Green, Dublin 2, Ireland (a division of Penguin Books Ltd).
Penguin Group (Australia), 250 Camberwell Road, Camberwell, Victoria 3124, Australia (a division of Pearson Australia Group Pty Ltd).
Penguin Books India Pvt Ltd, 11 Community Centre, Panchsheel Park, New Delhi - 110 017, India.
Penguin Group (NZ), 67 Apollo Drive, Rosedale, North Shore 0632, New Zealand (a division of Pearson New Zealand Ltd).
Penguin Books (South Africa) (Pty) Ltd, 24 Sturdee Avenue, Rosebank, Johannesburg 2196, South Africa.
Penguin Books Ltd, Registered Offices: 80 Strand, London WC2R 0RL, England.

Design by Semadar Megged. Text set in 18-point Paradigm. The artist used oil paint to create the illustrations for this book.

Library of Congress Cataloging-in-Publication Data
Blake, Robert J. Painter and Ugly / Robert J. Blake. p. cm. Summary: Painter and Ugly, two sled dogs who are inseparable best friends, are put on different teams for the Junior Iditarod, but they manage to find their way back to one another for the big race. 1. Sled dogs—Juvenile fiction. [1. Sled dogs—Fiction. 2. Dogs—Fiction. 3. Iditarod (Race)—Fiction. 4. Sled dog racing—Fiction. 5. Best friends—Fiction. 6. Friendship—Fiction. 7. Alaska—Fiction.] I. Title. PZ10.3.B5815Pai 2011 [E]—dc22
2010005395

ISBN 978-0-399-24323-3
1 3 5 7 9 10 8 6 4 2